Street by Street

LEICESTER
MARKET HARBOROUGH

LUTTERWORTH, OADBY, SYSTON, WIGSTON

Anstey, Birstall, Blaby, Broughton Astley, Cosby, Countesthorpe, Earl Shilton, Fleckney, Groby, Kibworth Beauchamp, Kirby Muxloe, Markfield, Narborough, Ratby, Stoney Stanton, Thurnby

3rd edition July 2008
© Automobile Association Developments Limited 2008

Original edition printed August 2003

This product includes map data licensed from Ordnance Survey® with the permission of the Controller of Her Majesty's Stationery Office. © Crown copyright 2008. All rights reserved. Licence number 100021153.

The copyright in all PAF is owned by Royal Mail Group plc.

Published by AA Publishing (a trading name of Automobile Association Developments Limited, whose registered office is Fanum House, Basing View, Basingstoke, Hampshire RG21 4EA. Registered number 1878835).

Produced by the Mapping Services Department of The Automobile Association. (A03713)

A CIP Catalogue record for this book is available from the British Library.

Printed by Oriental Press in Dubai

The contents of this atlas are believed to be correct at the time of the latest revision. However, the publishers cannot be held responsible or liable for any loss or damage occasioned to any person acting or refraining from action as a result of any use or reliance on any material in this atlas, nor for any errors, omissions or changes in such material. This does not affect your statutory rights. The publishers would welcome information to correct any errors or omissions and to keep this atlas up to date. Please write to Publishing, The Automobile Association, Fanum House (FH12), Basing View, Basingstoke, Hampshire, RG21 4EA. E-mail: streetbystreet@theaa.com

Ref: ML225y

Key to map pages	ii-iii
Key to map symbols	iv-1
Enlarged map pages	2-3
Main map pages	4-85
Index – towns & villages	86
Index – streets	86-98
Index – featured places	99-100
Acknowledgements	100

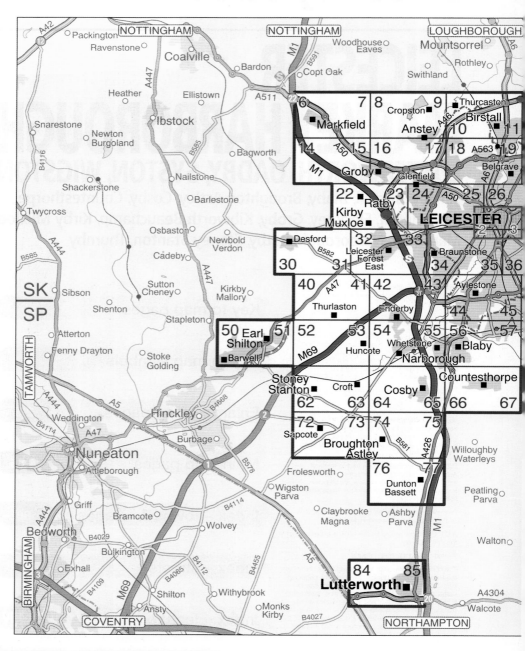

Scale of enlarged map pages **1:10,000** 6.3 inches to 1 mile

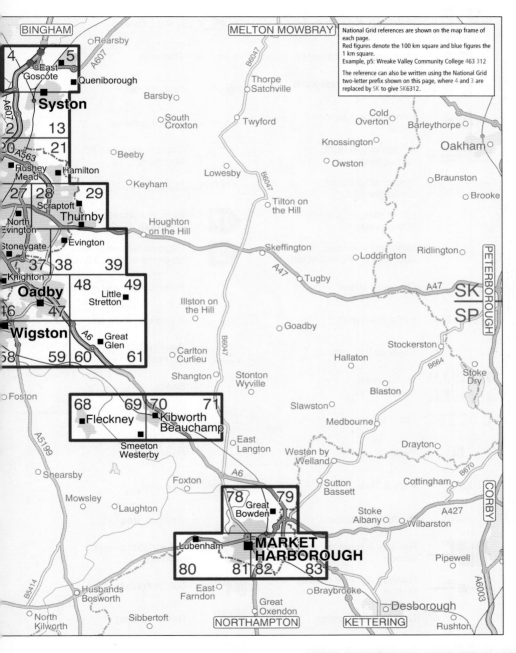

National Grid references are shown on the map frame of each page.
Red figures denote the 100 km square and blue figures the 1 km square.
Example, p5: Wreake Valley Community College 463 312

The reference can also be written using the National Grid two-letter prefix shown on this page, where 4 and 3 are replaced by SK to give SK6312.

BINGHAM

Rearsby

MELTON MOWBRAY

A607

4   5

East Goscote   Queniborough

Thorpe Satchville

Barsby

SYSTON

2   13

South Croxton

Twyford

Cold Overton

Barleythorpe

Knossington

Oakham

20   21

A563

Beeby

Lowesby

Owston

Braunston

Rushey Mead   Hamilton

Keyham

Tilton on the Hill

Brooke

27   28   29

Scraptoft

Thurnby

Houghton on the Hill

Skeffington

Loddington

Ridlington

North Evington

Stoneygate

Evington

A47

Tugby

A47

SK

SP

PETERBOROUGH

37   38   39

Knighton

Illston on the Hill

Oadby

48   49

Little Stretton

Goadby

Stockerston

Stoke Dry

B664

16   47

Wigston

A6

Great Glen

Hallaton

Blaston

58   59   60   61

Carlton Curlieu

Shangton

Stonton Wyville

Slawston

Medbourne

Drayton

68   69   70   71

Fleckney

Kibworth Beauchamp

East Langton

Weston by Welland

Cottingham

CORBY

Smeeton Westerby

A6

Shearsby

Foxton

Sutton Bassett

Mowsley

Laughton

78   79

Great Bowden

Stoke Albany

A427

Wilbarston

MARKET HARBOROUGH

Lubenham

Pipewell

80   81   82   83

Husbands Bosworth

East Farndon

Braybrooke

Desborough

North Kilworth

Sibbertoft

Great Oxendon

NORTHAMPTON

KETTERING

Rushton

4.2 inches to 1 mile   **Scale of main map pages**   **1:15,000**

0   1/4   miles   1/2   3/4

0   1/4   1/2   kilometres   3/4   1   1 1/4

Junction 9 — Motorway & junction

Services — Motorway service area

Primary road single/dual carriageway

Services — Primary road service area

A road single/dual carriageway

B road single/dual carriageway

Other road single/dual carriageway

Minor/private road, access may be restricted

One-way street

Pedestrian area

Track or footpath

Road under construction

Road tunnel

P — Parking

P+ — Park & Ride

Bus/coach station

Railway & main railway station

Railway & minor railway station

Underground station

Light railway & station

Preserved private railway

LC — Level crossing

Tramway

Ferry route

Airport runway

County, administrative boundary

Mounds

17 — Page continuation 1:15,000

3 — Page continuation to enlarged scale 1:10,000

River/canal, lake, pier

Aqueduct, lock, weir

465
Winter Hill — Peak (with height in metres)

Beach

Woodland

Park

Cemetery

Built-up area

Industrial/business building

Leisure building

Retail building

Other building

⊓⊓⊓⊓⊓⊓	City wall		♟	Castle
A&E	Hospital with 24-hour A&E department		🏛	Historic house or building
PO	Post Office		Wakehurst Place (NT)	National Trust property
📖	Public library		Ⓜ	Museum or art gallery
𝑖	Tourist Information Centre		🦅	Roman antiquity
𝑖	Seasonal Tourist Information Centre		⊥	Ancient site, battlefield or monument
⛽ ⛽	Petrol station, 24 hour Major suppliers only		🏭	Industrial interest
✝	Church/chapel		✳	Garden
🚻	Public toilets		◉	Garden Centre Garden Centre Association Member
♿	Toilet with disabled facilities		🌳	Garden Centre Wyevale Garden Centre
PH	Public house AA recommended		🌲🌲	Arboretum
🍴	Restaurant AA inspected		🐄	Farm or animal centre
Madeira Hotel ▬	Hotel AA inspected		🦌	Zoological or wildlife collection
🎭	Theatre or performing arts centre		🐦	Bird collection
🎥	Cinema		🐋	Nature reserve
⚑	Golf course		🐟	Aquarium
▲	Camping AA inspected		V	Visitor or heritage centre
🚐	Caravan site AA inspected		♉	Country park
▲🚐	Camping & caravan site AA inspected		◠	Cave
🎡	Theme park		✵	Windmill
🏛	Abbey, cathedral or priory		🛢	Distillery, brewery or vineyard

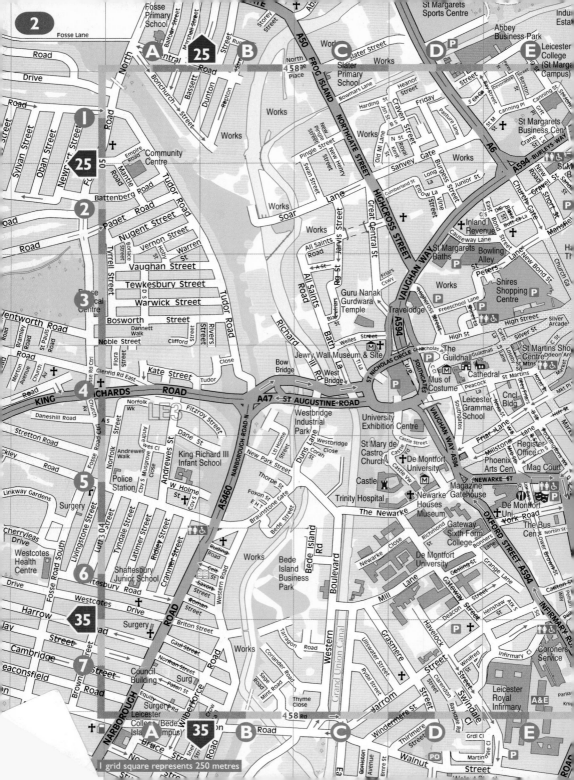

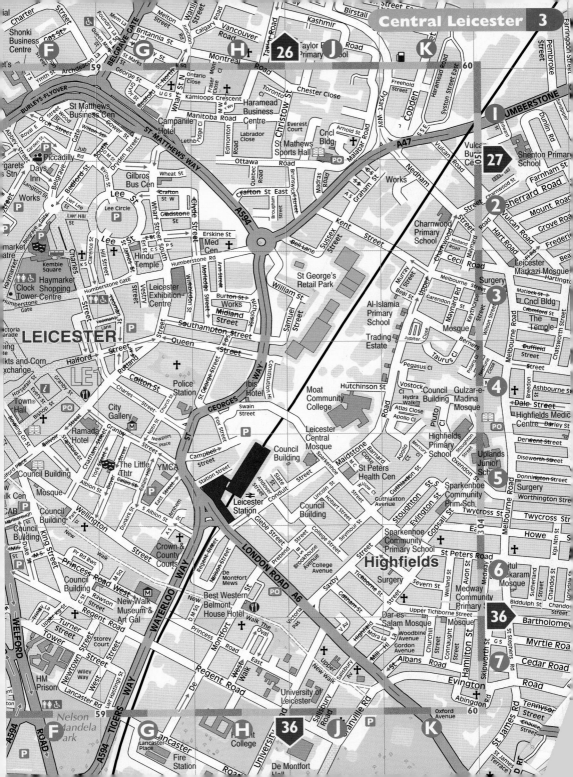

4

A   461   B   Glebe Lodge C   62   D

Humble Lane

14

Cossington
CE Primary
School

Cossington

1

Homestead
Close
Fisher
Close

Hall Cl

Bennett's Lane
Humble Lane

Back Lane
M Rd
Middlefield
Road

Blackberry Lane

Glebe Lodge
Farm

Home Farm

Wreake House
Farm

Lane

Main Street

tts Lane

2

A607 SYSTON ROAD

Syston Road

13

Grange

Chestnut Farm

COSSINGTON
LANE

A607

Lewin Bridge

3

A46

Fosse Way

4

Works

St Pe
& St
Prima

312

Meadow Lane

Meadow Lane

Ind
Est

High Street

Works

5

Grand Union Canal

The
Half Cft

Industrial
Estate

Harcourt
Close

Turn St

Brook St

A46

461

A6u

Glebe Way

Glebe Way

Moorland Rd

Swallow Drive

Teal Way

Swift Close

Mallard Drive

62

Necton St

West St

North

St Peter's Street

Broad Street

Melton Road

A   Wanlip Road   B   **12**   C   D

Martin Drive

Glebe
Way

Cygnet Clos

Blackthorn

St columbans

Iona Rd

Priory
Clos

Lindisfarne
Road

Abbotts

Willow
Walk

Gorse
Lane

Fosse Way

Wolsey
Way

Cranmer
Dr

Hardwick Cr

Chatsworth
Dr

Wanlip

Glebe
Way

earth

Avenue

Road

Syston
Station

Taylor Cl

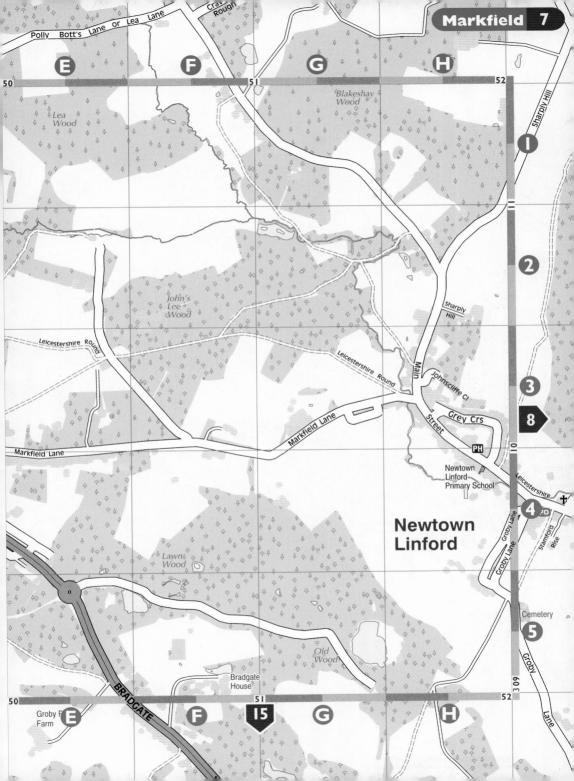

Polly Bott's Lane or Lea Lane

Crav... Rough

E F G H

50 51 52

Lea Wood

Blakeshay Wood

I

John's Lee Wood

2

Sharply Hill

Leicestershire Round

Main Street

Johnscliffe Cl

3

8

Grey Crs

Markfield Lane

PH

Markfield Lane

Newtown Linford Primary School

Leicestershire

4

Newtown Linford

Lawn Wood

Groby Lane

Stamford Rise

Cemetery

5

Old Wood

Groby Lane

Bradgate House

BRADGATE

50 51 52

Groby P... Farm

E F G H

I5

Sharply Hill

309

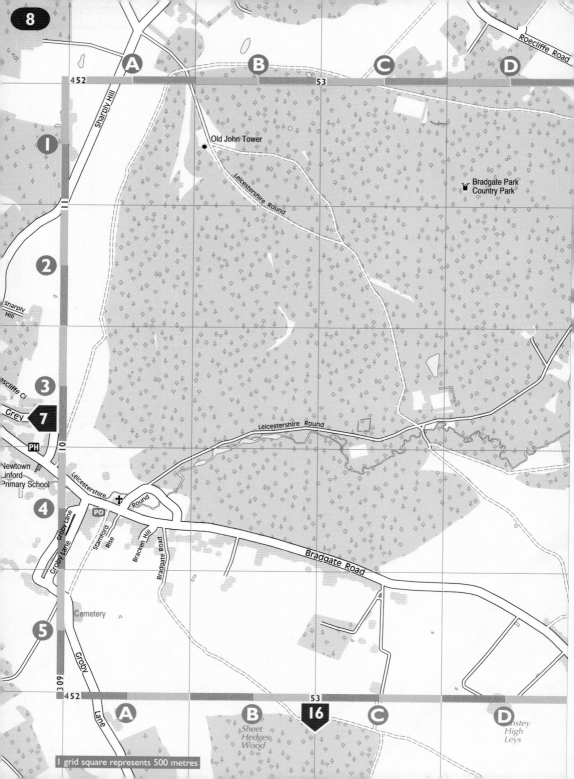

8

452

A   B   53   C   D

Roecliffe Road

Sharply Hill

1

Old John Tower

Leicestershire Round

Bradgate Park
Country Park

Sharply
Hill

2

oscliffe Cl

3

Grey **7**

PH

Leicestershire Round

Newtown
Linford
Primary School

Leicestershire

Round

4

PO

Stamford
Rise

Bracken Hill

Bradgate Road

Groby Lane

Cemetery

5

Groby

Lane

309

452

A   Lane   B   53   **16**   C   D   nstey
High
Leys

Sheet
Hedges
Wood

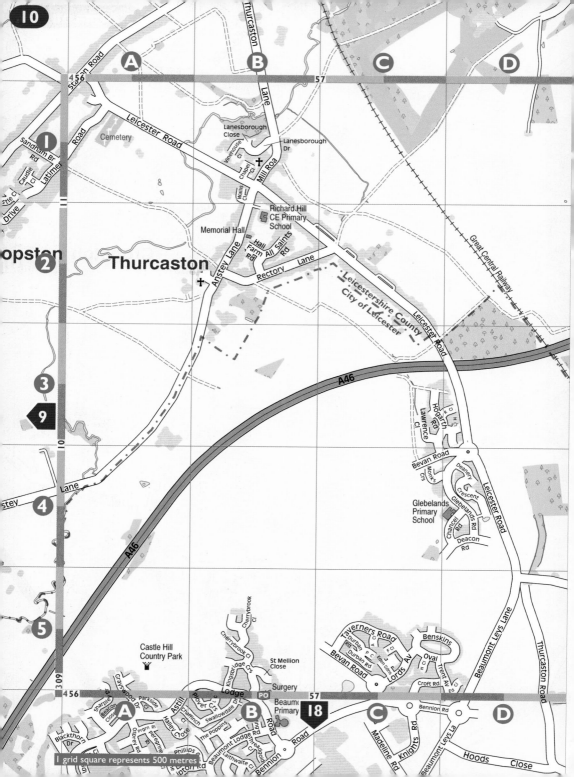

E F G H

I

A6

Wanlip
Hill

Council
Building

A46

Fillingate

Rectory
Road

Church
Road

2 Wan

Rectory Rd

Wanlip
Lane

Riverside
Ms

A46

A6 LOUGHBOROUGH ROAD

Connery Leys Rd

Longslade
Community
College

Stonehill
High School

Russ
Way

3

Melba Wy

12

Birch Tree
Av

Myrtle Av

Allington
Dr

Worcester Av

Malling Cl

Harrowgate Drive

Lime Tree
Av

Acacia Av

Dalby Av

Highgate
Av

Ryegate
Crs

Ambergate Dr

Sandgate
Av

Lyngate
Av

Sycamore Rd

Bentley
Rd

Holly Tree
Av

Hawth Cl

Thorn

Allington Drive

Blenheim Road

Worcester Av

4

Briargate
Dr

Woodgate Drive

Moorgate Av

Denegate
Avenue

Wellgate
Avenue

Brdg Cl

Rose Tree Av

Windmill Av

Kswc Cl

Queensgate Dr

Westgate
Av

PO

Castlegate Av

Saltersgate Drive

Colindale Av

Iris Av

Stonehill Avenue

Gwendolin Avenue

Laxton
Cl

Kingsgate Avenue

Heathgate

The Meadway

Hill Rise

Nfield
Av

Paget Av

Meadow Lane

Fieldgate Crs

Greengate
Medical
Centre

L Rd

The
Wayne

Lambourne Rd

Greengate Lane

Walnut Av

Spinney
Rise

Poplar Av

Sibson
Rd

PO

Wanlip Avenue

Wanlip Lane

Bramley Road

Orchard Road

5

Greengate Lane

Cem

Highcliffe
Primary
School

Hallam Av

Avenue

The Crossways

Rd

Riverside
Community
Primary School

Elmfield

Cliffwood Av

Cedar Av

Firfield Av

Lawn Av

Oakfield

L Wd

Fielding

Beechfield Av

Council
Building

Farm

Whiles La

Netherhall La

Johnson Road

Copeland R

59

BIRSTALL

A6 LOUGHBOROUGH ROAD

Council
Building

309

60

E

Cliffe Road

F

Goscote
Rd

Henson Cl

19

Walker Road

G

School Lane

Curzon Rd

tall Road

Church
Hl

Mill Cl

H

▶ Golf Course

Park Road

The
Drive

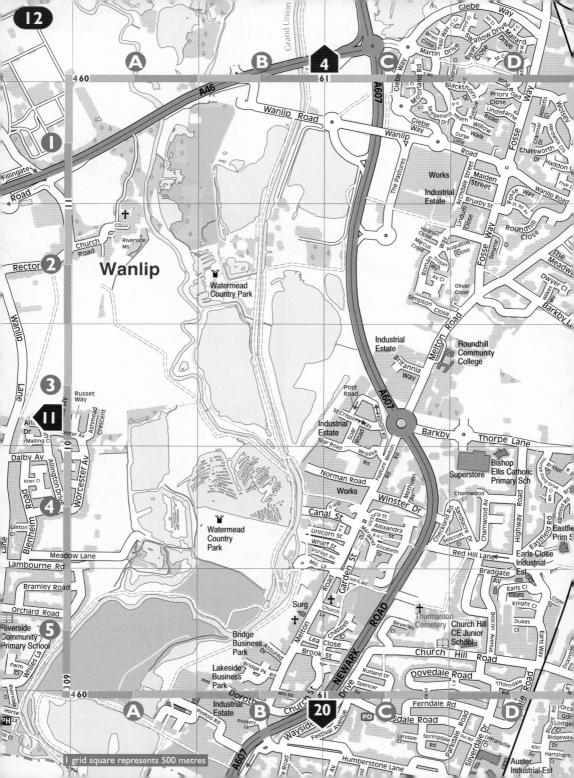

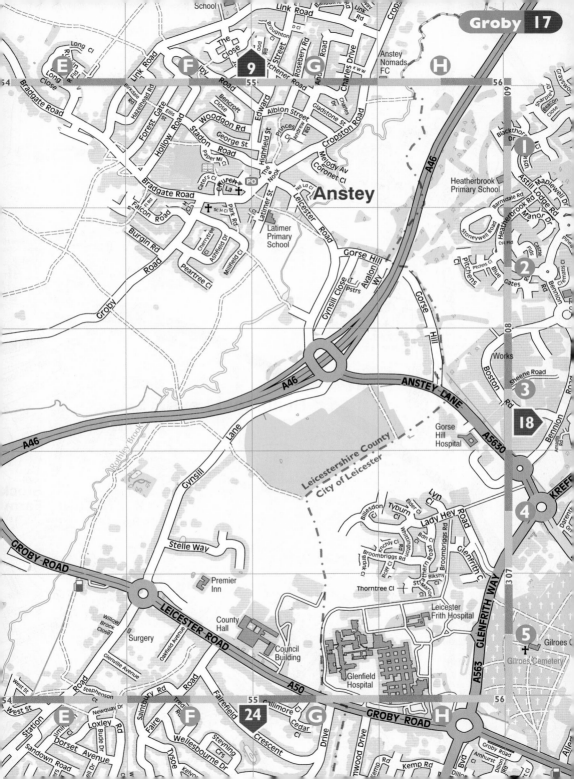

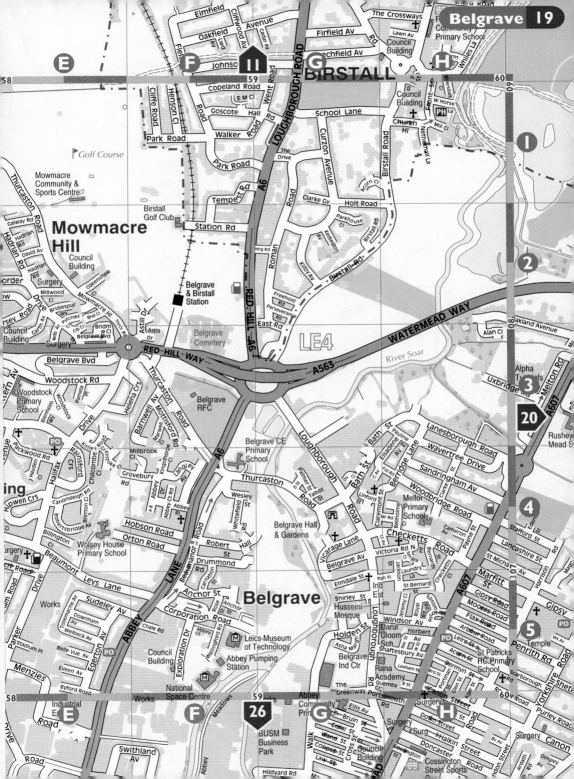

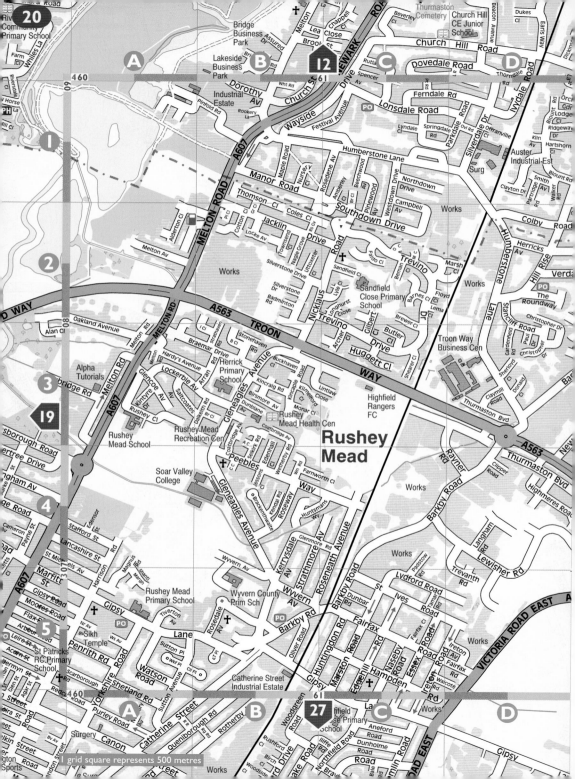

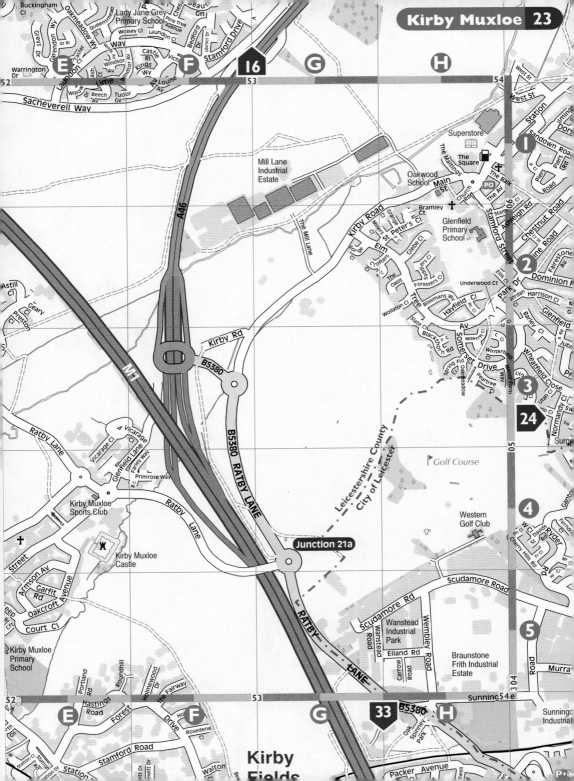

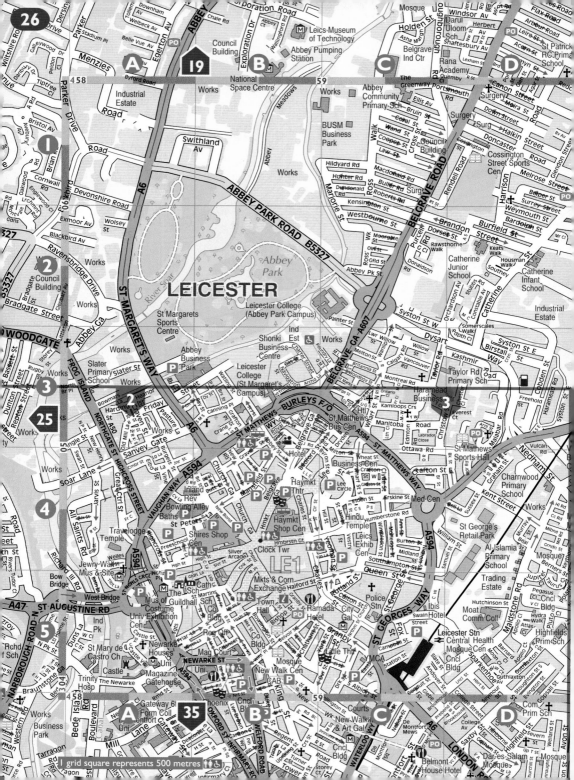

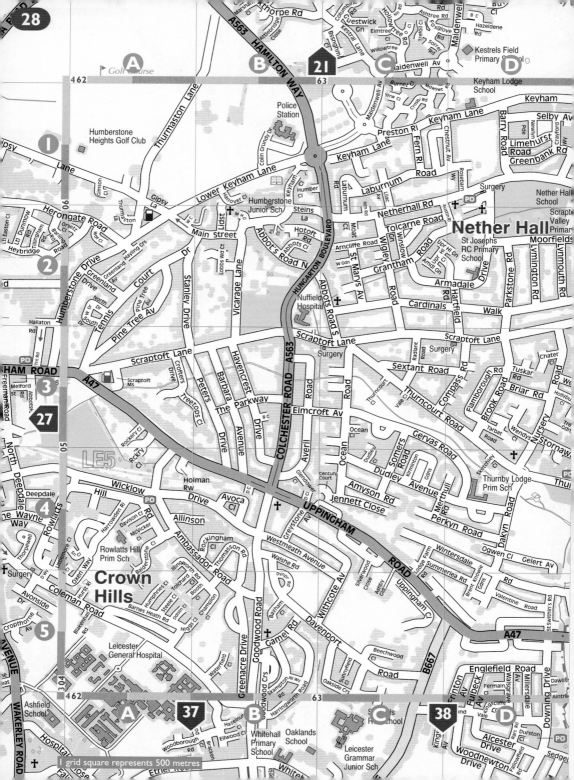

E F G 22 H

49 50 51

Gullet
Link

Elms
Farm

I

Park House
Farm

2

Oaks
Farm

04

03

Stud Farm

LANE

3

32

B582

Forest House

4

Alder
Hall

LEICESTER LANE

HINCKLEY ROAD

302

B582

5

A47

Thurlaston Lodge
Farm

DESFORD ROAD

Peckleton   Lane

49 50 51

E F G 41 H

Old
Brake

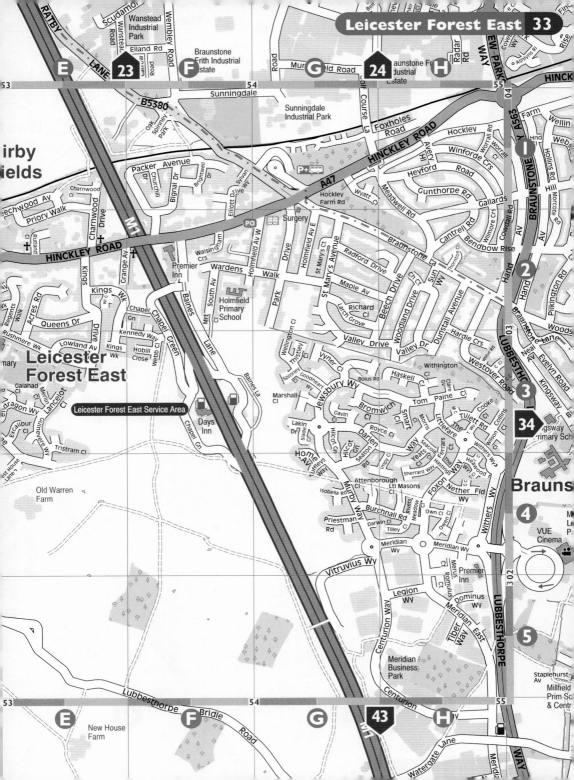

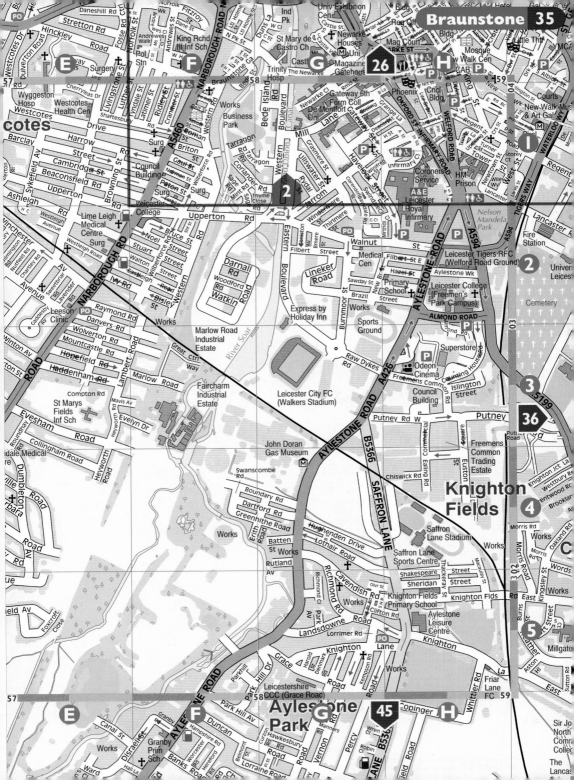

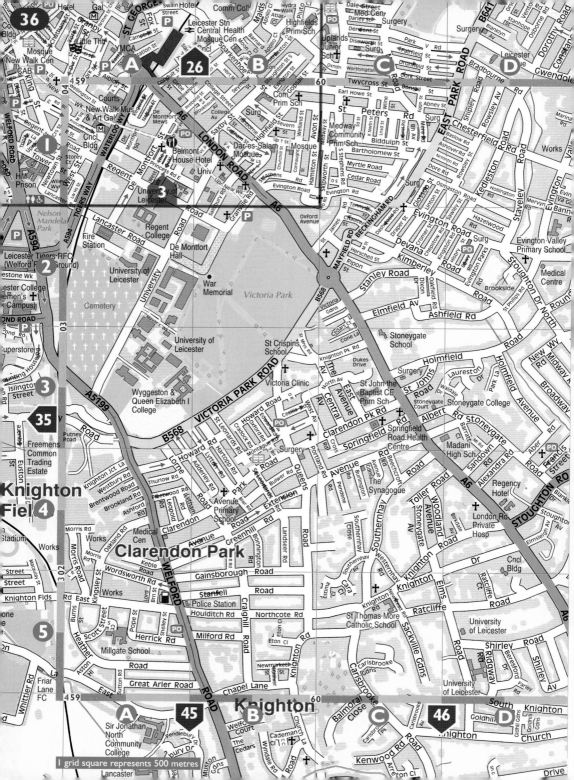

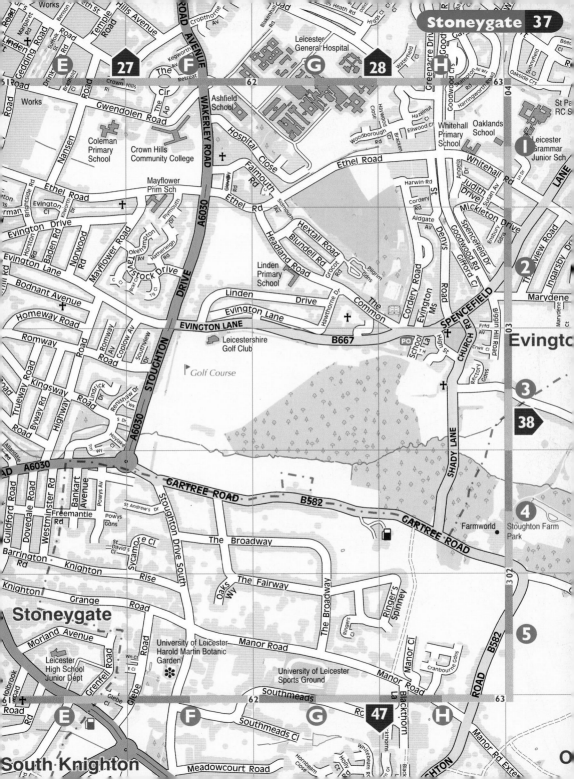

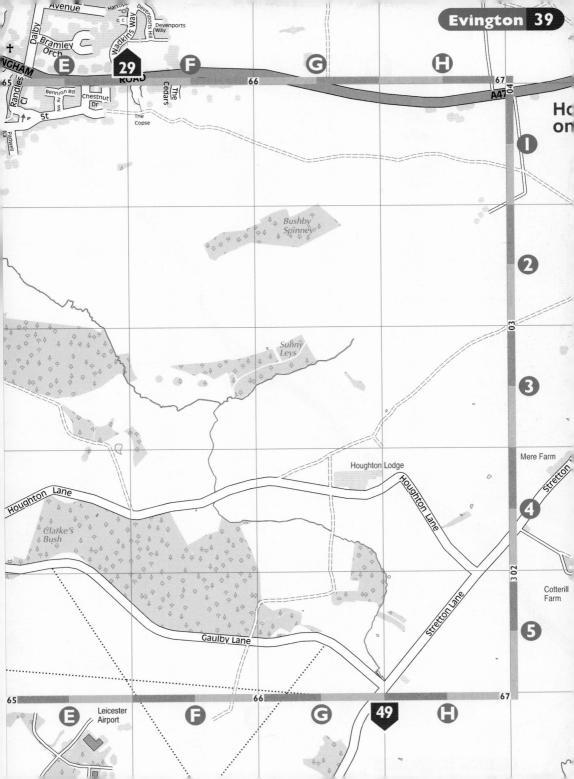

Avenue

Dalby

Bramley
Orch

Hartop
G C

Devenports
Hill

Devenports
Way

Wadkins Way

NGHAM

E

29
ROAD

Randles

65

St

Bennion Rd

Chestnut
Dr

The Cedars

F

The
Copse

66

G

A47
04

H

67

Padwell
Ra

Nw Av

I

Ho
on

Bushby
Spinney

2

03

Sunny
Leys

3

Mere Farm

Houghton Lodge

Stretton

4

Houghton   Lane

Houghton Lane

Clarke's
Bush

Cotterill
Farm

3 02

5

Gaulby Lane

Stretton Lane

65

66

49

67

E

Leicester
Airport

F

G

H

40

A   30   B   C   D

Works

448   49   Peckleton   Lane

Peckleton Common

1

Peckleton Lane
Business Park

Old
Brake

Dan's

Lane

010

2

Stretchnook
Farm

Roundabout
Spinney

ROAD

HINCKLEY

3

A47 LEICESTER ROAD

LEICESTER

Knoll Farm

Desford

Road

300

4

RD

Bassett
Farm

Clump
Farm

Bungalow
Farm

Desford Road

HINCKLEY ROAD

5

Hill
Farm

Moat
Close

299

Earl Shilton Road

448   49

A   B   52   C   D

I grid square represents 500 metres

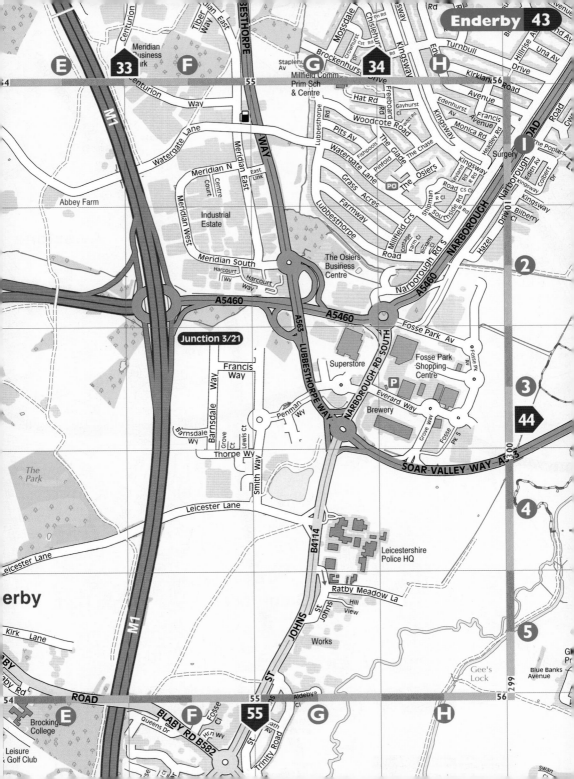

I grid square represents 500 metres

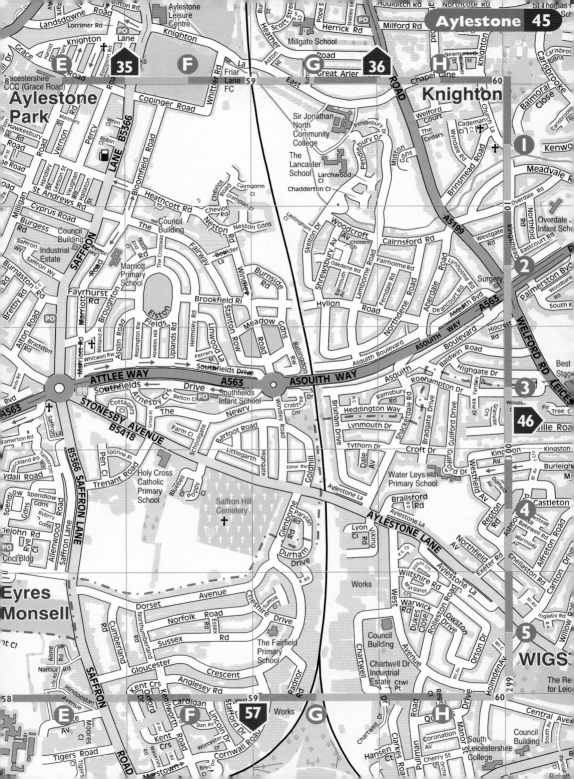

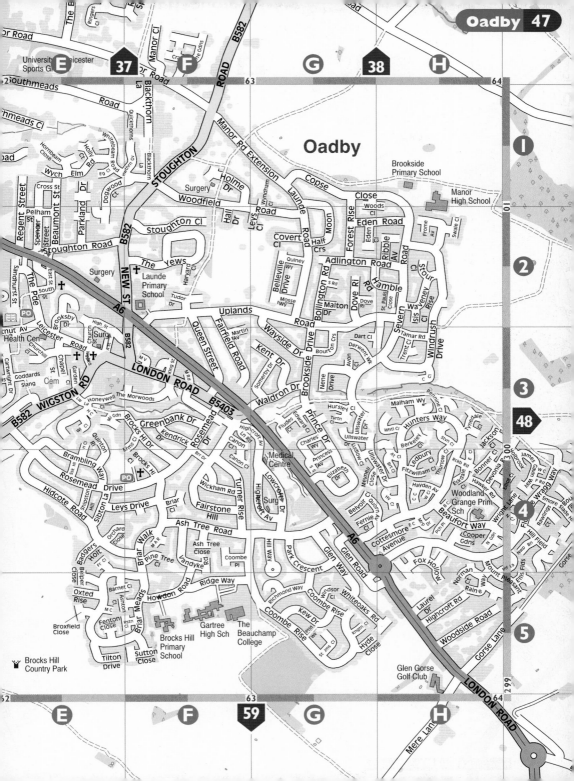

48

A **B** **38** **C** **D**

Gaulby Lane

464
65

1

Leicester Airport

Manor High School

Swale Cl

Cartree Road

2

Oadby Lodge Farm

Drive

Great Stretton +

3

47

Woodlands Ct

The Celandine Cl

The Spinney

Willow Herb Cl

Jacksdale

Bonner

Devonia Rd

James Gavin Way

Holbrook

Wright Lane

Eliiot Rd

Rawlins

The Pastures

Pipistrelle Way

Boulton Court

Chestnut Dr

Chestnut Drive

Chestnut Dr

The Av

4

Woodland Grange Prim Sch

Beaufort Way

Cooper Gdns

Hawker

Escdale

Thurow

Rickby Rd

Stvn Cl

Florence Wragg Way

Hill Field

Smore Side Hi

Ellis Flds

Gorse Lane

Glen Gorse

5

Norman Way

Mount Pleasant

Raine

Woodside Road

Gorse Lane

Hawthorne Cl

Sycamore Cl

River Sence

Stretton Hall Drive

LONDON ROAD

464
299

Chestnut Drive

A **B** **60** **C** **D**
65

Stre

1 grid square represents 500 metres

Stretton

E **39** F G H

6 67 68

Gaulby Lane

Mere Road

Cartree Road

I

Norton Gorse

2

Little Stretton

Kings Norton Lodge

Cornelias

3

Cartree Road

4

un Road

Stackley House

The Cottage

5

E F **61** G H

66 67 68

010

300

299

Brockey Farm

Brooklands Farm

Kirkby Road

A 44 4 B 45 C D

1

Barwell Fields Farm

Brockey Farm

White House Farm

2

The Brockey

Elwell

3

Glebe Farm

Bardon Road

Braddgate Road

Pearl Tree Cl

Apple Tree Cl

Yew Tree Cl

W T Cl

Willow Tree Cl

Ww T Cl

Frst Cl

Peckleton Cl

Ashleigh Gdns

Farm Road

William Bradford Community College

Charnwood Road The Drive Heath Lane

Berrywell Dr

Barwell

Stfrn Cl

Gartree Crescent

Heath Lane Sout

Harvey Cl

Byron Street Masefield Cl

Newlands Prim Sch PO

Belle Vue Rd Norton Rd

Mallory St

Rd

Field Way

HINCKLEY ROAD

Ross

Howard Close

ormnd

Aylesby Wy

W C Dr

Myrtle Cl

Nl

Cem

Regent St

Newlands Rd

Frisby Rd

First Vw Moore

Red Hall Rd

T C C

Queensway

Chesterfield Rd

Meadow Rd

Heathfield High School

A47

Doctors Fields

Hilyon Crs

Laburnum

Nursery Gdns

Balmoral Rd

En Rd

Oakdale Rd

Spilingham Av

Coronation Rd

Hc

Stapleton Lane

Russell

Cumberland

Hazel

Adrian Dr

Olyn Cl

Kirkby Road

Brockey Cl

Oxford St

Grg Wrd Ct

St George

Hastings

Shenton Rd

Mount Av

Ns Rd

T C O

Greenhill Dr

Holly La

Mayfield Wy

Ambled

4

Cedar

Kerry Cl

Holloway Cl

Penny La

Stfrd

Friswell La

Twnnd Rd

Barwell Inf Sch

East Cl

King St

Red Hall Dr

Shilton

Road

Elmshrst La

Leicester Rd

B581

Elmdale Rd

Birch Cl

Elmestho

Hereford Close

Ayrshire

Angus Cl

Bank Ter

Barwell Medical Centre

Chapel Street Works

Queen St

Hill St

Dawson's Lane

Hawthorne Way

CARRS HILL

The Crs

5

Boston Wy

Washington Av

Blackburn Rd

C Crs

Ln Rd

The Barracks

Stanley St

Barwell CE Jun Sch

PO

Queen St

Vw Wy

Inglenook

A47

Maryland Close

Moat Way

Ind Est

St Mary's Court

Chapel

Lane

Dovecote Wy

The Lane

Croft

Adct Cl

Church

LEICESTER ROAD

ELMESTHORPE LANE

A 44 4 B 45 C D

Mill Street

High Street

Ive Ivens Farm

Ivens Close

Common

The Crs

Billington Road W

Mary's Av

Crabtree Rd

Waterfall

Wensleydale

Wl Cl

Av

Wat

Moore La

G St La

1 grid square represents 500 metres

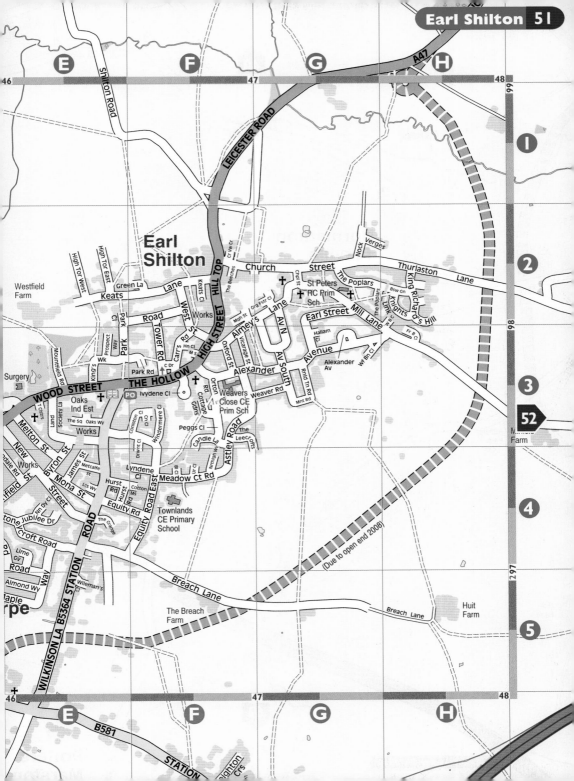

E F G H

A47

46 47 48

99

I

2

98

Shilton Road

LEICESTER ROAD

Earl Shilton

Westfield Farm

High Tor West

High Tor East

Green La

Keats Lane

Keats

Keats Cl

HILL TOP

West St

Works

The Beeches

Ct VW Cr

Church Street

Chpl St

St Peters RC Prim Sch

Nock Verges

Thurlaston Lane

King Richard's Hill

The Poplars

The Poplars

Bsw on

Knights Link

3

97

Park

Cl

Road

Prospect Way

Tower Rd

Carr's Rd

Hn Cl

C Dr

M St

Almey's Lane

Orton CI

St Osyth

AV N

Vicarage St

Earl Street

Mill Lane

Hallam CI

Fr B

W B Cl

52

Surgery

Mountfield Rd

King's

Wk

Park Rd

WOOD STREET

THE HOLLOW

PO

Ivydene Cl

Orton Rd

Cottage Gdns

Alexander

Weavers Close CE Prim Sch

Weaver Rd

Avenue

Alexander Av

Rnld Tm Rd

Mnt Rd

WF Bn Cl

M. Farm

Oaks Ind Est

T Clark's

Society La

Oaks Wy

The Sq

Works

J & G

Coniston CI

Windermere CI

Drwnt CI

Peggs CI

Candle La

Nrthgh Wy

The Leecrofts

Astley Road

Melton St

Byron St

New Works

James St

Metcalfe St

Lcs Wy

Lyndene CI

Bl CI

Ln CI

Meadow Ct Rd

4

nndale Rd

St

Mona Street

Hurst Rd

Hurst Rd

Cotton Ms

Equity Rd

Townlands CE Primary School

toney Jubilee Dr

Bn C

The Grange

Road

Equity Road East

(Due to open end 2008)

Croft Road

Lime Gv

rpe

New Road

Almond Wy

Way

WILKINSON LA B5364 STATION Road

Wileman's

Breach Lane

The Breach Farm

Breach Lane

Huit Farm

5

E F G H

46 47 48

B581

STATION

eighton Crs

52

A   B   **40**   C   D

448   49

Farm

Earl Shilton Road

Moat Close

1

99

Earl Shilton Road

LE9
Normanton Turville

Dairy Farm

2

Lane

98

3

51

Watery Gate Lane

Mirfield Farm

Pingle Lane

4

Mill Lane

297

Huit Farm

5

M69

448   49

A   B   **62**   C   D

Pingle

Potters Marston

1 grid square represents 500 metres

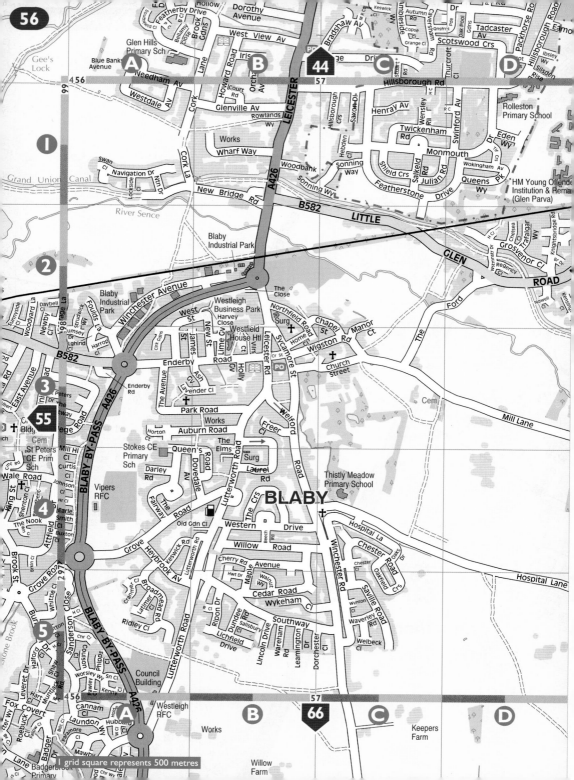

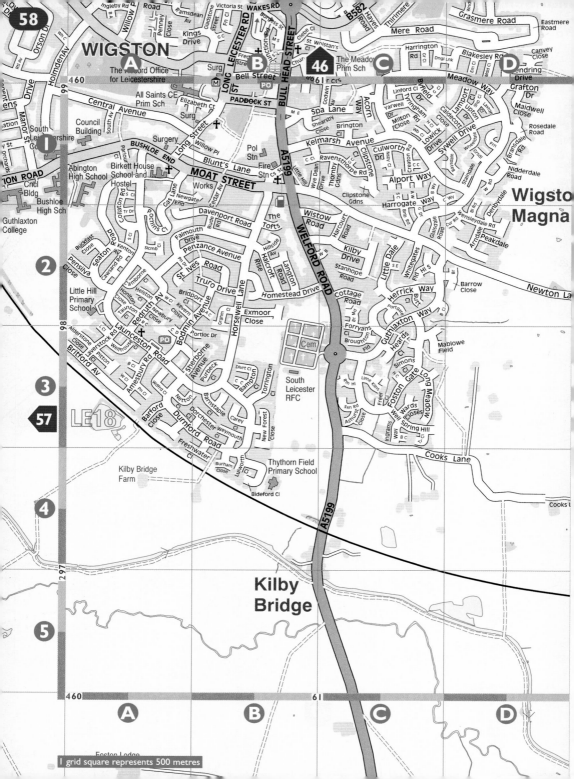

Broxfield Close

Fenton Close

Brstn Cl

Briar

Brocks Hill Primary School

Tilton Drive

Sutton Close

Gartree High Sch

The Beauchamp College

Combe Rise

Hyde Close

St Jms Cl

Kngtn Cl

Glen Gorse Golf Club

Brocks Hill Country

LONDON ROAD

Mere Lane

E **F** 47 **G** **H**

62 63 64 66

I

A6

Golf Course

Seven Oaks Farm

2

98

Highfield Farm

3

60

Lane

4

Glebe Farm

Glen Road

The Square

Post Office La

Wistow Road

297

New Har

5

Manor House

62 63 64

E **F** **G** **H**

Wain Bridge

Grand Union Ca

Newton
Harcourt

The
Woodlands

1 grid square represents 500 metres

Road

E

F

49

G

H

66

67

68

99

I

L

ark

Scotland

Coverside Road

Solmey View

The Chase

Stonehill Drive

Fernie Dene

Woodbury Rise

St Cuthbert's CE Prim Sch

Hilltop Avenue

Cherry Grove

St Thomas's Road

Glen Oaks

Washbrook Lane

Burton Overy

Baileys Lane

Elms Lane

2

98

Main Street

Back La

Carlton Lane

Car

Road

Bell La

The Gravel

3

Great Glen

Works

Burton Brook

4

Great Glen House

Burton Grange

Mayns Lane

297

5

A6

6

E

F

G

H

67

68

London Road

Burton Brook

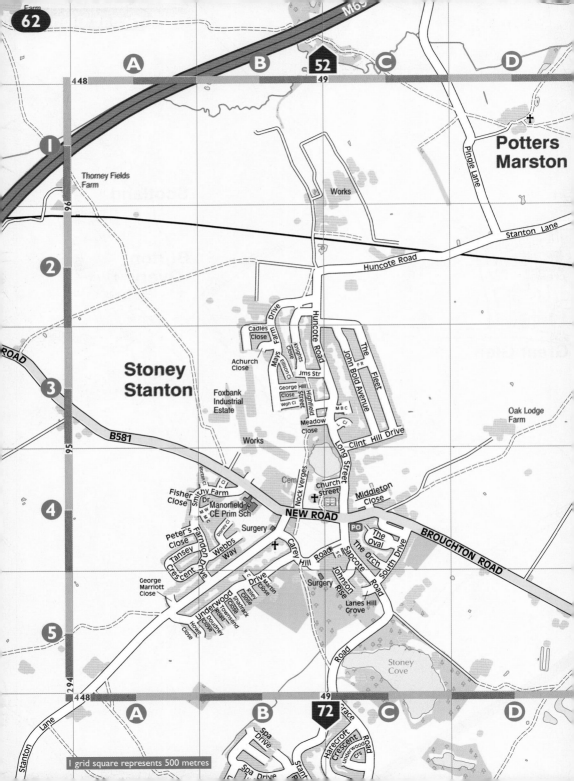

A   448   **B**   **52**   49   **C**   **D**

M69

I 96

Thorney Fields Farm

Potters Marston

Stanton Lane

Works

Huncote Road

2 95

Stoney Stanton

Cadles Close

Achurch Close

Foxbank Industrial Estate

Mays Farm Drive

Knights Close

Ellison Cl

Jms Str

Huncote Road

George Hill Close

Wgn Cl

Highfield Street

Meadow Close

The Fleet

F R

John Bold Avenue

M B C

L Cl

Oak Lodge Farm

3 ROAD

B581

Works

Clint Hill Drive

4

Fisher Close

Smithy Farm

Dr

M W M Cl

Peter's Close

Tansey

Farndon Drive

Crescent

Disney Cl

Webbs Way

Manorfield CE Prim Sch

Surgery

Nock Verges

Cem

Church Street

Long Street

Middleton Close

NEW ROAD

PO

The Oval

The Orch

South Drive

BROUGHTON ROAD

George Marriott Close

Underwood Drive

Martin Close

Riley Close

Sherrack Close

Townsend Road

Courtney Close

Howe Close

Carey Hill Road

Surgery

Johnson Rise

Sapcote Road

Lanes Hill Grove

5 294

Road

Stoney Cove

448   **A**   **B**   **72**   49   **C**   **D**

Stanton Lane

Spa Drive

Spa Drive

Harecroft Crescent

Stant

Terrace

Underwood CFS

Road

I grid square represents 500 metres

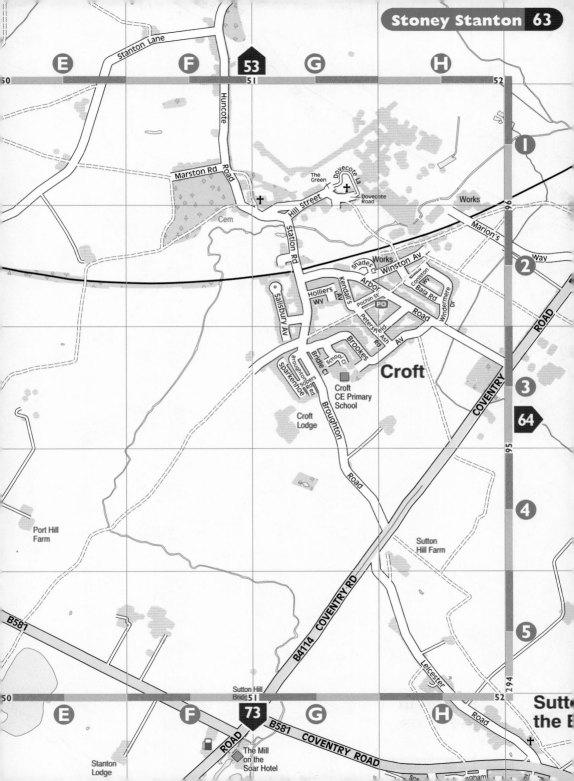

E F 53 G H

Stanton Lane

Huncote Road

Marston Rd

The Green

Dovecote La

Dovecote Road

Cem

Hill Street

Station Rd

Works

Marion's

Way

Works

Shades

Winston Av

Arbor

Coniston

Wy

Bala Rd

Windermere Dr

Salisbury Av

Holliers Wy

Kendall's Av

Pochin St

PO

Road

Petersfield Rd

Ash Av

Brookes

School Cl

Bridle Cl

Broughton Rd

Ropers Rd

Sparkenhoe

Croft

Croft CE Primary School

Croft Lodge

Broughton Road

COVENTRY ROAD

Port Hill Farm

Sutton Hill Farm

B581

B4114 COVENTRY RD

Leicester Road

Sutton Hill Bridge 51

The Mill on the Soar Hotel

Stanton Lodge

Road

B581 COVENTRY ROAD

Sutton the B

I

2

3

64

4

5

294

96

95

E F 73 G H

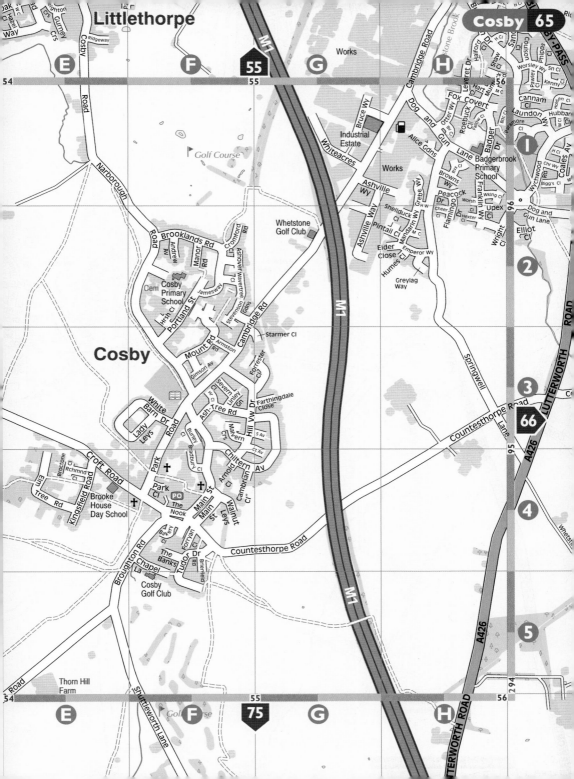

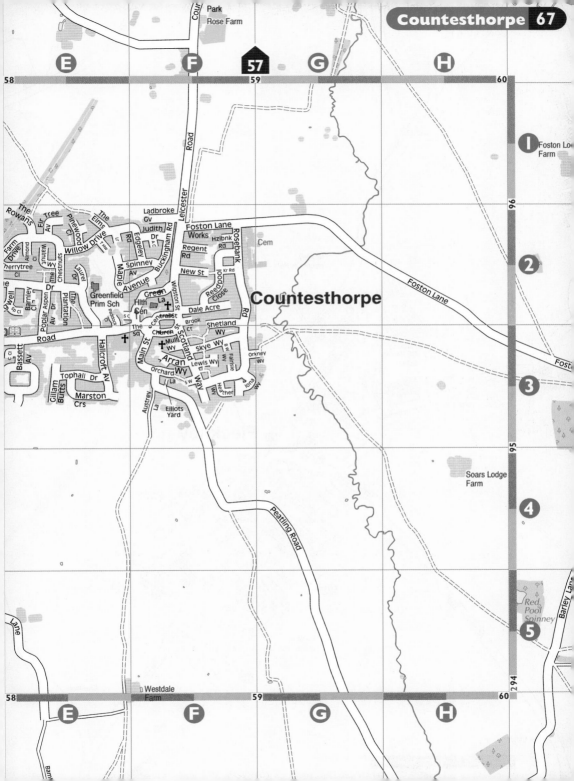

Park
Rose Farm

E F **57** G H

58 59 60

I Foston Lo
Farm

96

The
Rowans
Fir Tree
Pinewood
The Elms
Ladbroke
Gv
Judith
Dr

Leicester Road

Foston Lane

2

Farm
Drive
Willow Drive
Walnut
Almond
Edgeley
Rd
Buckingham Rd
Works
Regent
Rd
Hzlbnk
Rd
Rosebank
Cem

Foston Lane

Cherrytree
Cl
The
Chestnuts
Laurel
Spinney
Av
Maple
New St
Kr Rd

Countesthorpe

Barley
Dr
Poplar
The
plantation
Av
Aspen
Greenfield
Prim Sch
Avenue
Green
Hlth
Cen
La
Paddock
Central St
Wistow St
Reedpool
Close
Dale Acre
Rd

well
Cl
Bassett
Av
Road
Hallcroft
Av
The
Sq
Main St
Church
Mull
Wy
Scotland
Skye Wy
Brook
Ct
Shetland
Wy
B W
Orkney
Wy

95

Tophall
Dr
Gillam
Butts
Marston
Crs
Arran
Wy
Orchard
La
Austrey
La
Lewis Wy
Fairisle
Heather
S W
Iona
Wy

3

Elliots
Yard

Soars Lodge
Farm

4

Peatling Road

Lane

Red
Pool
Spinney

Barley Lane

5

294

Westdale
Farm

58 59 60

E F G H

Fost

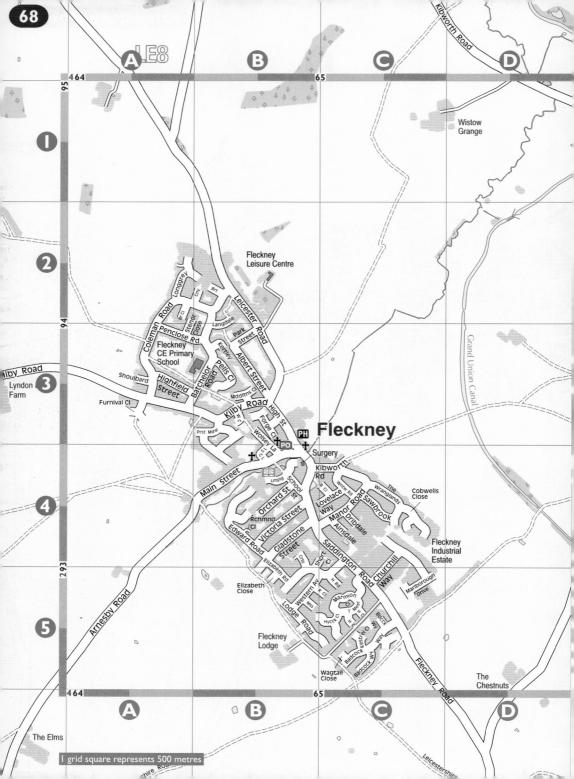

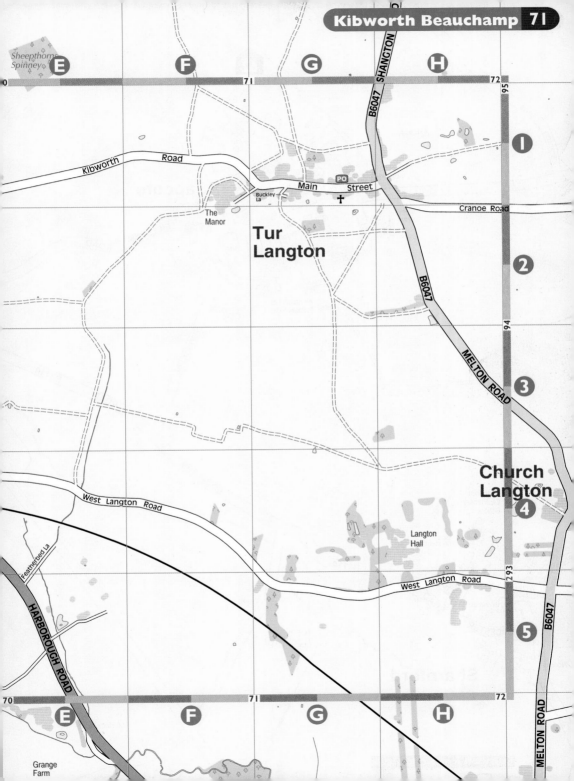

Sheepthorne Spinney

E **F** **G** **H**

0   71   72   95

I

Kibworth   Road

SHANGTON

B6047

Buckley La

Main   Street   PO   ✝

Cranoe Road

The Manor

Tur Langton

2

B6047

94

MELTON ROAD

3

Church Langton

West   Langton   Road

4

Langton Hall

Featherbed La

93

West   Langton   Road

HARBOROUGH ROAD

5

B6047

70   71   72

E **F** **G** **H**

Grange Farm

MELTON ROAD

Sapcote

Sharnford

LE10

The Homestead

River Soar

Springfield Farm

Sharnford CE Primary School

All Saints CE Primary School

Cem

Pougher Close

Wesley Cl

Brown's Close

Mill Close

Livesey Drive

Hinckley Road

Spa Drive

Spa Drive

Stanton Road

Sapcote Road

Grace Road

Harecroft Crescent

Underwood CFS

Frewen Drive

Penfield Close

Buckwell Rd

Mnr Rd

Kirby Close

Church St

Neville Close

Smith Close

Mt Gdns

Church St

Castle Close

Park Road

Bassett Lane

Cook's Lane

New Walk

Morley Rd

Calvert

Crescent

B4669 LEICESTER ROAD

Sharnford Road

COVENTRY ROAD B4114

B4114

Stanton Lane

Aston Lane

Holyoak Dr

Park W

Henson Way

Brookfield

Halls Crescent

Halls CFS

Mill

St Helen's Cl

Chapel La

Chapel St

ROAD

LEICESTER

Sharnbrook Gdns

School La

High Lees

Fosse Cl

Works

Works

Works

Stoney Cove

PO

PO

62

448   95

49

94

448

49

E F 63 G H

B581

B4114 COVE

Leicester Road

0 51 52 95

Sutton Bridge

Sutto
the E

B581 COVENTRY ROAD

COVENTRY ROAD

Stanton Lodge

The Mill on the Soar Hotel

I

Soar
Mill La

Gr Av

Uppingham Dr

Whitby Cl

Melton Dr

K Cl

S C

Warwick Road

Warwick Road

Coventry

Lichfield Avenue

Works

COVENTRY

COVENTRY

Road

Merton Cl

The Av

Orchard R

High Cl

Crs

Estley Rd

Whinham Av

Malling Avenue

Denison R

Amsden

2

Baldwin Rd

Cr

Gorham Rd

Blenheim

Bramley

Grange Rd

Glebe Rd

Cm Av

Coventry Rd

Primethorpe

Orchard C Primary School

294

3

74

Fosse Farm

Sutton Lodge

Lodge Farm

Cem

Frol

4

293

Leire Lane

The Bungalow

5

Lodge Farm

Lodge Farm Cottages

Broughton Road

Broughton Lane

50 51 52

E F G H

Frolesworth Lodge

74

A   B   **64**   C   D

452   53

Sutton in the Elms

I

Broughton Astley

Cottage Lane
Industrial Estate

Thomas Estley
Community
College

Old Mill
Co Prim
Sch

73

Orchard CE
Primary School

Lodge
Farm

Mill
Farm

Cem

The
Bungalow

Arkwright
Cottages

Hallbrook Primary
School

Muncaster
Cl

76

452   53

A   B   **76**   C   D

I grid square represents 500 metres

Valley View

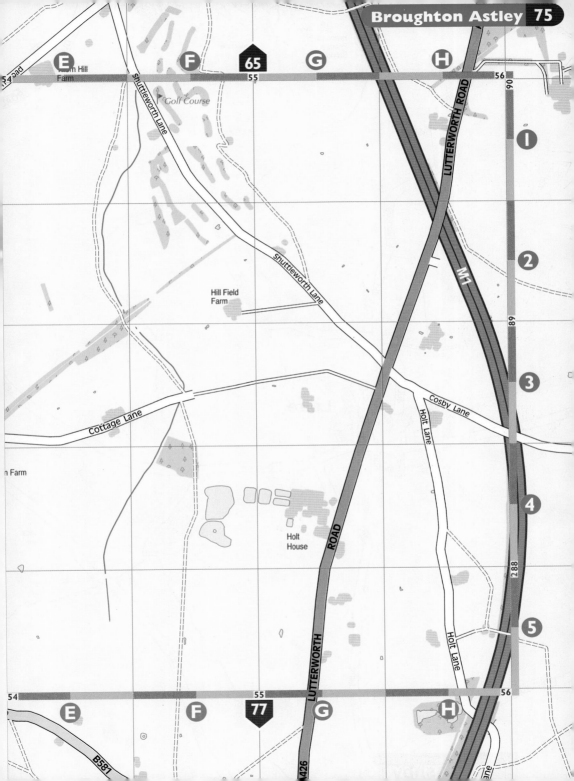

452

A

Broughton Lane

Hallbrook
Primary
School

Crowfoo
Murray
Plough Pinel
Ceveze Way
Juncaster
Cotsbrook Way
Speer

Cran
Fxglv

B

Benford
Cl

74

53

C

Orchid
Pl

Dunton Road

DU

D

ROAD

1

16

Valley View
Farm

Stemborough Lane

2

White
House
Close

Andrews Cl

Broughton Lane

Back Lane

Back Lane

3

Station Lane

Main Lane

Walgs
Orch
Ardn St

Leire

St Peter's
Cl

Road

90

Leir

St Margarets
Dr

Little
La
The
Gn

Dunton   Road

Leire

4

Leire Lane

Lodge
Farm

5

Froleswort

289

452

Road

Leire Lane

Dunt

Lane

53

A

B

C

D

I grid square represents 500 metres

Ashby

E F **75** G H

54 55 56

I

91

B591

BROUGHTON LANE

A426

M1

Holt Lane

Ashby Magna

2

Old Forge

Peveril Rd

COOPER'S LANE

Station Road

Elfin Gv

LUTTERWORTH

Dunton Bassett

Elwells Av

Main St

Chapel Close

Wakes Cl

PO

Bennetts Hl

Dunton Bassett Prim Sch

The Mt

Little Lunnon

Loves Lane

Church

Church Cl

Church Lane

Lane

Oak Spinney

3

90

Gilmorton Rd

4

Low Spinney Farm

M1

LUTTERWORTH ROAD

5

Gilmorton

289

Ashby Lodge

426

E F G H

54 55 56

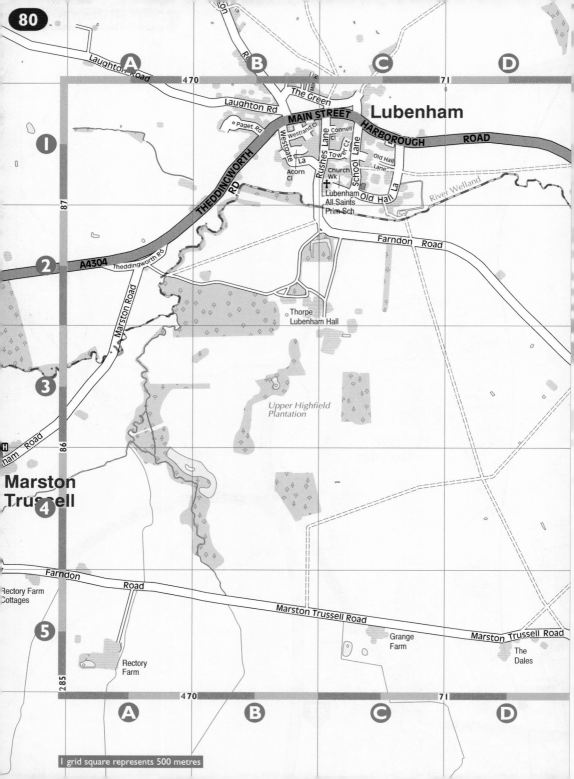

Southleigh Gv
Fairway
Fairfield
Brooke House Colle
Heygate
Orch St
Shrpsnr Pl
Roman Way
Saxon St
Hill
Conduit

E   72   **F**   **78**   **G**   73   **H**   **I**

Adamswood Cl
Spinney Cl
Fieldhead Cl
Knoll Street
Highcross St
Logan St
Morley St
Spencer St
Harcourt St
East Street
Hearth Street
Market Harborough CE Primary School
Works
Old School
Nelson St
Highfield St
St
High St The So
Three Swans Htl
Talbot
Works
Symington Wy
M

Brookfield Road
The Pstrs
Gardiner Street
Wartnaby Street
Charles St
Clarke Street
Mkt Harborough District Hospital
St Josephs RC Prim Sch
Theatre
Brooklands Gdns
Superstore
Westfield Cl

A4304 LUBENHAM HILL   COVENTRY ROAD A4304
Medical Centre
Yeomanry Ct
Walcot Rd
Springfield
Springfield Crs
Nithside

Riley Cl
Millers Gdns
Springhill
Rhodes Cl
VIEW
Elm Dr
Willow Crs
Farndale
Welland Park Community College
Nithsdal
2
Auriga
The
NORTHAMPTON

MARKET HARBOROUGH
Rugby Close
Summers
Pear Tree Gdns
Pride
Road
Fairfax
Naseby Cl
Newcombe St
Cross St
Patrick St
Gladstone St
Granville Street
Street

Road
Astley Cl
De Lisle
Stuart
Ireton Road
Ireton Rd
Bath Road
Works
Caxton St
Clipston Street
Crosby Rd
Lathkill
3

Works
LE16
Western   Avenue
PO Sq
Lenthall
Green La
Hurlingham Rd
Haddonian Rd
Tungstone

Leicestershire County
Northamptonshire County
Essex Gdns
Cromwell Gdns
Balfour Gdns
Howard Wy
Huntingdon Gdns
Rupert Road
Rowan
Rd
Ansuk
82
borough Leisure Centre

Farndon Road
Fleetwood Gdns
Howard Wy
Rochester Gdns
Bishop
Selby Cl
Dallison Cl
Club House

Butler Cl
Strttn
Hrtsn Cl
Maurice Rd
Rainsborough
Crescent
Gardens
Argyle Pk
Vaughan Cl
4
worth FC

Watson Av
Barnaby Rd
Gerrard Gdns
Lindsey Gdns
Ritchie Pk
Farndon Fields Primary School

Lubenham Road
Harborough Road
The Iealand
Brierley Farm
Hopton Flds

Street
Main
New House Farm
Home Farm Cl

5

Golf Course
Market Harborough Golf Club
HARBOROUGH

East Farndon
E   72   **F**   **G**   73   **H**   285

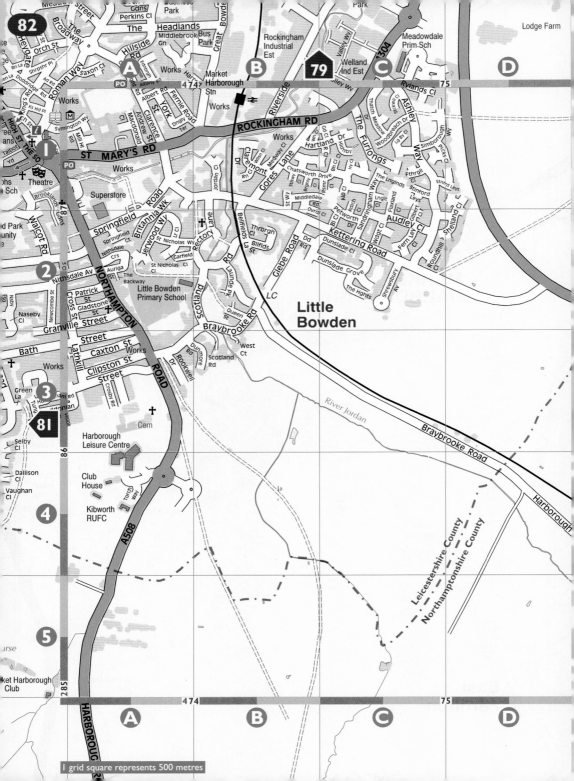

A427

Lingley Lane

Church Lane

G

H **Dingley**

E F

76 77

Dingley
Lodge

MAIN

ROAD A427

I

Woodlands

Home
Close

Braybrooke Road

Dingley
Warren

87

2

Dingley
Wood

HARBOROUGH ROAD

3

86

HARBOROUGH

4

Commons
Farm

ROAD

Road

5

Braybrooke
Lower Lodge

285

76 77

E F G H

Church
Close

84

Springfields Farm

Bitteswell Lodge

Woodby Lane

I

Hawke Way

Boulevard

Harrier Parkway

2

Vulcan Way

Hunter

Wellington Pkwy

Field Farm

Blakenhall Farm

85

3

Hunter Bvd

Magna Park Distribution Centre

Wellington Parkway

4

Hunter Boulevard

Wellington Parkway

Shackelton Wy

Hunter Bvd

COVENTRY ROAD A4303

Wood Bridge

284

Padge Hall Farm

Glebe Fm

B4027

5

ROAD

Moorbarns Farm

451 52

A B C D

1 grid square represents 500 metres

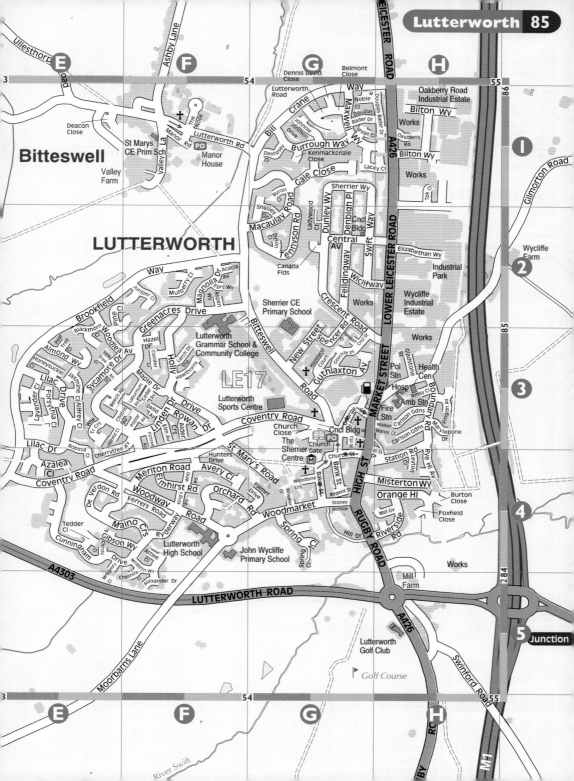

Anstey 17 C1
Aylestone 44 D2
Aylestone Park 45 E1
Barkby 13 H4
Barkby Thorpe 13 F5
Barwell 50 A3
Beaumont Leys 18 B3
Belgrave 19 F5
Birstall 11 G5
Bitteswell 85 E1
Blaby 56 B4
Bondman Hays 14 C4
Braunstone 34 A4
Broughton Astley 74 C3
Burton Overy 61 H2
Bushby 29 H5
Church Langton 71 H4
Clarendon Park 36 A4
Cosby 65 E3
Cossington 4 A1
Countesthorpe 67 F2

Croft 63 H3
Cropston 9 H2
Crown Hills 28 A5
Desford 30 C2
Dunton Bassett 77 E2
Earl Shilton 51 F2
East Farndon 81 E5
East Goscote 5 H1
Elmesthorpe 50 D5
Enderby 42 D5
Evington 38 A3
Eyres Monsell 44 D5
Field Head 6 D4
Fleckney 68 B3
Glenfield 24 A2
Glen Parva 44 B5
Great Bowden 79 F3
Great Glen 61 E3
Great Stretton 48 C2
Groby 16 B3
Hamilton 21 H3

Highfields 3 J6
Humberstone 27 H5
Huncote 53 H4
Kibworth Beauchamp 70 B4
Kibworth Harcourt 70 B1
Kilby Bridge 58 B5
Kirby Fields 32 D1
Kirby Muxloe 45 H1
Knighton 45 H1
Knighton Fields 35 H4
Leicester 3 F3
Leicester Forest East 33 E3
Leire 76 B5
Little Bowden 82 B2
Little Stretton 49 G3
Littlethorpe 55 E5
Lubenham 80 C1
Lutterworth 85 E2
Market Harborough 81 E2
Markfield 6 A5
Mowmacre Hill 19 E2

Narborough 54 A3
Nether Hall 28 D2
New Parks 24 D3
Newton Harcourt 60 A5
Newtown Linford 7 H4
Normanton Turville 52 B2
North Evington 27 G4
Oadby 47 G1
Potters Marston 62 D1
Primethorpe 73 H2
Queniborough 5 H4
Ratby 22 C2
Red Hill 54 C3
Rushey Mead 20 C3
Sapcote 72 C1
Scotland 61 H1
Scraptoft 29 E2
Sharnford 72 A5
Smeeton Westerby 69 H5
South Knighton 46 B1
South Wigston 57 F2

Spinney Hills 27 E5
Stocking Farm 18 D4
Stoneygate 37 E5
Stoney Stanton 62 A3
Stoughton 38 C4
Sutton in the Elms 74 A1
Syston 11 E5
Thurcaston 10 A2
Thurlaston 41 F5
Thurmaston 13 E5
Thurnby 29 E5
Tur Langton 71 G2
Wanlip 11 E3
Westcotes 34 D1
Western Park 24 D4
Whetstone 55 C4
Wigston 46 A5
Wigston Magna 58 D1
The Woodlands 60 C5

USING THE STREET INDEX

Street names are listed alphabetically. Each street name is followed by its postal town or area locality, the Postcode District, the page number, and the reference to the square in which the name is found.

Standard index entries are shown as follows:

Abbey Ct LEIN LE4.................. 19 F5

Street names and selected addresses not shown on the map due to scale restrictions are shown in the index with an asterisk:

The Arcade WGSTN LE18 * 46 B5

GENERAL ABBREVIATIONS

ACC...ACCESS	CTYD...COURTYARD	HLS...HILLS	MWY...MOTORWAY	SE...SOUTH EAST
ALY...ALLEY	CUTT...CUTTINGS	HO...HOUSE	N...NORTH	SER...SERVICE AREA
AP...APPROACH	CV...COVE	HOL...HOLLOW	NE...NORTH EAST	SH...SHORE
AR...ARCADE	CYN...CANYON	HOSP...HOSPITAL	NW...NORTH WEST	SHOP...SHOPPING
ASS...ASSOCIATION	DEPT...DEPARTMENT	HRB...HARBOUR	O/P...OVERPASS	SKWY...SKYWAY
AV...AVENUE	DL...DALE	HTH...HEATH	OFF...OFFICE	SMT...SUMMIT
BCH...BEACH	DM...DAM	HTS...HEIGHTS	ORCH...ORCHARD	SOC...SOCIETY
BLDS...BUILDINGS	DR...DRIVE	HVN...HAVEN	OV...OVAL	SP...SPUR
BND...BEND	DRO...DROVE	HWY...HIGHWAY	PAL...PALACE	SPR...SPRING
BNK...BANK	DRY...DRIVEWAY	IMP...IMPERIAL	PAS...PASSAGE	SQ...SQUARE
BR...BRIDGE	DWGS...DWELLINGS	IN...INLET	PAV...PAVILION	ST...STREET
BRK...BROOK	E...EAST	IND EST...INDUSTRIAL ESTATE	PDE...PARADE	STN...STATION
BTM...BOTTOM	EMB...EMBANKMENT	INF...INFIRMARY	PH...PUBLIC HOUSE	STRD...STRAND
BUS...BUSINESS	EMBY...EMBASSY	INFO...INFORMATION	PK...PARK	SW...SOUTH WEST
BVD...BOULEVARD	ESP...ESPLANADE	INT...INTERCHANGE	PKWY...PARKWAY	TDG...TRADING
BY...BYPASS	EST...ESTATE	IS...ISLAND	PL...PLACE	TER...TERRACE
CATH...CATHEDRAL	EX...EXCHANGE	JCT...JUNCTION	PLN...PLAIN	THWY...THROUGHWAY
CEM...CEMETERY	EXPY...EXPRESSWAY	JTY...JETTY	PLNS...PLAINS	TNL...TUNNEL
CEN...CENTRE	EXT...EXTENSION	KG...KING	PLZ...PLAZA	TOLL...TOLLWAY
CFT...CROFT	F/O...FLYOVER	KNL...KNOLL	POL...POLICE STATION	TPK...TURNPIKE
CH...CHURCH	FC...FOOTBALL CLUB	L...LAKE	PR...PRINCE	TR...TRACK
CHA...CHASE	FK...FORK	LA...LANE	PREC...PRECINCT	TRL...TRAIL
CHYD...CHURCHYARD	FLD...FIELD	LDG...LODGE	PREP...PREPARATORY	TWR...TOWER
CIR...CIRCLE	FLDS...FIELDS	LGT...LIGHT	PRIM...PRIMARY	U/P...UNDERPASS
CIRC...CIRCUS	FLS...FALLS	LK...LOCK	PROM...PROMENADE	UNI...UNIVERSITY
CL...CLOSE	FM...FARM	LKS...LAKES	PRS...PRINCESS	UPR...UPPER
CLFS...CLIFFS	FT...FORT	LNDG...LANDING	PRT...PORT	V...VALE
CMP...CAMP	FWY...FREEWAY	LTL...LITTLE	PT...POINT	VA...VALLEY
CNR...CORNER	FY...FERRY	LWR...LOWER	PTH...PATH	VIAD...VIADUCT
CO...COUNTY	GA...GATE	MAG...MAGISTRATE	PZ...PIAZZA	VIL...VILLA
COLL...COLLEGE	GAL...GALLERY	MAN...MANSIONS	QD...QUADRANT	VIS...VISTA
COM...COMMON	GDN...GARDEN	MD...MEAD	QU...QUEEN	VLG...VILLAGE
COMM...COMMISSION	GDNS...GARDENS	MDW...MEADOWS	QY...QUAY	VLS...VILLAS
CON...CONVENT	GLD...GLADE	MEM...MEMORIAL	R...RIVER	VW...VIEW
COT...COTTAGE	GLN...GLEN	MI...MILL	RBT...ROUNDABOUT	W...WEST
COTS...COTTAGES	GN...GREEN	MKT...MARKET	RD...ROAD	WD...WOOD
CP...CAPE	GND...GROUND	MKTS...MARKETS	RDG...RIDGE	WHF...WHARF
CPS...COPSE	GRA...GRANGE	ML...MALL	REP...REPUBLIC	WK...WALK
CR...CREEK	GRG...GARAGE	MNR...MANOR	RES...RESERVOIR	WKS...WALKS
CREM...CREMATORIUM	GT...GREAT	MS...MEWS	RFC...RUGBY FOOTBALL CLUB	WLS...WELLS
CRS...CRESCENT	GTWY...GATEWAY	MSN...MISSION	RI...RISE	WY...WAY
CSWY...CAUSEWAY	GV...GROVE	MT...MOUNT	RP...RAMP	YD...YARD
CT...COURT	HGR...HIGHER	MTN...MOUNTAIN	RW...ROW	YHA...YOUTH HOSTEL
CTRL...CENTRAL	HL...HILL	MTS...MOUNTAINS	S...SOUTH	
CTS...COURTS		MUS...MUSEUM	SCH...SCHOOL	

POSTCODE TOWNS AND AREA ABBREVIATIONS

COAL...Coalville	LEI...Leicester	LUTT...Lutterworth	RLEINE/SYS...Rural Leicester north & east/Syston
END/NAR...Enderby/Narborough	LEIE...Leicester east	LUTT...Lutterworth	RLEIS/BBY...Rural Leicester south/Blaby
GBY/RBY...Groby/Ratby	LEIN...Leicester north	MKTHBORO...Market Harborough	RLEIW/BAR...Rural Leicester west/Barwell
HINC...Hinckley	LEIS...Leicester south	RLBORO...Rural Loughborough	WGSTN...Wigston
	LEIW...Leicester west		

Index – streets

A

Abbey Ct LEIN LE4.................. 19 F5
Abbey Court Rd LEIN LE4 .. 19 F4
Abbey Dr LEIN LE4 .... 19 F4
Abbey Ga LEIN LE4 .... 26 A3
Abbey La LEIN LE4 .... 19 E5
Abbey Mdw LEIN LE4 .... 26 B1
Abbeymead Rd LEIN LE4 .. 19 F4
Abbey Park Rd LEIN LE4 ...... 26 B1

Abbey Park St LEIN LE4 ...... 26 C2
Abbey Ri LEIN LE4 .... 19 F4
Abbey Rd END/NAR LE19 ... 55 F2
Abbey St LEI LE1 .... 3 F1
   MKTHBORO 81 H1
Abbots Cl LEIE LE5 .... 28 B2
Abbotsford Rd LEIE LE5 .... 28 B2
Abbots's Rd North LEIE LE5 ... 28 B2
Abbots Rd South LEIE LE5 .. 28 B2
Abbotts Cl RLEINE/SYS LE7 ... 12 C1

Aber Rd LEIS LE2 .... 36 D3
Abingdon Rd LEIS LE2 .... 3 K7
Abney St LEIE LE5 .... 36 C1
Acacia Av LEIW LE3 .... 11 H4
   LUTT LE17 .... 85 F2
Acacia Cl LEIW LE3 .... 32 D5
Acan Wy END/NAR LE19 .... 54 C4
Acer Cl END/NAR LE19 ...... 54 C4
   LEIN LE4 .... 18 C3
Achurch Cl RLEIW/BAR LE9 .. 62 B3
Acorn Cl LEIN LE4 .... 19 G1
   MKTHBORO 80 B1

Acorn St LEIN LE4 .... 19 H5
Acorn Wy WGSTN LE18 ..... 58 C1
Acre Rd LEIE LE3 .... 33 E2
Adam & Eve St
   MKTHBORO 78 D5
Adamswood Cl
   MKTHBORO 81 H1
Adcock Rd LEIW LE3 .... 25 F3
Adcote Cl RLEIW/BAR LE9 .. 50 A5
Adderley Rd LEIS LE2 .... 36 B4
Adelaide Cl LEIN LE4 .... 10 C5
Adlington Rd LEIS LE2 ...... 47 G2

Adrian Dr RLEIW/BAR LE9 .. 50 A4
Agar St LEIN LE4 .... 26 D1
Aikman Av LEIW LE3 .... 24 D2
Aikman Cl LEIW LE3 .... 25 E3
Ainsdale RLEIS/BBY LE8 .... 68 C4
Ainsdale Rd LEIW LE3 .... 25 E5
Aintree Cl LEIE LE5 .... 38 B1
Aintree Crs LEIS LE2 .... 47 H4
Airedale Cl LUTT LE17 .... 76 B5
Aisne Rd LEIS LE2 .... 45 E5
Alan Cl LEIN LE4 .... 19 H5
Aland Gdns RLEIW/BAR LE9 .. 74 C3

Albany Rd MKTHBORO LE16 78 D5
Alberta St LEIE LE5 3 J2
Albert Ct RLEIS/BBY LE8 55 H3
Albert Rd LEIS LE2 36 C3
MKTHBORO LE16 82 A1
Albert St RLEINE/SYS LE7 13 F1
RLEIS/BBY LE8 68 B3
RLEIS/BBY LE8 70 A1
Albion St LEI LE1 3 F5
LEIS LE2 47 E3
RLEINE/SYS LE7 5 E5
RLEINE/SYS LE7 17 G1
WGSTN LE18 57 F1
Alcester Dr LEIE LE5 38 B1
Alcott Cl LEIW LE3 25 E5
Aldeby Cl END/NAR LE19 55 G1
LEIS LE2 44 B4
Alder Cl LEIW LE3 32 D3
Alder Crs LUTT LE17 85 F3
Alderleigh Rd LEIS LE2 57 E2
Alderstone Cl WGSTN LE18 58 A3
Alderton Cl LEIN LE4 20 A2
Aldgate Av LEIE LE5 37 H2
Alexander Av END/NAR LE19 42 C5
RLEIW/BAR LE9 51 F3
Alexander Dr LUTT LE17 85 F5
Alexander St LEIW LE3 2 C3
Alexandra Rd LEIS LE2 36 D4
Alexandra St END/NAR LE19 55 E3
LEIN LE4 12 C4
Alfreton Rd WGSTN LE18 46 A4
Alice Gdns RLEIS/BBY LE8 65 H1
Allandale Rd LEIS LE2 37 E3
Allenwood Rd LEIS LE2 45 E4
Allerton Dr LEIW LE3 25 E1
Allexton Gdns LEIW LE3 24 B4
Allfrey Cl LUTT LE17 85 E3
Alliance Rd LEIW LE3 24 A3
Allington Dr LEIN LE4 11 H3
Allington St LEIN LE4 26 D2
Allinson Cl LEIE LE5 28 A4
Alloway Cl LEIN LE4 20 B3
All Saints Cl RLEIW/BAR LE9 72 B2
All Saints Rd LEIW LE3 2 C2
RLEINE/SYS LE7 10 B2
Alma St LEIW LE3 25 G4
Almey's La RLEIW/BAR LE9 51 F3
Almond Cl RLEIS/BBY LE8 67 E2
Almond Rd LEIS LE2 35 H2
Almond Wy LUTT LE17 85 E3
RLEIW/BAR LE9 51 E5
Alport Wy WGSTN LE18 58 C1
Altar Stones La COAL LE67 6 A1
Althorp Cl LEIS LE2 44 B3
MKTHBORO LE16 82 C1
Alton Rd LEIS LE2 45 E3
Alvaston Rd LEIW LE3 34 D4
Alvecote Rd LEIS LE2 44 D3
Alvington Wy
MKTHBORO LE16 78 B4
Alyssum Wy END/NAR LE19 54 B2
Amadis Rd LEIN LE4 18 A3
Amanda Rd LEIS LE2 44 B4
Ambassador Rd LEIE LE5 28 A4
Amber Gate Cl
RLEIW/BAR LE9 74 C3
Ambergate Dr LEIN LE4 11 F4
Amberley Cl LEIN LE4 20 C1
Ambler Cl WGSTN LE18 58 B2
Ambleside RLEIW/BAR LE9 50 C4
Ambleside Cl LEIS LE2 44 C5
Ambleside Dr LEIS LE2 44 C5
Ambleside Wy LEIS LE2 44 C5
Ambrose Cl LEIW LE3 25 F4
Amersham Rd LEIN LE4 25 H1
Amesbury Rd WGSTN LE18 58 A3
Amhurst Cl LEIW LE3 24 D1
Amos Rd LEIW LE3 24 B4
Amsden Ri RLEIW/BAR LE9 73 H2
Amyson Rd LEIE LE5 28 C4
Amy St LEIW LE3 44 A1
Anchor St LEIN LE4 19 F5
Andover St LEIS LE2 3 H5
Andrew Av RLEIW/BAR LE9 65 F2
Andrewes Cl LEIW LE3 2 A4
Andrewes St LEIW LE3 2 A5
Andrewes Wk LEIW LE3 2 A5
Andrew Macdonald Cl
MKTHBORO LE16 82 A1
Andrew Rd RLEINE/SYS LE7 17 G1
Andrews Cl LUTT LE17 76 B2
Aneford Rd LEIN LE4 27 G1
Angela Dr LEIE LE5 37 H1
Anglesey Rd WGSTN LE18 45 F5
Angus Cl RLEINE/SYS LE7 29 F4
Angus Rd RLEIW/BAR LE9 50 A5
Ann St LEI LE1 3 H3
Anstey La GBY/RBY LE6 16 C4
LEIN LE4 25 F1
RLEINE/SYS LE7 9 H4
Anthony Cl RLEINE/SYS LE7 12 C2
Anthony Dr RLEINE/SYS LE7 29 F5
Anthony Rd LEIN LE4 25 H1
Antringham Cl LEIE LE5 21 F5
Apollo Cl LEIS LE2 3 K4
Apollo Ct LEIS LE2 3 K5
Appleby Cl LEIW LE3 24 A5
Appleby Rd LEIN LE4 13 E5
Appleton Av LEIN LE4 18 D3
Apple Tree Cl RLEIW/BAR LE9 50 B2
The Approach LEIE LE5 37 F1
Aquitaine Cl END/NAR LE19 42 C5
Arbor Rd RLEIW/BAR LE9 63 G2
Arbour Rd LEIN LE4 19 H5
The Arcade WGSTN LE18 * 46 B5
Archdale St RLEINE/SYS LE7 12 D2
Archdeacon La LEI LE1 3 F1
Archer Cl LEIN LE4 20 C3
Archery Cl RLEIS/BBY LE8 67 F2
Archway Rd LEIE LE5 29 E1
Ardath Rd LEIN LE4 27 E1
Arden Av LEIW LE3 34 B3
Arden Cl MKTHBORO LE16 79 E5
Arden Wy MKTHBORO LE16 78 D4
Ardern Ter LEIW LE3 34 C3
Argyle Pk MKTHBORO LE16 81 H4
Armadale Dr LEIE LE5 28 C2
Armadale Gn LEIE LE5 28 C2
Armson Av RLEIW/BAR LE9 23 E5
Armston Rd RLEIW/BAR LE9 65 F3
Arncliffe Rd LEIE LE5 28 C2
Arndale WGSTN LE18 58 D2
Arnesby Crs LEIS LE2 45 F3
Arnesby Rd RLEIS/BBY LE8 68 A5
Arnhem St LEI LE1 3 G5
Arnold Av WGSTN LE18 57 G2
Arnold Cl RLEIW/BAR LE9 65 F4
Arnold St LEI LE1 3 J1
Arran Rd LEIN LE4 20 B3
Arran Wy RLEIS/BBY LE8 67 F3
Arreton Cl LEIS LE2 46 A1
Arum Wy LEIW LE3 24 B4
Ascot Rd LEIN LE4 19 H5
Asfordby St LEIE LE5 27 F4
Asha Margh LEIN LE4 19 G5
Ashbourne Rd WGSTN LE18 46 A4
Ashbourne St LEIS LE2 27 E5
Ashby Gld LEIE LE5 28 C5
Ashby Ri RLEIS/BBY LE8 60 D2
Ashby Rd COAL LE67 6 B2
Ash Cl GBY/RBY LE6 22 B1
Ashclose Av LEIS LE2 46 A1
Ash Ct GBY/RBY LE6 16 A5
Ashdown Av LEIW LE3 25 F4
Ashdown Rd WGSTN LE18 46 B4
Ash Dr RLEINE/SYS LE7 13 F2
Ashfield Dr RLEINE/SYS LE7 17 F2
Ashfield Rd LEIN LE4 12 D4
LEIS LE2 36 C2
MKTHBORO LE16 78 C5
Ashford Rd LEIS LE2 36 A4
Ash Gv RLEIS/BBY LE8 56 B3
Ashington Cl LEIW LE3 25 F2
Ashlands Wy END/NAR LE19 54 B2
Ashleigh Dr LUTT LE17 85 E3
Ashleigh Gdns LEIW LE3 * 35 E2
RLEIW/BAR LE9 50 C3
Ashleigh Rd LEIW LE3 23 H2
LEIW LE3 35 E1
Ashley Wy MKTHBORO LE16 82 C1
Ashlyns Ri LEIW LE3 24 C5
Ashmead Crs LEIN LE4 12 A3
Ashover Cl RLEIW/BAR LE9 65 F2
Ashover Rd LEIE LE5 36 C1
Ash Rd RLEIW/BAR LE9 50 D4
RLEIW/BAR LE9 63 H3
Ash St LEIE LE5 27 E3
Ashthorpe Rd LEIW LE3 34 C1
Ashton Cl LEIS LE2 47 E5
WGSTN LE18 * 58 A2
Ash Tree Cl LEIS LE2 47 F4
Ashtree Rd LEIE LE5 21 G5
Ash Tree Rd LEIS LE2 47 F4
Ash-Tree Rd RLEIW/BAR LE9 65 F3
Ashurst Cl WGSTN LE18 58 C3
Ashurst Rd LEIW LE3 34 B5
Ashville Wy RLEIS/BBY LE8 65 G1
Ashwell St LEI LE1 3 G6
Askrigg Wy WGSTN LE18 58 C1
Aspen Dr RLEIS/BBY LE8 67 E2
Aspen Wy LUTT LE17 85 F2
Asplin Rd LEIS LE2 45 E3
Asquith Bvd LEIS LE2 45 G3
Asquith Wy LEIS LE2 45 G3
Assured Dr LEIN LE4 12 B5
Astill Cl GBY/RBY LE6 23 E2
Astill Dr LEIN LE4 19 F3
Astill Lodge Rd LEIN LE4 18 A1
Astley Cl LEIW LE3 34 D2
MKTHBORO LE16 81 G3
Astley Rd RLEIW/BAR LE9 51 F4
Aston Hl LEIS LE2 36 A5
Atherstone Cl LEIS LE2 47 H4
Atkinson St LEIE LE5 27 F4
Atkins St LEIS LE2 2 E6
Atlas Cl LEIS LE2 3 K4
Attenborough Cl LEIW LE3 33 G4
WGSTN LE18 46 C4
Attfield Dr RLEIS/BBY LE8 55 H4
Attingham Cl LEIN LE4 27 F2
Attlebridge Cl LEIE LE5 21 F5
Attlee Cl LUTT LE17 85 F4
Attlee Wy LEIS LE2 45 E3
Auburn Rd RLEIS/BBY LE8 56 A3
Auden Cl LEIN LE4 18 B5
Audley Cl MKTHBORO LE16 82 C2
Audley End LEIW LE3 34 C4
Augusta Cl LEIW LE3 24 A4
Augustus Cl RLEINE/SYS LE7 12 C2
Auriga St MKTHBORO LE16 82 A2
Austin Ri LEIE LE5 28 C1
Austins Cl MKTHBORO LE16 81 G1
Austrey La RLEIS/BBY LE8 67 F3
Austwick Cl LEIN LE4 18 C4
Autumn Rd LEIS LE2 44 C5
Avalon Wy RLEINE/SYS LE7 17 G2
Avebury Av LEIN LE4 25 G1
Avenue Cl RLEINE/SYS LE7 5 G4
Avenue Gdns LEIS LE2 36 C4
Avenue North
RLEIW/BAR LE9 51 G2
Avenue Rd LEIS LE2 36 C4
RLEINE/SYS LE7 5 H4
Avenue Rd Extension
LEIS LE2 36 A4
Avenue South
RLEIW/BAR LE9 51 G3
The Avenue LEIS LE2 36 C3
LEIS LE2 48 C4
LEIW LE3 23 H1
RLEIS/BBY LE8 56 A3
RLEIW/BAR LE9 74 A2
Averil Rd LEIE LE5 28 B4
Avery Cl LUTT LE17 85 F4
Avery Dr COAL LE67 6 B3
RLEINE/SYS LE7 5 E5
Avery Hl LEIW LE3 33 H1
Avington Cl LEIW LE3 18 A5
Avoca Cl LEIE LE5 28 B4
Avon Cl LEIS LE2 47 G3
Avondale Rd WGSTN LE18 46 B5
Avon Dr RLEIS/BBY LE8 55 H4
Avon Rd LEIW LE3 34 A3
Avonside Dr LEIE LE5 27 H5
Avon St LEIS LE2 3 K6
Axbridge Cl LEIN LE4 25 H1
Aylestone Dr LEIS LE2 44 D3
Aylestone La LEIS LE2 45 G4
Aylestone Rd LEIS LE2 44 C2
Aylestone Wk LEIS LE2 35 H2
Aylmer Rd LEIW LE3 34 B1
Ayrshire Cl RLEIW/BAR LE9 50 A5
Aysgarth Rd LEIN LE4 18 C4
Ayston Rd LEIW LE3 34 C4
Azalea Cl LUTT LE17 85 E4

B

Babingdon Rw LEIS LE2 45 G3
Babingley Dr LEIN LE4 18 D5
Back La LUTT LE17 76 A3
RLEINE/SYS LE7 4 A2
RLEIS/BBY LE8 61 H3
The Backway
MKTHBORO LE16 82 A2
Badcock Wy RLEIS/BBY LE8 68 C5
Baddely Dr WGSTN LE18 45 H4
Baden Rd LEIE LE5 37 E2
Badger Cl END/NAR LE19 54 C4
Badger Dr RLEIS/BBY LE8 65 H1
Badger's Cnr RLEINE/SYS LE7 5 G1
Badgers Holt LEIS LE2 47 E4
Badminton Rd LEIN LE4 20 B2
RLEINE/SYS LE7 5 E4
Baggrave St LEIE LE5 27 F4
Baileys La RLEIS/BBY LE8 61 H2
Bainbridge Rd LEIW LE3 34 D4
WGSTN LE18 58 C2
Baines La LEIW LE3 33 F2
Baker St LUTT LE17 85 G4
Bakers Wy LEIE LE5 21 H4
Bakery Cl RLEIW/BAR LE9 65 F4
Bakewell Rd WGSTN LE18 46 A4
Bakewell St LEIS LE2 27 E4
Bala Rd RLEIW/BAR LE9 63 H2
Balcombe Av LEIW LE3 25 F4
Balderstone Cl LEIE LE5 28 A5
Baldwin Av WGSTN LE18 57 G2
Baldwin Ri RLEIW/BAR LE9 73 H2
Baldwin Rd LEIS LE2 45 H3
Bale Rd LEIN LE4 27 G1
Balfour Gdns
MKTHBORO LE16 81 G3
Balfour St LEIW LE3 25 H3
Balisfire Gv LEIN LE4 18 B4
The Balk LEIW LE3 23 H1
Balladine Rd RLEINE/SYS LE7 9 G5
Ballards Cl LEIN LE4 18 B4
Ballater Cl LEIE LE5 38 B2
Balliol Av RLEINE/SYS LE7 13 G2
Balmoral Cl LEIS LE2 46 A1
MKTHBORO LE16 82 C2
Balmoral Dr LEIW LE3 34 A3
Balmoral Rd RLEIW/BAR LE9 50 D4
Bambrook Cl RLEIW/BAR LE9 30 B2
Bamburgh Cl
MKTHBORO LE16 82 C1
Bambury La RLEIS/BBY LE8 66 D5
Bampton Cl WGSTN LE18 58 B3
Bankart Av LEIS LE2 37 E4
Bankfield Dr
MKTHBORO LE16 79 E4
Bankside LEIE LE5 29 E2
Banks Rd LEIS LE2 44 D1
The Banks RLEIW/BAR LE9 65 F4
Bank St LUTT LE17 85 G4
Bank Ter RLEIW/BAR LE9 50 A5
Bannerman Rd LEIE LE5 36 D2
Bannister Rd LEIW LE3 43 H2
Bantlam La END/NAR LE19 42 D5
Barbara Av LEIE LE5 28 B3
RLEIW/BAR LE9 32 C2
Barbara Cl END/NAR LE19 42 C5
Barbara Rd LEIW LE3 34 D4
Barclay St LEIW LE3 35 E1
Bardolph St LEIN LE4 26 D2
Bardolph St East LEIN LE4 27 E2
Bardon Cl LEIW LE3 17 H4
Bardon Rd RLEIW/BAR LE9 50 B3
Barfoot Cl RLEIS/BBY LE8 68 A2
Barfoot Rd LEIS LE2 45 F3
Barford Cl WGSTN LE18 58 A3
Barge Cl WGSTN LE18 57 G3
Barkby La RLEINE/SYS LE7 12 D2
Barkby Rd LEIN LE4 20 B5
RLEINE/SYS LE7 13 F1
Barkby Thorpe La LEIN LE4 12 C3
Barkbythorpe Rd LEIN LE4 20 D3
Barker St LEIE LE5 27 F3
Barkford Cl RLEINE/SYS LE7 29 E1
Barley Cl LEIW LE3 24 A2
Barleyman Cl LEIE LE5 21 G4
Barling Rd LEIE LE5 27 H2
Barmouth Av LEIS LE2 45 G2
Barnard Cl LEIS LE2 3 J5
Barnard Gdns
MKTHBORO LE16 81 G4
Barnby Av WGSTN LE18 46 A4
Barn Cl WGSTN LE18 58 C3
Barnes Cl LEIN LE4 20 C2
RLEIS/BBY LE8 69 H3
Barnes Heath Rd LEIE LE5 28 A5
Barnet Cl LEIS LE2 47 E5
Barnett Cl RLEINE/SYS LE7 4 A2
Barnfield Cl RLEIS/BBY LE8 60 D2
Barngate Cl LEIN LE4 11 F4
Barnley Cl RLEIS/BBY LE8 67 E2
Barns Cl RLEIW/BAR LE9 22 C5
Barnsdale Rd LEIN LE4 17 H2
Barnsdale Wy
END/NAR LE19 43 F3
Barnstaple Cl WGSTN LE18 58 B3
Barnstaple Rd LEIE LE5 38 B2
Barns Wy RLEIW/BAR LE9 30 C1
Barn Wy COAL LE67 6 C4
Barnwell Av LEIN LE4 19 F3
Baronet Wy LEIE LE5 29 E1
Barons Cl RLEIW/BAR LE9 22 C5
Barons Ct RLEIW/BAR LE9 22 C5
The Barracks RLEIW/BAR LE9 50 A5
Barratt Cl LEIS LE2 36 D3
Barrington Rd LEIS LE2 37 E4
Barrow Cl WGSTN LE18 58 D2
Barry Cl RLEIW/BAR LE9 32 C2
Barry Dr RLEINE/SYS LE7 5 E5
RLEIW/BAR LE9 32 C2
Barry Rd LEIE LE5 28 D1
Barston St LEI LE1 2 E1
Bartholomew St LEIS LE2 36 C1
Barton Cl GBY/RBY LE6 22 D3
WGSTN LE18 * 58 A2
Barton Rd LEIW LE3 25 G2
Barwell Rd RLEIW/BAR LE9 22 D5
Baslow Rd LEIE LE5 36 C1
Bassett Av RLEIS/BBY LE8 67 E3
Bassett La RLEIW/BAR LE9 72 B2
Bassett St LEIW LE3 2 A1
WGSTN LE18 57 F2
Batchelor Rd RLEIS/BBY LE8 68 B3
Bateman Rd LEIW LE3 25 E3
Bates Cl MKTHBORO LE16 78 C3
Bath Cl RLEIW/BAR LE9 72 B1
Bath La LEIW LE3 2 C3
Bath St LEIN LE4 19 G3
MKTHBORO LE16 81 H3
RLEINE/SYS LE7 4 D5
Bathurst Rd LEIE LE5 38 B1
Battenberg Rd LEIW LE3 25 G4
Batten St LEIS LE2 35 G4
Battersbee Rd LEIW LE3 24 C2
Battersbee Wy LEIW LE3 24 C2
Baxters Cl LEIN LE4 18 B5
Bayberry Gdns LEIS LE2 45 E4
Baycliff Cl LEIW LE3 25 F2
Bayham Cl LEIE LE5 28 B5
Baysdale WGSTN LE18 58 D1
Baysdale Rd LEIS LE2 2 D7
Bay St LEI LE1 2 D1
Bayswater Dr LEIS LE2 56 D2
Beacon Av LEIN LE4 12 D5
Beacon Cl COAL LE67 6 C3
GBY/RBY LE6 16 B5
LEIN LE4 18 A1
Beaconsfield Rd LEIW LE3 35 E1
Beaker Cl RLEIS/BBY LE8 69 H5
Beal St LEIS LE2 3 K3
Beatrice Rd LEIW LE3 25 F3
Beatty Av LEIE LE5 27 G3
Beatty Rd LEIE LE5 27 G3
RLEINE/SYS LE7 5 E5
Beauchamp Rd
RLEIS/BBY LE8 69 H3
Beaufort Cl LEIS LE2 47 H4
RLEIW/BAR LE9 30 B3
Beaufort Rd LEIW LE3 34 C4
Beaufort Wy LEIS LE2 47 H4
Beaumanor Rd LEIN LE4 19 F5
Beaumont Gn GBY/RBY LE6 16 B5
Beaumont Leys Cl LEIN LE4 18 D4
Beaumont Leys La LEIN LE4 18 C2
Beaumont Lodge Rd
LEIN LE4 18 B1
Beaumont Rd LEIE LE5 27 E4
Beaumont St LEIS LE2 47 E2
Beaumont Wy LEIN LE4 18 A2
Beauville Dr LEIN LE4 18 A4
Beaver Cl RLEIS/BBY LE8 65 H1
Beck Cl LEIS LE2 44 A5
Beckett Rd LEIE LE5 27 G2
Beckingham Rd LEIS LE2 36 C2
Bedale Dr LEIN LE4 18 C2
Bede Island Rd LEIS LE2 2 C6
Bede St LEIW LE3 2 B6
Bedford Cl RLEIW/BAR LE9 30 B2
Bedford Dr GBY/RBY LE6 16 B5
Bedford Rd WGSTN LE18 45 G5
Bedford St North LEI LE1 3 G1
Bedford St South LEI LE1 3 F2
Beeby Cl RLEINE/SYS LE7 13 G1
Beeby Rd LEIE LE5 27 F4
RLEINE/SYS LE7 13 H4
RLEINE/SYS LE7 29 G2
Beech Av GBY/RBY LE6 23 E1
LUTT LE17 85 E3
Beech Cl COAL LE67 6 C4
Beechcroft Av LEIW LE3 34 C5
Beechcroft Rd LEIS LE2 36 C4
Beech Dr LEIW LE3 33 H2
RLEINE/SYS LE7 13 F2
The Beeches RLEIW/BAR LE9 51 F2
Beechfield Av LEIN LE4 11 G5
Beechfield Cl RLEIS/BBY LE8 60 D2
Beechings Cl RLEIS/BBY LE8 66 C3
Beech Rd RLEIS/BBY LE8 56 B4
Beech St LEIE LE5 27 E3
Beech Tree Cl RLEIS/BBY LE8 70 A1
Beech Wy RLEIW/BAR LE9 30 A2
Beechwood Av LEIN LE4 20 C1
LEIW LE3 32 D2
RLEINE/SYS LE7 5 G4
RLEIW/BAR LE9 32 D1
Beechwood Cl LEIE LE5 28 C5
Beechwood Rd
END/NAR LE19 54 D5
Beggar's La END/NAR LE19 42 B2
LEIW LE3 32 C3
Begonia Cl LEIW LE3 32 D3
Belfry Dr LEIW LE3 24 A5
Belgrave Av LEIN LE4 19 G4
Belgrave Bvd LEIN LE4 18 C2
Belgrave Ga LEI LE1 3 F2
Belgrave Rd LEIN LE4 26 C2
Bellamy Cl LEIS LE2 44 A5
Bell Cl GBY/RBY LE6 22 D2
RLEIW/BAR LE9 74 C5
Belleville Dr LEIS LE2 47 G2
Belle Vue Av LEIN LE4 19 E5
Belle Vue Rd RLEIW/BAR LE9 50 C3
Bellfields La
MKTHBORO LE16 82 B2
Bellfields St
MKTHBORO LE16 82 B2
Bellflower Rd LEIE LE5 21 F5
Bellholme Cl LEIN LE4 19 H4
Bell La END/NAR LE19 55 E4
LEIE LE5 3 J2
RLEIS/BBY LE8 61 H3
Bell St LUTT LE17 85 G4
WGSTN LE18 46 B5
Bell Vw END/NAR LE19 * 55 E3
Belmont St LEIS LE2 44 D1
Belper Cl LEIS LE2 47 E4
WGSTN LE18 57 G3
Belper St LEIN LE4 26 D1
Belton Cl LEIS LE2 45 F3
Belton Rd LEIW LE3 34 C5
Belvoir Cl LEIS LE2 47 G4
RLEIW/BAR LE9 30 B2
Belvoir Dr LEIS LE2 44 C2
RLEINE/SYS LE7 5 F5
Belvoir Dr East LEIS LE2 44 D2
Belvoir St LEI LE1 3 F4
Beman Cl LEIN LE4 20 C2
Bembridge Cl LEIW LE3 25 H2
Bembridge Rd LEIW LE3 25 G2
Bencroft Cl RLEINE/SYS LE7 17 F1
Bendbow Ri LEIW LE3 33 H2
Benford Cl RLEIW/BAR LE9 74 B5
Bennett Ri RLEIW/BAR LE9 54 A3
Bennetts Hl LUTT LE17 77 F2
Bennett's La RLEINE/SYS LE7 4 A1
Bennett Wy WGSTN LE18 57 G1
Bennion Rd LEIN LE4 18 A3
RLEINE/SYS LE7 39 E1
Benskins Ov LEIN LE4 10 C5
Benskyn Cl RLEIS/BBY LE8 66 D2
Benson St LEIE LE5 27 G5
Bentinghouse Rd LEIS LE2 44 D4
Bentley Rd LEIN LE4 11 G4
Beresford Dr LEIS LE2 36 D5
Berford Cl RLEIW/BAR LE9 74 B4
Berkeley Cl LEIS LE2 47 H3
Berkley St LEI LE1 2 D1
Berkshire Rd LEIS LE2 44 D1
Berners St LEIS LE2 3 K3
Berridge Dr LEIS LE2 47 F4
Berridge La LEIN LE4 19 H4
Berridge St LEI LE1 2 E4
Berrington Cl LEIE LE5 27 G2
Berry Cl MKTHBORO LE16 79 E4
Berry's La GBY/RBY LE6 22 C2
Berrywell Dr RLEIW/BAR LE9 50 A3
Bessingham Cl LEIE LE5 21 G5
Best Cl WGSTN LE18 57 F2
Bestwood Cl LEIW LE3 25 F1
Beth-el WGSTN LE18 * 58 A3
Bevan Rd LEIN LE4 10 C5
Beverley Av LEIN LE4 26 D1
Beverley Cl LEIN LE4 12 C5
Beverley Dr RLEIW/BAR LE9 74 A1
Bevington Cl GBY/RBY LE6 22 B1
Bewcastle Gv LEIN LE4 18 D2
Bewicke Rd LEIW LE3 34 D3
Bexhill Ri LEIE LE5 29 E3
Biam Wy LEIW LE3 34 C5
Biddle Rd END/NAR LE19 55 E5
LEIW LE3 25 F3
Biddulph Av LEIS LE2 36 C1
Biddulph St LEIS LE2 36 C1
Bideford Cl WGSTN LE18 58 B4
Bideford Rd LEIE LE5 38 B2
Bidford Cl LEIW LE3 34 A3
Bidford Rd LEIW LE3 34 A3
Biggin Hill Rd LEIE LE5 37 H2
Bigg's Cl RLEIS/BBY LE8 66 A1
Bignal Dr LEIW LE3 33 F1
Bilberry Cl LEIW LE3 44 A2
Bill Crane Wy LUTT LE17 85 G1
Billesdon Cl LEIW LE3 17 G4
Billington Cl LEIN LE4 19 E4
Bilsdale Rd WGSTN LE18 58 D2
Bilton Wy LUTT LE17 85 H1
Bindley La RLEIS/BBY LE8 60 C2
Bingley Rd END/NAR LE19 54 D5
Bintree Cl LEIE LE5 21 F5
Birch Cl COAL LE67 14 C1
LEIN LE4 27 F1
RLEIW/BAR LE9 50 D5
Birchfield Av COAL LE67 6 B4
Birch Tree Av LEIN LE4 11 G3
Birch Tree Gdns
MKTHBORO LE16 78 D5
Birchtree Rd WGSTN LE18 46 B4
Birchwood Cl LEIW LE3 32 D3
RLEINE/SYS LE7 13 G1
Birdie Cl RLEIS/BBY LE8 70 B3
Birds Nest Av LEIW LE3 24 D2
Birkby Cl LEIE LE5 21 G4
Birkdale Av LEIS LE2 36 D4
Birkdale Rd RLEINE/SYS LE7 17 E1
Birkenshaw Rd LEIW LE3 25 E1
Birsmore Av LEIN LE4 20 B3
Birstall Rd LEIN LE4 19 G2
Birstall St LEI LE1 26 D3
Birstow Crs LEIN LE4 18 D2
Birtley Coppice
MKTHBORO LE16 78 B5
Bishop Cl MKTHBORO LE16 81 H4
Bishopdale Rd LEIN LE4 18 C4
Bishop St LEI LE1 3 F4
Bisley St LEIW LE3 35 F2
Bitteswell Rd LUTT LE17 85 G2

Blaby By-Pass
RLEIS/BBY LE8 56 A5
Blaby Rd END/NAR LE19 42 D5
END/NAR LE19 55 F1
WGSTN LE18 57 G2
Blackberry La
RLEINE/SYS LE7 4 B1
Blackbird Av LEIN LE4 25 H2
Blackbird Rd LEIN LE4 25 H2
LEIW LE3 25 G3
Blackburn Rd
RLEIW/BAR LE9 50 A5
Blackett Av LEIW LE3 25 E2
Blackfriars St LEIW LE3 2 C3
Blackmore Dr LEIW LE3 25 E5
Blacksmiths La
RLEIS/BBY LE8 69 H5
Blackthorn Cl LUTT LE17 85 E3
Blackthorn Dr LEIN LE4 17 H1
RLEINE/SYS LE7 12 C1
Blackthorn La LEIS LE2 37 H5
Blackthorn Rd LEIW LE3 23 H3
Blackwell Cl WGSTN LE18 58 C2
Bladen Cl RLEIS/BBY LE8 66 D2
Blairmore Rd LEIW LE3 24 A4
Blaise Gv LEIN LE4 27 F1
Blake Ct END/NAR LE19 42 C5
Blakenhall Cl END/NAR LE19 54 B3
Blakenhall Rd LEIE LE5 28 A5
Blakeshay Cl LEIW LE3 17 H5
Blakesley Rd WGSTN LE18 46 D5
Blake St LEI LE1 2 E2
Bland Rd LEIW LE3 24 D2
Blankley Dr LEIS LE2 36 D4
Blanklyn Av LEIE LE5 27 F5
Blaydon Cl LEIW LE3 25 F2
Bleasby Cl LEIN LE4 21 E3
Blenheim Cl WGSTN LE18 57 F3
Blenheim Crs
RLEIW/BAR LE9 73 H2
Blenheim Rd LEIN LE4 11 H4
Blenheim Wy LEIN LE4 19 E3
MKTHBORO LE16 78 C4
Blissett Rd LEIW LE3 25 E3
Bloomfield Rd LEIS LE2 45 F1
Blossom Rd LEIW LE3 34 C1
The Blossoms COAL LE67 14 C1
Blount Rd LEIN LE4 20 D1
Bloxams Cl LEIW LE3 43 H2
Bloxham Rd LEIW LE3 25 F3
Blue Banks Av LEIS LE2 44 A5
Bluebell Cl RLEINE/SYS LE7 5 H3
RLEIW/BAR LE9 23 F4
Bluebell Dr GBY/RBY LE6 16 C4
LEIS LE2 45 F4
Blue Gates Rd LEIN LE4 17 H2
Blue Pots Cl LEIW LE3 32 C3
Blundell Rd LEIE LE5 37 G2
Blunt's La WGSTN LE18 58 B1
Bodenham Cl WGSTN LE18 58 A3
Bodicoat Cl RLEIS/BBY LE8 65 H1
Bodmin Av WGSTN LE18 58 A3
Bodnant Av LEIE LE5 37 E2
Bodycote Cl RLEIW/BAR LE9 74 B4
Bollington Rd LEIS LE2 47 G2
Bolsover St LEIE LE5 27 G4
Bolton Rd LEIW LE3 25 G5
Bolus Rd LEIW LE3 33 G3
Bonchurch St LEIW LE3 2 A1
Bondman Cl LEIN LE4 19 E2
Bonner Cl LEIS LE2 47 H4
Bonners La LEI LE1 2 D6
Bonney Rd LEIW LE3 25 E1
Bonnington Rd LEIS LE2 36 B4
Bonsall St LEIE LE5 36 C1
Bonville Pl LEIW LE3 34 D4
Booth Cl LEIE LE5 28 B5
Bordeaux Cl END/NAR LE19 42 C5
Border Dr LEIN LE4 18 D2
Borlace St LEIW LE3 2 A2
Borrowcup Cl
RLEIS/BBY LE8 66 C2
Borrowdale Cl
RLEIW/BAR LE9 51 F4
Boston Rd LEIN LE4 17 H3
Boswell St END/NAR LE19 54 C2
Bosworth Gn
RLEIW/BAR LE9 51 H2
Bosworth St LEIW LE3 2 A3
Boulder La LEIS LE2 45 F2
Boulter Crs WGSTN LE18 46 B5
Boulton Ct LEIS LE2 48 A4
Boundary Rd LEIS LE2 35 F4
LUTT LE17 85 H3
Bourton Crs LEIS LE2 47 G3
Bow Br LEIW LE3 2 B4
Bowden La
MKTHBORO LE16 78 C5
Bowden Rdg
MKTHBORO LE16 79 E4
Bowhill Gv LEIE LE5 29 E4
Bowling Green St LEI LE1 3 F4
Bowmans Wy LEIW LE3 23 H2
Bowmars La LEIW LE3 2 C1
Boyers Wk LEIW LE3 32 D2
Boynton Rd LEIW LE3 34 C1
Brabazon Cl LEIS LE2 46 D3
Brabazon Rd LEIS LE2 46 D2
Bracken Cl LEIE LE5 37 H1
LEIW LE3 32 D3
Bracken Dl RLEINE/SYS LE7 5 H2
Brackenfield Wy LEIN LE4 12 D4
Bracken Hl GBY/RBY LE6 8 A4
Brackenthwaite LEIN LE4 20 B4
Bracken Wy COAL LE67 6 C3
Bradbourne Rd LEIE LE5 27 F5
Bradbury Cl RLEIW/BAR LE9 65 F3
Bradfield Cl LEIE LE5 37 E1
Bradgate Av LEIN LE4 12 D5
Bradgate Cl RLEINE/SYS LE7 29 E5
Bradgate Dr GBY/RBY LE6 22 C1
WGSTN LE18 45 H3
Bradgate Hl COAL LE67 7 E5
Bradgate Rd COAL LE67 6 C3
GBY/RBY LE6 8 A5
RLEIW/BAR LE9 50 B3
Bradgate St LEIN LE4 25 H2
Brading Rd LEIW LE3 25 G2
Bradshaw Av LEIS LE2 44 C5
Bradstone Cl RLEIW/BAR LE9 74 D4
Bradston Rd LEIS LE2 45 E3
Braemar Dr LEIN LE4 20 A3
Brailsford Rd WGSTN LE18 45 H4
Bramall Ct LEIE LE5 27 G2
Bramall Rd LEIE LE5 27 F3
Bramber Cl LEIN LE4 20 C1
Bramble Cl LEIE LE5 21 H5
LEIW LE3 24 B3
Bramble Wy LEIW LE3 34 C4
Brambling Rd LEIE LE5 27 F4
Brambling Wy LEIS LE2 47 E4
Bramcote Rd LEIW LE3 34 D5
WGSTN LE18 46 A5
Bramham Cl LEIW LE3 25 E1
Bramley Cl RLEIW/BAR LE9 74 A3
Bramley Ct LEIW LE3 23 H2
Bramley Orch
RLEINE/SYS LE7 29 G5
Bramley Rd LEIN LE4 11 H5
LEIW LE3 25 G5
Brampton Av LEIW LE3 25 E4
Brampton Wy LEIS LE2 46 D2
Brancaster Cl LEIN LE4 18 D5
Brandon St LEIN LE4 26 C2
Bransdale Rd WGSTN LE18 58 D1
Branting Hl GBY/RBY LE6 16 D4
Branting Hill Av LEIW LE3 16 D5
Branting Hill Gv LEIW LE3 16 D5
Bratmyr RLEIS/BBY LE8 68 B2
Braunstone Av LEIW LE3 34 B3
Braunstone Cl LEIW LE3 34 B4
Braunstone Ga LEIW LE3 2 B5
Braunstone La LEIW LE3 33 H2
Braunstone La East
LEIW LE3 34 D5
Braunstone Wy LEIW LE3 34 A2
Braybrooke Rd LEIN LE4 27 G1
MKTHBORO LE16 82 B2
Braymish Cl RLEIS/BBY LE8 70 B3
Brazil St LEIS LE2 35 G2
Breach La RLEIW/BAR LE9 51 F5
Brecon Cl WGSTN LE18 57 F1
Breedon Av WGSTN LE18 46 A5
Breedon St LEIS LE2 27 E5
Brent Knowle Gdns LEIE LE5 28 D5
Brentwood Rd LEIS LE2 36 A4
Bretby Rd LEIS LE2 45 E2
Brettell Rd LEIS LE2 44 D4
Bretton Cl LEIN LE4 19 E4
Brewer Cl LEIN LE4 20 C2
Brex Ri LEIW LE3 24 B4
Brian Rd LEIN LE4 25 H1
Brians Cl RLEINE/SYS LE7 5 F5
The Brianway LEIE LE5 27 H3
Briar Cl LEIS LE2 47 F4
Briarfield Dr LEIE LE5 29 E1
Briargate Dr LEIN LE4 11 E4
Briar Meads LEIS LE2 47 F5
Briar Rd LEIE LE5 28 D3
Briar Wk LEIS LE2 47 F4
Brickman Cl LEIW LE3 32 C3
Bridevale Rd LEIS LE2 45 E3
Bridge Cl LEIN LE4 12 D4
Bridgemere Cl LEIS LE2 44 B4
Bridge Park Rd LEIN LE4 12 B5
Bridge Rd LEIE LE5 27 F3
Bridgewater Dr
RLEIS/BBY LE8 60 D2
Bridge Wy RLEIS/BBY LE8 55 H5
Bridle Cl RLEIW/BAR LE9 63 G3
Bridlespur Wy LEIN LE4 19 E2
The Bridle LEIS LE2 44 B4
Bridport Cl WGSTN LE18 58 A2
Brierfield Rd RLEIW/BAR LE9 65 F4
Briers Cl END/NAR LE19 54 D4
Brighton Av RLEINE/SYS LE7 5 F5
WGSTN LE18 46 A3
Brighton Cl WGSTN LE18 46 A3
Brighton Rd LEIE LE5 27 F2
Brightside Rd LEIE LE5 37 E2
Brightwell Dr LEIW LE3 33 F1
Brindley Ri LEIE LE5 29 E1
Bringhurst Rd LEIW LE3 24 B3
Brington Cl WGSTN LE18 58 C1
Brinsmead Rd LEIS LE2 45 H1
Bristol Av LEIN LE4 25 H1
Britannia St LEI LE1 26 C3
Britannia Wk
MKTHBORO LE16 82 A2
Britannia Wy LEIN LE4 12 C3
Britford Av WGSTN LE18 57 H3
Briton St LEIW LE3 2 A7
Brixham Dr LEIS LE2 45 G3
Brixworth Ri LEIE LE5 29 E4
Broad Av LEIE LE5 27 H5
Broadbent Cl RLEIS/BBY LE8 55 H4
Broadfield Wy
RLEIS/BBY LE8 66 C2
Broadford Cl LEIN LE4 20 B3
Broadgate Cl LEIN LE4 11 G4
Broadhurst St LEIN LE4 19 H5
Broad Meadow WGSTN LE18 58 C2
Broadmead Rd
RLEIS/BBY LE8 56 A5
Broadnook Cl LEIW LE3 17 G4
Broad St END/NAR LE19 42 D5
RLEINE/SYS LE7 13 E1
Broadway RLEINE/SYS LE7 13 E1
Broadway Furlong
RLEINE/SYS LE7 9 G5
Broadway Rd LEIE LE5 36 D3
The Broadway LEIS LE2 37 F4
MKTHBORO LE16 78 D5
Brockenhurst Dr LEIW LE3 34 A5
Brockey Cl RLEIW/BAR LE9 50 B4
Brocklesby Wy LEIE LE5 29 E2
Brocks Hill Cl LEIS LE2 47 F4
Brocks Hill Dr LEIS LE2 47 E3
Broctone Cl RLEIW/BAR LE9 74 D4
Broctone Dr RLEIW/BAR LE9 74 A2
Brompton Rd LEIE LE5 21 G4
Bromwich Cl LEIW LE3 33 G3
Bronte Cl LEIW LE3 34 C1
Bronze WGSTN LE18 58 D2
Brook Ct RLEIS/BBY LE8 67 F2
Brookdale Rd LEIW LE3 24 B5
Brook Dr GBY/RBY LE6 22 C3
Brookes Av RLEIW/BAR LE9 63 G3
Brookfield HINC LE10 72 A4
Brookfield Av
RLEINE/SYS LE7 5 E5
Brookfield Ri LEIS LE2 45 F2
Brookfield Rd
MKTHBORO LE16 81 F1
Brookfield St
RLEINE/SYS LE7 13 F1
Brookfield Wy LUTT LE17 85 E2
RLEIS/BBY LE8 70 B3
Brook Gdns LEIS LE2 44 B5
Brookhouse Av LEIS LE2 3 J6
Brookhouse St LEIS LE2 3 J6
Brookland Rd LEIS LE2 36 A4
Brooklands Cl RLEIS/BBY LE8 55 H5
RLEIW/BAR LE9 74 B3
Brooklands Gdns
MKTHBORO LE16 81 H1
Brooklands Rd
RLEIW/BAR LE9 65 F2
Brook Rd LEIE LE5 28 D3
Brooksby Dr LEIS LE2 47 E3
Brooksby St LEIS LE2 35 G4
Brookside LEIS LE2 36 D2
RLEINE/SYS LE7 4 D5
RLEIS/BBY LE8 55 H5
Brookside Dr LEIS LE2 47 G3
Brookside Gdns
RLEIS/BBY LE8 * 68 B4
Brook St END/NAR LE19 42 D5
LEIN LE4 12 B5
RLEINE/SYS LE7 4 D5
RLEIS/BBY LE8 55 H4
RLEIW/BAR LE9 53 H4
Broombriggs Rd LEIW LE3 17 G4
Broome Av RLEINE/SYS LE7 5 H1
Broome La RLEINE/SYS LE7 5 H1
Broomfield RLEINE/SYS LE7 5 H2
Broomhills Rd
END/NAR LE19 54 B3
Broomleys RLEIS/BBY LE8 66 D2
Broom Wy END/NAR LE19 54 B2
Brougham St LEI LE1 3 H2
Broughton Cl RLEINE/SYS LE7 9 G5
Broughton Fld WGSTN LE18 58 C3
Broughton La LUTT LE17 76 A2
RLEIW/BAR LE9 74 A5
Broughton Rd LEIS LE2 45 E2
RLEIW/BAR LE9 74 D1
Broughton Wy
RLEIW/BAR LE9 74 B2
Browning St END/NAR LE19 54 C2
LEIW LE3 35 E1
Brown's Cl RLEIW/BAR LE9 72 C1
Browns Wy RLEIS/BBY LE8 65 H1
Broxburn Cl LEIN LE4 20 B3
Broxfield Cl LEIS LE2 47 E5
Bruce St LEIW LE3 35 F2
Bruce Wy RLEIS/BBY LE8 65 G1
Bruin St LEIN LE4 26 C1
Bruins Wk LEIS LE2 46 D3
Brunel Av LEIW LE3 25 E1
Brunswick St LEI LE1 3 J2
Bruxby St RLEINE/SYS LE7 34 C1
Bryngarth Crs LEIE LE5 28 B3
Bryony Rd LEIE LE5 21 H5
Buckfast Cl LEIE LE5 37 F2
WGSTN LE18 58 A2
Buckhaven Cl LEIN LE4 20 B3
Buckingham Cl GBY/RBY LE6 16 A5
Buckingham Dr LEIS LE2 44 B3
Buckingham Rd
RLEIS/BBY LE8 67 F2
Buckland Rd LEIE LE5 27 F2
Buckley La RLEIS/BBY LE8 71 G1
Buckminster Rd LEIW LE3 25 G2
Buckwell Rd RLEIW/BAR LE9 72 B1
Bude Dr LEIW LE3 24 A1
Bude Rd WGSTN LE18 58 B2
Buller Rd LEIN LE4 26 C1
Buller St RLEIS/BBY LE8 69 H3
Bull Head St WGSTN LE18 58 B1
Bulwer Rd LEIS LE2 35 F3
Burchnall Rd LEIW LE3 33 G4
Burdet Cl LEIW LE3 34 A4
Burdett Wy LEIN LE4 18 D3
Burdock Cl LEIE LE5 21 H5
Burfield St LEIN LE4 26 D2
Burgess Rd LEIS LE2 45 E2
Burgess St LEI LE1 2 D1
WGSTN LE18 46 B5
Burghley Cl
MKTHBORO LE16 82 B1
Burgin Rd RLEINE/SYS LE7 17 F2
Burleigh Av WGSTN LE18 46 A4
Burley Cl RLEIW/BAR LE9 30 B2
RLEIW/BAR LE9 65 F3
Burleys F/O LEI LE1 3 F1
Burleys Wy LEI LE1 2 E1
Burlington Rd LEIS LE2 36 C4
Burnaby Av LEIE LE5 27 F4
Burnaston Rd LEIS LE2 45 E2
Burnell Rd LEIW LE3 34 D3
Burneston Wy WGSTN LE18 58 C1
Burnet Cl LEIE LE5 21 G5
Burnham Cl WGSTN LE18 58 B4
Burnham Dr LEIN LE4 18 D5
RLEIS/BBY LE8 55 H5
Burnmill Rd
MKTHBORO LE16 78 C4
Burnmoor St LEIS LE2 35 G3
Burnside Rd LEIS LE2 45 G2
RLEIW/BAR LE9 74 B4
Burns St END/NAR LE19 54 C2
LEIS LE2 36 A5
Burroughs Rd GBY/RBY LE6 22 A1
Burrough Wy LUTT LE17 85 G1
Burrows Cl END/NAR LE19 54 D4
The Burrows END/NAR LE19 54 B3
RLEINE/SYS LE7 5 F2
Bursdon Cl LEIW LE3 24 B4
Bursom Rd LEIN LE4 18 B1
Burton Cl LEIS LE2 47 H4
LUTT LE17 85 H4
Burton St LEI LE1 3 H3
Buscot Cl LEIN LE4 27 F2
Bushby Rd LEIE LE5 27 F3
Bushey Cl END/NAR LE19 54 D3
Bush Lock Cl WGSTN LE18 57 G3
Bushloe End WGSTN LE18 58 A1
Bushnell Cl RLEIW/BAR LE9 74 C5
Butcombe Rd LEIN LE4 25 H1
Bute Wy RLEIS/BBY LE8 67 F3
Butler Cl GBY/RBY LE6 22 D2
LEIN LE4 20 C3
Butler Gdns
MKTHBORO LE16 81 F3
Butt Cl WGSTN LE18 58 C2
Butt Close La LEI LE1 2 E2
Buttercup Cl END/NAR LE19 54 C2
GBY/RBY LE6 16 C4
Buttermere St LEIS LE2 35 G2
Butterwick Dr LEIN LE4 18 C3
Buxton Cl RLEIS/BBY LE8 55 H4
Buxton St LEIS LE2 27 E4
Buzzard Cl RLEIW/BAR LE9 74 B2
Byfield Dr WGSTN LE18 46 C5
Byford Rd LEIN LE4 19 E5
Byre Crs RLEIW/BAR LE9 74 B4
Byron Cl END/NAR LE19 54 C1
LUTT LE17 85 G1
RLEIS/BBY LE8 68 B4
Byron St LEI LE1 3 G2
RLEIW/BAR LE9 50 B3
Byway Rd LEIE LE5 37 E3

C

Cademan Cl LEIS LE2 45 H1
Cadles Cl RLEIW/BAR LE9 62 B3
Cairngorm Cl LEIS LE2 45 F1
Cairns Cl LEIW LE3 43 H1
Cairnsford Rd LEIS LE2 45 H2
Calais Hl LEI LE1 3 G5
Calais St LEI LE1 3 G5
Caldecote Rd LEIW LE3 34 C4
Caldecott Cl WGSTN LE18 58 C1
Calder Rd LEIN LE4 18 C4
Caledine Rd LEIW LE3 24 D2
Calgary Rd LEI LE1 26 C3
Callan Cl END/NAR LE19 54 C3
Calver Hey Rd LEIN LE4 18 A4
Calvert Crs RLEIW/BAR LE9 72 C2
Calverton Av WGSTN LE18 46 A4
Calverton Cl GBY/RBY LE6 22 D2
Camborne Cl WGSTN LE18 58 A2
Cambrian Cl RLEIW/BAR LE9 65 F4
Cambridge Cl
RLEINE/SYS LE7 13 F1
Cambridge Dr
RLEIW/BAR LE9 30 A2
Cambridge Rd
RLEIW/BAR LE9 65 F3
Cambridge St LEIW LE3 35 E1
Camden Rd LEIW LE3 34 C4
Camden St LEI LE1 3 G2
Camellia Cl END/NAR LE19 54 B2
Camelot Wy END/NAR LE19 54 C2
Cameron Av LEIN LE4 19 H4
Camfield Ri LEIS LE2 44 D4
Campbell Av LEIN LE4 20 C1
Campbell St LEIS LE2 3 G5
Campion Cl END/NAR LE19 54 C3
Camville Rd LEIW LE3 34 B1
Canada Flds LUTT LE17 85 G2
Canal St LEIN LE4 12 B4
LEIS LE2 44 C1
WGSTN LE18 57 F3
Candle La RLEIW/BAR LE9 51 F3
Cank St LEI LE1 2 E3
Cannam Cl RLEIS/BBY LE8 66 A1
Canning Pl LEI LE1 2 E1
Canning St LEI LE1 2 E1
Cannock St LEIN LE4 21 E4
Canon Cl LEIS LE2 47 F3
Canons Cl END/NAR LE19 54 D3
Canonsleigh Rd LEIN LE4 19 E4
Canon St LEIN LE4 19 H5
Canterbury Ter LEIW LE3 34 D2
Cantrell Rd LEIW LE3 33 H2
Canvey Cl WGSTN LE18 46 D5
Capers Cl END/NAR LE19 42 C5
Capesthorne Cl LEIE LE5 27 F2
Cara Cl LEIS LE2 36 C5
Carbery Cl LEIS LE2 47 H4
Cardigan Dr WGSTN LE18 57 F1
Cardinal Cl GBY/RBY LE6 22 D2
Cardinals Wk LEIE LE5 28 C2
Carey Cl WGSTN LE18 58 B3
Carey Hill Rd RLEIW/BAR LE9 62 B4
Carey Rd RLEIW/BAR LE9 53 H4
Careys Cl LEI LE1 2 D4
Carfax Av LEIS LE2 46 D1
Carisbrooke Av LEIS LE2 46 A1
Carisbrooke Gdns LEIS LE2 36 C5
Carisbrooke Pk LEIS LE2 46 A1
Carisbrooke Rd LEIS LE2 36 C5
Carlisle St LEIW LE3 25 F5
Carlson Gdns LUTT LE17 85 H3
Carl St LEIS LE2 44 C2
Carlton Av END/NAR LE19 55 E3
Carlton Ct LEIW LE3 24 B2
Carlton Dr WGSTN LE18 46 A5
Carlton Gdns RLEIS/BBY LE8 60 D4
Carlton La RLEIS/BBY LE8 61 H3
Carlton St LEI LE1 2 E6
Carmen Gv GBY/RBY LE6 15 H4
Carnation Cl LEIW LE3 32 D3
Carnation St LEIN LE4 19 F5
Carnoustie Rd LEIW LE3 24 B4
Caroline Ct LEIS LE2 45 E2
Carpenter's Cl LEIW LE3 23 H3
Carpe Rd LEIN LE4 27 F1
Carrington Rd LEIE LE5 21 G4
Carrow Rd LEIW LE3 23 H5
Carr's Dr RLEIW/BAR LE9 51 F3
Carrs Hl RLEIW/BAR LE9 50 C5
Carr's Rd RLEIW/BAR LE9 51 F3
Carter Cl END/NAR LE19 42 C5
Carter St LEIN LE4 27 E2
Carts La LEI LE1 2 E3
Cartwright Dr LEIS LE2 47 E3
Carty Rd LEIE LE5 21 G4
Carvers Cnr LEIS LE2 * 44 B5
Cashmore Vw LEIN LE4 18 D3
Castell Dr GBY/RBY LE6 16 B4
Castle Cl RLEIW/BAR LE9 72 B2
Castle Flds LEIN LE4 17 H2
Castleford Rd LEIW LE3 34 A5
Castlegate Av LEIN LE4 11 F4
Castle Ri GBY/RBY LE6 16 B5
Castle Rd RLEIW/BAR LE9 22 D5
Castle St LEI LE1 2 D5
Castleton Rd WGSTN LE18 46 A4
Castle Vw LEI LE1 2 D5
Castle Yd LEI LE1 2 D5
Caswell Cl LEIN LE4 18 D3
Caters Cl RLEINE/SYS LE7 17 F1
Catesby St LEIW LE3 2 A5
Catherine St LEI LE1 26 D2
Cathkin Cl LEIW LE3 24 B5
Caudle Cl RLEINE/SYS LE7 9 H1
Causeway La LEI LE1 2 D2
RLEINE/SYS LE7 9 F2
Cavendish Rd LEIS LE2 35 G5
Caversham Rd LEIS LE2 44 C5
Cawsand Rd WGSTN LE18 58 A2
Cawston Cl LEIE LE5 21 F5
Caxton St MKTHBORO LE16 82 A3
Cecilia Rd LEIS LE2 36 B3
Cecil Rd LEIS LE2 3 K3
Cedar Av LEIN LE4 11 G5
LUTT LE17 85 F3
WGSTN LE18 58 B2
Cedar Cl LEIW LE3 24 C1
RLEIS/BBY LE8 69 H3
Cedar Ct GBY/RBY LE6 16 B5
Cedar Crs END/NAR LE19 54 D4
Cedar Dr RLEINE/SYS LE7 13 F2
Cedar Rd LEIS LE2 36 C1
RLEIS/BBY LE8 56 B5
RLEIW/BAR LE9 50 D4
Cedars Ct LEIS LE2 36 C3
The Cedars LEIS LE2 45 H1
RLEINE/SYS LE7 39 F1
Cedarwood Cl LEIN LE4 27 F1
Celandine Cl LEIS LE2 48 A4
Celandine Rd LEIE LE5 21 G5
Celt St LEIW LE3 2 B6
Cemetery Rd RLEIS/BBY LE8 55 H4
Central Av LEIS LE2 36 C3
LUTT LE17 85 C2
RLEINE/SYS LE7 5 E5
WGSTN LE18 58 A1
Central Cl RLEIS/BBY LE8 55 H3
Central Rd LEIW LE3 25 H3
Central St RLEIS/BBY LE8 67 F3
Centre Ct END/NAR LE19 43 F1
Centurion Wy
END/NAR LE19 33 H5
Century Ct LEIE LE5 28 C4
Chadderton Cl LEIS LE2 45 G1
Chadwell Rd LEIW LE3 24 C3
Chaffinch Cl LEIN LE4 18 A1
Chainama Cl LEIW LE3 24 A4
Chale Rd LEIN LE4 19 F5
Chalvington Cl LEIE LE5 38 A2
Chambers Cl COAL LE67 6 D4
Champion Cl LEIE LE5 28 B5
Chancel Rd LEIN LE4 10 D4
Chancery Pl LEI LE1 * 2 E4
Chancery St LEI LE1 2 E5
Chantry Cl RLEIW/BAR LE9 53 G3
Chapel Cl LUTT LE17 77 F2
RLEINE/SYS LE7 4 D5
RLEINE/SYS LE7 10 B1
Chapel Gn LEIW LE3 33 F3
Chapel Hl GBY/RBY LE6 16 A4
Chapel La GBY/RBY LE6 22 C2
HINC LE10 72 A5
LEIS LE2 45 H1
RLEIW/BAR LE9 30 B1
RLEIW/BAR LE9 65 F4
Chapel St END/NAR LE19 42 C5
HINC LE10 72 A5
LEIS LE2 47 E3
LUTT LE17 85 G3
RLEINE/SYS LE7 4 D5
RLEIS/BBY LE8 56 B2
RLEIW/BAR LE9 50 A5
Chaplin Ct LEIW LE3 33 H2
Chappell Cl LEIN LE4 12 C5
Charlecote Av LEIW LE3 34 A4
Charles Dr RLEINE/SYS LE7 17 G1
Charles St LEI LE1 3 F2
MKTHBORO LE16 81 G1
Charleston Crs
RLEIW/BAR LE9 50 A5
Charles' Wy LEIS LE2 47 G3
Charles Wy RLEIS/BBY LE8 66 A1
Charlock Rd LEIE LE5 21 H5
Charlton Cl RLEIS/BBY LE8 56 A5
Charnor Rd LEIW LE3 24 C2
Charnwood GBY/RBY LE6 22 B1

Charnwood Av *LEIN* LE4 ...... 12 D4
  RLEIS/BBY LE8 .... 55 H5
Charnwood Cl *LEIN* LE4 ..... 12 D4
  LEIW LE3 .... 33 E1
Charnwood Dr *COAL* LE67 ..... 6 D4
  LEIW LE3 .... 33 E2
  RLEINE/SYS LE7 .... 29 F5
Charnwood Rd
  RLEINE/SYS LE7 .... 9 F5
  RLEIW/BAR LE9 .... 50 B3
Charter St *LEI* LE1 .... 26 B5
Chartley Rd *LEIW* LE3 .... 35 E2
Chartwell Dr *WGSTN* LE18 .... 57 C1
Chartwell Point *WGSTN* LE18 .. 45 H5
The Chase *COAL* LE67 ....
   .... 43 H1
  RLEINE/SYS LE7 .... 5 G1
  RLEIS/BBY LE8 .... 61 E2
Chater Cl *LEIE* LE5 .... 28 D3
  MKTHBORO LE16 .... 79 E5
Chatham St *LEI* LE1 .... 3 F5
Chatsworth Av *LEIE* LE18 .... 57 G2
Chatsworth Dr
  MKTHBORO LE16 .... 82 B1
  RLEINE/SYS LE7 .... 12 D1
Chatsworth St *LEIS* LE2 ..... 27 E5
Chatteris Av *LEIS* LE2 .... 38 B2
Chaucer St *END/NAR* LE19 .... 54 C2
  LEIS LE2 .... 36 C2
Checketts Cl *LEIN* LE4 .... 19 H5
Checketts Rd *LEIN* LE4 .... 19 H4
Checkland Rd *LEIN* LE4 ...... 12 C4
Cheddar Rd *WGSTN* LE18 ..... 46 C5
Cheer Cl *RLEIS/BBY* LE8 ..... 65 H2
Chellaston Rd *WGSTN* LE18 ... 46 A4
Chelsea Cl *LEIS* LE2 .... 56 C2
Cheltenham Rd *LEIN* LE4 ...... 18 C5
Cheney End *RLEIW/BAR* LE9 .. 53 H3
Cheney Rd *LEIN* LE4 .... 21 E2
Chepstow Rd *LEIS* LE2 .... 36 C2
Cheriton Rd *LEIS* LE2 .... 44 D3
Cherrybrook Cl *LEIN* LE4 .... 10 E5
Cherry Dr *RLEINE/SYS* LE7 ... 13 F2
Cherry Gv *RLEIS/BBY* LE8 .... 61 E3
Cherry Hills Rd *LEIW* LE3 .... 24 A4
Cherryleas Dr *LEIW* LE3 ..... 35 E1
Cherry St *WGSTN* LE18 .... 57 H1
Cherrytree Av *LUTT* LE17 .... 85 E4
Cherry Tree Av
  RLEIW/BAR LE9 .... 32 C2
Cherrytree Cl
  RLEINE/SYS LE7 .... 17 F2
  RLEIS/BBY LE8 .... 66 D2
Cherry Tree Dr
  RLEIW/BAR LE9 .... 50 B3
Cherry Tree Gv
  END/NAR LE19 .... 42 C5
Cheshire Cl *LUTT* LE17 .... 85 F2
Cheshire Dr *WGSTN* LE18 .... 45 F5
Cheshire Gdns *LEIS* LE2 ..... 44 D1
Cheshire Rd *LEIS* LE2 .... 44 D1
Chester Cl *LEI* LE1 .... 3 J1
Chesterfield Rd *LEIE* LE5 .... 36 D1
Chesterfield Wy
  RLEIW/BAR LE9 .... 50 C4
Chester Rd *RLEIS/BBY* LE8 ... 56 C4
Chestnut Av *LEIE* LE5 .... 28 C1
  LEIS LE2 .... 46 D5
  LUTT LE17 .... 85 E3
Chestnut Cl *END/NAR* LE19 .. 54 D5
  RLEINE/SYS LE7 .... 9 F3
  RLEIW/BAR LE9 .... 74 C4
Chestnut Dr *LEIS* LE2 .... 60 B1
Chestnut Rd *LEIW* LE3 .... 39 E1
The Chestnuts *LEIW* LE3 ..... 24 A2
The Chestnuts
  RLEIS/BBY LE8 .... 67 E2
Chestnut Wk *COAL* LE67 ..... 14 C1
  GBY/RBY LE6 .... 16 B5
Chestnut Wy *RLEINE/SYS* LE7 .. 5 H2
Chettle Rd *LEIW* LE3 .... 25 F2
Chevin Av *LEIW* LE3 .... 24 B5
Cheviot Rd *LEIS* LE2 .... 44 C2
Chilcombe Cl *LEIN* LE4 ...... 19 E4
Chiltern Av *RLEIW/BAR* LE9 .. 50 C4
Chiltern Cl *MKTHBORO* LE16 .. 78 D4
Chiltern Gn *LEIS* LE2 .... 45 G2
Chislehurst Av *LEIW* LE3 .... 35 H4
Chiswick Rd *LEIE* LE5 .... 35 H4
Chitterman Wy *LUTT* LE17 ... 85 G1
Chorley Wood Rd *LEIE* LE5 .. 38 B1
Christopher Cl
  RLEIS/BBY LE8 .... 67 E3
Christopher Dr *LEIN* LE4 .... 20 D2
Christow St *LEI* LE1 .... 3 H1
Church Av *LEIW* LE3 .... 25 G5
Church Cl *LUTT* LE17 .... 77 F3
  LUTT LE17 .... 85 G5
  RLEINE/SYS LE7 .... 5 H2
  RLEIS/BBY LE8 .... 70 A2
  RLEIW/BAR LE9 .... 50 A5
  RLEIW/BAR LE9 .... 74 B5
Church Dr *COAL* LE67 .... 6 B4
Church Ga *LEI* LE1 .... 2 E2
  LUTT LE17 .... 85 G5
Church Hi *LEIN* LE4 .... 19 H1
  RLEINE/SYS LE7 .... 29 F2
Church Hill Rd *LEIN* LE4 ..... 12 C5
Churchill Cl *LEIS* LE2 .... 47 E3
  LUTT LE17 .... 85 E4
Churchill Dr *LEIW* LE3 .... 33 F1
Churchill St *LEIS* LE2 .... 3 K7
Churchill Wy *RLEIS/BBY* LE8 .. 66 B4
Church La *END/NAR* LE19 .... 55 E3
  GBY/RBY LE6 .... 22 C2
  LEIN LE4 .... 12 B5
  LEIS LE2 .... 45 H1
  LUTT LE17 .... 77 F3
  MKTHBORO LE16 .... 83 H1
  RLEINE/SYS LE7 .... 17 F1

  RLEIS/BBY LE7 .... 38 D1
  RLEIS/BBY LE8 .... 55 H4
  RLEIS/BBY LE8 .... 68 B4
  RLEIW/BAR LE9 .... 30 B2
  RLEIW/BAR LE9 .... 50 A5
Church Nook *WGSTN* LE18 ... 46 B5
Church Ponds Cl
  GBY/RBY LE6 .... 22 D2
Church Rd *LEIE* LE5 .... 37 H5
  LEIS LE2 .... 44 C2
  LEIW LE3 .... 23 H1
  RLEINE/SYS LE7 .... 12 A2
  RLEIS/BBY LE8 .... 60 C3
  RLEIS/BBY LE8 .... 65 H5
  RLEIW/BAR LE9 .... 22 D5
Church Sq *MKTHBORO* LE16 .. 81 H1
Church St *LEI* LE1 .... 3 G4
  LEIN LE4 .... 20 B1
  LEIE LE5 .... 47 E5
  LUTT LE17 .... 77 F3
  MKTHBORO LE16 .... 81 H1
  RLEIS/BBY LE8 .... 56 C3
  RLEIW/BAR LE9 .... 41 E5
  RLEIW/BAR LE9 .... 51 F2
  RLEIW/BAR LE9 .... 74 A5
Church Vw *END/NAR* LE19 .... 55 E5
Church Wk *MKTHBORO* LE16 .. 80 C1
Churchward Av *LEIN* LE4 ..... 18 C3
The Circle *LEIE* LE5 .... 27 H5
Clarefield Rd *LEIW* LE3 ...... 25 F5
Clare Gv *LEIW* LE3 .... 33 H3
Claremont Dr
  MKTHBORO LE16 .... 82 B1
Claremont St *LEIN* LE4 ...... 19 G4
Clarence Rd *END/NAR* LE19 .. 55 F1
Clarence St *LEI* LE1 .... 3 G4
  MKTHBORO LE16 .... 82 A1
Clarendon Park Rd *LEIS* LE2 .. 36 A4
Clarendon St *LEIS* LE2 .... 2 D7
Clarke Gv *LEIN* LE4 .... 19 G1
Clarkes Rd *WGSTN* LE18 ..... 57 H1
Clarke St *LEIN* LE4 .... 19 H4
  MKTHBORO LE16 .... 82 D4
Clark Gdns *RLEIS/BBY* LE8 ... 56 A3
Claybrook Av *LEIW* LE3 ...... 34 C5
Claydon Rd *LEIE* LE5 .... 27 G2
Claymill Rd *LEIN* LE4 .... 20 D3
Clayton Dr *LEIN* LE4 .... 20 D1
Clear View Crs
  RLEIW/BAR LE9 .... 51 F2
Clematis Cl *LEIN* LE4 .... 18 A2
Clement Av *LEIN* LE4 .... 19 G4
Clevedon Crs *LEIN* LE4 ...... 27 G2
Cleveland Rd *WGSTN* LE18 ... 46 B5
Cleveleys Av *LEIW* LE3 ...... 34 C5
Cliffe House Ms
  RLEIS/BBY LE8 .... 55 H4
Cliffe Rd *LEIN* LE4 .... 19 F1
Clifford St *LEI* LE1 .... 2 A5
  WGSTN LE18 .... 57 F1
Cliffwood Av *LEIN* LE4 ...... 11 F5
Clifton Dr *WGSTN* LE18 ...... 57 C3
Clifton Rd *LEIS* LE2 .... 35 G5
Clint Hill Dr *RLEIW/BAR* LE9 .. 62 C4
Clipper Rd *LEIN* LE4 .... 26 C1
Clipstone Cl *LEIN* LE4 .... 18 B4
Clipstone Gdns *WGSTN* LE18 .. 58 C1
Clipstone St *MKTHBORO* LE16 .. 82 A3
The Cloisters *RLEIW/BAR* LE9 .. 51 E5
The Close *END/NAR* LE19 ..... 54 C1
  RLEINE/SYS LE7 .... 9 F2
  RLEIW/BAR LE9 .... 50 B4
Clovelly Rd *LEIE* LE5 .... 37 F1
  LEIS LE2 .... 24 B2
Clover Cl *END/NAR* LE19 ..... 54 C5
Cloverdale Rd *LEIE* LE5 ...... 21 G5
Clover Wy *RLEINE/SYS* LE7 .. 13 C2
Clumber Cl *RLEINE/SYS* LE7 .. 9 F1
Clumber Rd *LEIE* LE5 .... 27 G5
Clyde St *LEI* LE1 .... 3 H2
Coalbourn Cl *LEIN* LE4 ...... 19 E5
Coales Gdns *RLEIS/BBY* LE8 .. 66 A1
Coales Gdns
  MKTHBORO LE16 .... 78 B4
Coatbridge Av *LEIN* LE4 ..... 20 B3
Coates Av *LEIN* LE4 .... 25 E3
Cobwells Cl *RLEIS/BBY* LE8 .. 68 C4
Cokayne Rd *LEIN* LE4 .... 24 B4
Colbert Dr *LEIW* LE3 .... 44 A1
Colby Dr *LEIN* LE4 .... 21 H5
Colby Rd *LEIN* LE4 .... 20 D2
Colchester Rd *LEIE* LE5 ...... 28 B4
Colebrook Cl *LEIE* LE5 .... 37 E2
Coleford Rd *LEIN* LE4 .... 21 E2
Coleman Cl *LEIE* LE5 .... 27 H5
Coleman Rd *LEIE* LE5 .... 27 H5
  RLEIS/BBY LE8 .... 68 A3
Coleridge Dr *END/NAR* LE19 .. 42 D5
Coles Cl *LEIN* LE4 .... 20 B2
Colindale Av *LEIN* LE4 .... 11 G4
Colin Grundy Dr *LEIE* LE5 ... 28 C1
Collaton Rd *WGSTN* LE18 .... 58 A2
College Av *LEIS* LE2 .... 3 J6
College Cl *RLEINE/SYS* LE7 ... 13 F1
  RLEIS/BBY LE8 .... 55 H5
College St *LEIS* LE2 .... 3 J6
Collett Rd *LEIN* LE4 .... 18 C3
Collingham Rd *LEIW* LE3 .... 35 E3
Collin Pl *LEIN* LE4 .... 20 A5
Collins Cl *LEIW* LE3 .... 33 H3
Colne Cl *LEIS* LE2 .... 47 H3
Colsterdale Cl *LEIN* LE4 ..... 18 D2
Coltbeck Av *END/NAR* LE19 .. 54 C4
Colthurst Wy *LEIE* LE5 ...... 29 E4
Colton St *LEI* LE1 .... 3 G4
Coltsfoot Cl *LEIE* LE5 .... 21 G5
Coltsfoot Wy
  RLEIW/BAR LE9 .... 74 C5
Columbia Cl *END/NAR* LE19 .. 42 C5
Columbine Cl *LEIN* LE4 ...... 34 A3
Columbine Rd *LEIE* LE5 ...... 21 H4
Colwell Rd *LEIW* LE3 .... 25 H2

Combe Cl *LEIW* LE3 .... 25 G2
Comet Cl *LEIW* LE3 .... 25 F3
Commercial Sq *LEIS* LE5 ..... 35 H4
The Common *LEIE* LE5 .... 37 G2
  RLEIW/BAR LE9 .... 50 B5
Compass Rd *LEIE* LE5 .... 28 C3
Compton Dr *RLEIW/BAR* LE9 .. 53 H3
Compton Rd *LEIW* LE3 .... 34 B2
Conaglen Rd *LEIS* LE2 .... 44 B2
Condor Cl *RLEIW/BAR* LE9 ... 74 B2
Conduit St *LEIS* LE2 .... 3 H5
Cone La *LEIN* LE4 .... 36 C3
Coney La *END/NAR* LE19 ..... 55 E3
Coneygrey *RLEIS/BBY* LE8 .... 68 C2
Conifer Cl *LUTT* LE17 .... 85 F5
Coninsby Cl *LEIE* LE5 .... 34 D4
Coniston Av *LEIE* LE5 .... 35 G2
Coniston Cl *RLEIW/BAR* LE9 .. 51 F3
Coniston Wy *RLEIW/BAR* LE9 .. 51 F3
Connaught Rd
  MKTHBORO LE16 .... 78 D5
Connaught St *LEIS* LE2 .... 3 K7
Connell Cl *MKTHBORO* LE16 .. 80 C1
Connery Leys Rd *LEIN* LE4 ... 11 F3
Constable Av *LEIN* LE4 ...... 25 G3
Constance Rd *LEIE* LE5 ...... 27 F5
Constitution Hl *LEI* LE1 ..... 3 H4
Conway Rd *LEIN* LE4 .... 36 D2
Cooden Av *LEIW* LE3 .... 34 B4
Cooke Cl *LEIN* LE4 .... 12 D5
  LEIW LE3 .... 33 H4
Cooke's Dr *RLEIW/BAR* LE9 .. 74 A3
Cook's La *RLEIW/BAR* LE9 ... 72 B2
Cooks La *WGSTN* LE18 .... 58 C4
Cookson Rd *LEIN* LE4 .... 21 E2
Cooling Cl *LEIE* LE5 .... 27 H5
  LEIN LE4 .... 47 F4
Coombe Hi *LEIE* LE5 .... 47 F4
Coombe Ri *LEIE* LE5 .... 47 G5
Co-operation St
  END/NAR LE19 .... 42 D5
Cooper Cl *LEIS* LE2 .... 44 C2
Cooper Rd *LEIN* LE4 .... 19 G1
Cooper St *LEIN* LE4 .... 53 H3
Cooper Gdns *LEIS* LE2 ...... 47 H4
Cooper La *GBY/RBY* LE6 ..... 16 B5
Cooper's La *LUTT* LE17 ...... 77 F2
Cooper's Nook
  RLEINE/SYS LE7 .... 5 G2
Cooper St *LEIN* LE4 .... 26 C1
Copdale Rd *LEIE* LE5 .... 27 G5
Copeland Av *LEIN* LE4 .... 25 E1
Copeland Rd *LEIS* LE2 .... 19 F1
Copinger Rd *LEIS* LE2 .... 45 F1
Coplow Av *LEIE* LE5 .... 37 E3
Coplow Crs *RLEINE/SYS* LE7 .. 13 C2
Coppice Cl *LEIN* LE4 .... 13 E5
The Coppice *COAL* LE67 ..... 6 C4
  END/NAR LE19 .... 54 C3
  LEIN LE4 .... 13 E5
Copse Cl *LEIS* LE2 .... 44 C5
  LEIS LE2 .... 47 H3
  LEIW LE3 .... 32 C4
The Copse *RLEINE/SYS* LE7 .. 39 F1
Copthorne Cl *LEIS* LE2 ...... 24 B5
Copt Oak Rd *END/NAR* LE19 .. 54 B2
Corah St *LEIS* LE2 .... 2 C5
Cordery Rd *LEIE* LE5 .... 26 C1
Corbet Cl *LEIN* LE4 .... 18 B4
Cordelia Cl *LEIS* LE2 .... 27 G2
Cordery Rd *LEIE* LE5 .... 37 H2
Cordonnier Cl
  RLEIW/BAR LE9 .... 74 C5
Corfield Ri *LEIW* LE3 .... 34 A2
Coriander Rd *LEIE* LE5 .... 21 H4
Cork La *LEIS* LE2 .... 56 A1
Cork St *LEIE* LE5 .... 36 D1
Cornfield Cl *END/NAR* LE19 .. 55 E4
Cornfields *LEIS* LE2 .... 49 F3
Cornwallis Av *LEIN* LE4 ..... 18 B5
Cornwall Rd *LEIN* LE4 .... 19 G1
  WGSTN LE18 .... 57 F1
Cornwall St *END/NAR* LE19 .. 42 D5
Coronation Av
  RLEIW/BAR LE9 .... 74 A3
  WGSTN LE18 .... 57 H1
Coronation Rd
  RLEIW/BAR LE9 .... 50 D5
Coronet Cl *RLEINE/SYS* LE7 .. 17 G1
Corporation Rd *LEIN* LE4 .... 19 F5
Corshaw Wk *LEIN* LE4 ...... 27 F2
Cort Crs *LEIW* LE3 .... 34 A4
Cosby La *RLEIW/BAR* LE9 .... 75 H3
Cosby Rd *END/NAR* LE19 .... 55 E5
  RLEIS/BBY LE8 .... 66 B3
  RLEIW/BAR LE9 .... 74 B3
Cossington La
  RLEINE/SYS LE7 .... 4 D2
Cossington St *LEIN* LE4 ..... 26 D1
Cotley Rd *LEIN* LE4 .... 18 C2
Cotswold Av *RLEIW/BAR* LE9 .. 65 F4
Cottage Cl *GBY/RBY* LE6 .... 22 C1
Cottage Farm *RLEIS/BBY* LE8 .. 43 H2
Cottage Gdns
  RLEIW/BAR LE9 .... 51 F3
Cottage La *COAL* LE67 .... 6 A1
  RLEIW/BAR LE9 .... 30 B1
  RLEIW/BAR LE9 .... 74 C3
Cottage Rd *WGSTN* LE18 .... 58 C2
Cottage Wy *LEIW* LE3 .... 34 D5
Cottagers Cl *LEIS* LE2 .... 45 E3
Cottesbrooke Cl
  WGSTN LE18 .... 58 B1
Cottesmore Av *LEIE* LE5 .... 47 G4
Cottesmore Rd *LEIE* LE2 .... 27 F3
Cotton Cl *LEIN* LE4 .... 18 C2
Cotton Ms *LEIN* LE4 .... 51 F4
Coulson Cl *RLEIS/BBY* LE8 ... 56 A5
Coulter Cl *RLEINE/SYS* LE7 .. 29 F2
Council St *LUTT* LE17 .... 85 C3
Countesthorpe Rd
  RLEIW/BAR LE9 .... 65 F4
  LEIS LE2 .... 57 F2
Counting House Rd
  LEIS LE2 .... 35 H3

Countryman's Wy
  RLEINE/SYS LE7 .... 5 G1
Countryman Wy *COAL* LE67 .. 6 C4
Court Cl *RLEIW/BAR* LE9 ..... 23 E5
Courtenay Rd *LEIW* LE3 ..... 35 E2
Court Rd *LEIS* LE2 .... 56 B1
  RLEINE/SYS LE7 .... 5 H2
Coventry Rd *END/NAR* LE19 .. 54 D4
  HINC LE10 .... 72 C4
  LUTT LE17 .... 84 B3
  MKTHBORO LE16 .... 81 G2
Coventry St *LEIW* LE3 .... 35 E2
Coverdale Rd *WGSTN* LE18 .. 58 D2
Coverside Rd *RLEIS/BBY* LE8 .. 61 E2
Covert Cl *LEIS* LE2 .... 47 G2
  RLEINE/SYS LE7 .... 5 G2
Covert Wy *LEIW* LE3 .... 12 C1
Cow La *GBY/RBY* LE6 .... 14 C4
Cowley Wy *LEIN* LE4 .... 18 C4
Cowslip Cl *END/NAR* LE19 .. 54 B3
Crabtree Cnr *LEIS* LE2 ...... 47 H3
Cradock Rd *LEIS* LE2 .... 36 B5
Cradock St *LEIW* LE3 .... 3 J2
Crafton St East *LEI* LE1 ..... 3 H2
Crafton St West *LEI* LE1 .... 3 G2
Craftsmans Wy
  RLEINE/SYS LE7 .... 5 G2
Craig Gdns *LEIW* LE3 .... 24 B4
Craighill Rd *LEIS* LE2 .... 35 H3
Cranberry Cl *LEIW* LE3 ...... 33 H5
Cranbourne Gdns *LEIS* LE2 .. 37 H5
Cranbrook Rd
  RLEINE/SYS LE7 .... 29 F3
Crane-ley Rd *GBY/RBY* LE6 .. 16 A4
Cranesbill Rd *LEIE* LE5 ...... 28 C1
Crane St *LEI* LE1 .... 2 E2
Cranfield Rd *LEIE* LE5 ...... 44 D2
Cranmer Cl *RLEIS/BBY* LE8 .. 56 A5
Cranmer Dr *RLEINE/SYS* LE7 .. 13 C2
Cranmer St *LEIW* LE3 .... 2 A6
Cranoe Rd *RLEIS/BBY* LE8 ... 71 H2
Cransley Rd *LEIS* LE2 .... 21 G4
Cranstone Crs *LEIW* LE3 .... 24 A4
Crantock Cl *LEIE* LE5 .... 38 A2
Cranwell Cl *LEIE* LE5 .... 37 H3
Craven St *LEI* LE1 .... 2 D1
Crawford Cl *LEIW* LE3 ...... 25 H4
Crawford Rd *LEIN* LE4 ...... 26 C3
Crayford Wy *LEIE* LE5 ...... 28 D1
Craythorne Wy *WGSTN* LE18 .. 58 C1
Creaton Cl *WGSTN* LE18 .... 58 C1
Creaton Rd *WGSTN* LE18 ... 58 C1
Crediton Cl *WGSTN* LE18 .... 58 B3
Crescent Cl *MKTHBORO* LE16 .. 78 D5
Crescent Rd *LUTT* LE17 ..... 85 G2
Crescent St *LEI* LE1 .... 3 G4
The Crescent *LEI* LE1 * 3 F6
  MKTHBORO LE16 .... 78 D5
  RLEIS/BBY LE8 .... 56 B4
  RLEIS/BBY LE8 * 66 B4
  WGSTN LE18 .... 46 A4
The Crest *RLEIW/BAR* LE9 ... 74 C5
Cresswell Cl *LEIN* LE4 .... 21 E1
The Crestway *RLEIS/BBY* LE8 .. 55 H3
Crete Av *WGSTN* LE18 .... 57 E1
Critchlow Rd *RLEIW/BAR* LE9 .. 55 H3
Croft Av *LEIS* LE2 .... 50 B5
Croft Cl *RLEIW/BAR* LE9 ..... 50 B5
Croft Dr *WGSTN* LE18 .... 45 H4
Crofters Cl *LEIW* LE3 .... 23 C2
Crofters Dr *LEIS* LE2 .... 28 A3
Croft Hill Rd *RLEIW/BAR* LE9 .. 53 E5
Croft Rd *LEIN* LE4 .... 51 G5
  LEIN LE4 .... 10 B5
  LEIS LE2 .... 53 E1
The Croft *RLEIW/BAR* LE9 ... 22 D5
Croftway *COAL* LE67 .... 6 B4
Croft Wy *RLEIW/BAR* LE9 .... 74 C5
Cromarty Cl *LEIN* LE4 .... 20 B4
Cromer St *LEIS* LE2 .... 36 B5
Cromford Av *WGSTN* LE18 .. 57 C2
Cromford Rd *RLEIW/BAR* LE9 .. 65 F2
Cromford St *LEIS* LE2 .... 27 F4
Cromford Wy
  RLEIW/BAR LE9 .... 74 D5
Cromwell Crs
  MKTHBORO LE16 .... 81 G3
Cromwell Rd *RLEIS/BBY* LE8 .. 60 D3
Cropston Cl *LEIN* LE4 .... 20 C5
Cropston Rd *RLEINE/SYS* LE7 .. 17 G1
Cropthorne Av *LEIE* LE5 .... 27 G5
Crosby Rd *MKTHBORO* LE16 .. 82 A3
Cross Hedge Cl *LEIN* LE4 ... 18 C3
Cross Keys Gn *LEIE* LE5 .... 29 E3
Crossleys *RLEIS/BBY* LE8 .... 68 B4
Crossley St *LEIW* LE3 .... 26 A2
Cross Rd *LEIS* LE2 .... 36 C5
Cross St *END/NAR* LE19 ..... 55 H2
  LEIN LE4 .... 26 C1
  LEIS LE2 .... 47 E1
  MKTHBORO LE16 .... 81 H2
  RLEINE/SYS LE7 .... 13 F1
  RLEIS/BBY LE8 .... 56 B3
  RLEIW/BAR LE9 .... 58 B1
The Cross *END/NAR* LE19 ... 42 D5
The Crossways *LEIN* LE4 .... 11 G5
The Crossway *LEIS* LE2 ..... 45 F2
  LEIW LE3 .... 25 F5
Crowan Dr *WGSTN* LE18 .... 58 A3
Crowfoot Wy
  RLEIW/BAR LE9 .... 74 B5
Crowhurst Dr *RLEIW/BAR* LE9 .. 34 A5
Crow La *LEIN* LE4 .... 35 F2
Crown Cl *RLEIS/BBY* LE8 .... 60 D4
Crown Hills Av *LEIE* LE5 .... 27 G5
Crown Hills Ri *LEIE* LE5 .... 27 G5
Croyland Gn *LEIN* LE4 ...... 19 E4
Cufflin Cl *GBY/RBY* LE6 ..... 22 D2
Cuffling Cl *LEIW* LE3 .... 24 B4
Cuffling Dr *LEIW* LE3 .... 24 B4

Culham Av *LEIW* LE3 .... 27 F2
Culver Rd *LEIW* LE3 .... 25 G2
Culworth Dr *RLEIW/BAR* LE9 .. 58 C1
Cumberland Rd *WGSTN* LE18 .. 45 E5
Cumberland St *LEI* LE1 ...... 2 C2
Cumberland Wy
  RLEIW/BAR LE9 .... 50 A4
Cumberwell Dr
  END/NAR LE19 .... 55 E2
Cunningham Dr *LUTT* LE17 .. 85 E4
Curlew Cl *RLEINE/SYS* LE7 ... 4 C5
Curlew Wk *LEIE* LE5 * 28 D4
Curteys Cl *LEIN* LE4 .... 25 F3
Curtis Cl *RLEIS/BBY* LE8 .... 55 H4
Curzon Av *LEIN* LE4 .... 19 G1
  WGSTN LE18 .... 57 G2
Curzon Cl *RLEINE/SYS* LE7 .. 5 G2
Curzon St *LEI* LE1 .... 3 G4
  LEIS LE2 .... 45 E1
  LEIE LE5 .... 26 D3
Cutters Cl *END/NAR* LE19 ... 54 C4
The Cuttings *RLEINE/SYS* LE7 .. 29 F4
Cygnet Cl *RLEIW/BAR* LE9 ... 4 C5
Cyprus Rd *LEIS* LE2 .... 45 G2
Cyril St *LEIW* LE3 .... 34 C5

D

Dabey Cl *COAL* LE67 .... 6 B4
Daisy Cl *GBY/RBY* LE6 .... 16 C4
Dakyn Rd *LEIE* LE5 .... 28 D4
Dalby Av *LEIN* LE4 .... 11 H4
  RLEINE/SYS LE7 .... 29 G5
Dalby Rd *GBY/RBY* LE6 ...... 16 B4
Dalby Rd *RLEINE/SYS* LE7 ... 9 F5
Dale Acre *RLEIS/BBY* LE8 .... 67 F2
Dale Av *WGSTN* LE18 .... 45 G4
The Dales *RLEIS/BBY* LE8 .... 66 C2
Dale St *LEIS* LE2 .... 2 B5
Dalkeith Rd *LEIN* LE4 .... 20 B5
Dalby Ci *RLEINE/SYS* LE7 .... 13 F2
Dallison Cl *MKTHBORO* LE16 . 81 H4
Dalton Rd *LEIE* LE5 .... 21 H4
Danbury Dr *LEIN* LE4 .... 18 D5
Dandees Cl *COAL* LE67 ...... 6 C3
Danehurst Av *LEIW* LE3 ..... 25 F4
Daneshill Rd *LEIW* LE3 ...... 25 G5
Dane St *LEIW* LE3 .... 2 A4
Dannett St *LEIW* LE3 .... 2 A3
Dan's La *RLEIW/BAR* LE9 .... 40 B1
Danvers Rd *LEIW* LE3 .... 35 E2
Darby Wy *END/NAR* LE19 .... 54 C4
Darenth Dr *LEIE* LE4 .... 18 A4
Darien Wy *LEIW* LE3 .... 33 G3
Darker St *LEI* LE1 .... 2 E2
Darley Av *WGSTN* LE18 ...... 57 G2
Darley Rd *RLEIS/BBY* LE8 ... 56 A4
Darley St *LEIW* LE3 .... 27 E5
Darlington Rd *LEIE* LE5 ..... 35 F2
Darnall Rd *LEIS* LE2 .... 47 G3
Dartford Rd *LEIS* LE2 .... 35 F4
Darwen Cl *LEIW* LE3 .... 25 G5
Darwin Cl *LEIN* LE4 .... 25 F3
  RLEIW/BAR LE9 .... 74 B4
Dashwood Rd *LEIS* LE2 ...... 36 C2
Davenport Av *LEIS* LE2 ..... 46 D2
Davenport Rd *LEIE* LE5 ..... 28 B5
  WGSTN LE18 .... 58 B2
Davett Cl *LEIE* LE5 .... 28 B4
David Av *LEIN* LE4 .... 19 E2
Davies Cl *MKTHBORO* LE16 .. 78 B4
Davison Cl *LEIE* LE5 .... 28 A5
Dawlish Cl *LEIE* LE5 .... 28 D5
Dawson's La *RLEIW/BAR* LE9 .. 50 B5
Daybell Cl *RLEIS/BBY* LE8 ... 55 H2
Day St *LEIN* LE4 .... 19 G4
Deacon Cl *LUTT* LE17 .... 85 E1
Deacon Rd *MKTHBORO* LE16 . 78 B4
Deacon Cots
  RLEIW/BAR LE9 * 63 G2
Deacon Rd *LEIN* LE4 .... 19 G4
Deacon St *LEIS* LE2 .... 2 D7
Deancourt Rd *LEIE* LE2 ..... 45 H2
Deanery Crs *LEIN* LE4 .... 10 D4
Dean Rd *LEIN* LE4 .... 27 E1
Debdale La *RLEIS/BBY* LE8 .. 69 H5
Deene Cl *MKTHBORO* LE16 * .. 82 D1
Deepdale *LEIE* LE5 .... 27 H4
Delaware Rd *LEIE* LE5 .... 38 C2
De Lisle Cl *MKTHBORO* LE16 . 78 D4
De Montfort Ms *LEI* LE1 ..... 3 H6
De Montfort Sq *LEI* LE1 ..... 3 G7
De Montfort St *LEI* LE1 ...... 3 G7
Dempsey Cl *LUTT* LE17 ..... 85 G1
Denacre Av *WGSTN* LE18 .... 57 G2
Denbigh Pl *LUTT* LE17 .... 85 G2
Denbydale *WGSTN* LE18 ..... 58 D2
Denegate Av *LEIW* LE3 ...... 11 F4
Denham St *LEIW* LE3 .... 24 A4
Denis Cl *LEIW* LE3 .... 34 A3
Deniston Av *RLEIW/BAR* LE9 .. 73 H2
Denman La *RLEIW/BAR* LE9 .. 52 C5
Denmark Rd *LEIS* LE2 .... 35 G5
Denmead Av *WGSTN* LE18 ... 46 A5
Denton St *LEIS* LE2 .... 25 F5
Derby Cl *RLEIW/BAR* LE9 ... 23 E5
Dersingham Rd *LEIN* LE4 .... 18 D5
Derwent Rd *RLEIW/BAR* LE9 .. 74 B4
Derwent St *LEI* LE1 .... 27 E5
Derwent Wk *LEI* LE1 .... 47 G3
Desford La *RLEIW/BAR* LE9 .. 30 A3
  RLEIW/BAR LE9 .... 50 D5
Desford Rd *END/NAR* LE19 .. 54 D4
  END/NAR LE19 .... 40 D4
  RLEIW/BAR LE9 .... 50 B2
Devana Rd *LEIS* LE2 .... 36 C2
Devenports Hl
  RLEINE/SYS LE7 .... 29 H5

Devenports Wy
RLEINE/SYS LE7 29 H5
De Verdon Rd LUTT LE17 85 E4
Devitt Wy RLEIW/BAR LE9 74 B5
Devonia Rd LEIS LE2 47 H4
Devonshire Av WGSTN LE18 57 G2
Devonshire Rd LEIN LE4 26 A1
Devonshire St LEI LE1 2 E1
Devon Wy LEIE LE5 27 H5
Dickens Ct LEIW LE3 25 E5
The Dicken RLEIS/BBY LE8 55 H4
Dickinson Wy LEIN LE4 12 D5
Didsbury St LEIW LE3 34 A2
Digby Cl LEIW LE3 34 D1
Dillon Ri LEIW LE3 24 D2
Dillon Rd LEIW LE3 24 D1
Dillon Wy LEIW LE3 24 D1
Dimmingsdale Cl
RLEINE/SYS LE7 9 G5
Dingley Av LEIN LE4 27 E1
Dingley Link WGSTN LE18 46 C5
Dingley Rd MKTHBORO LE16 79 F3
Dingley Ter MKTHBORO LE16 82 A1
Diseworth St LEIS LE2 27 E5
Disney Cl RLEIW/BAR LE9 62 B4
Disraeli Cl RLEIS/BBY LE8 69 H3
Disraeli St LEIS LE2 44 C1
Ditchling Av LEIW LE3 25 E4
Dixon Dr LEIS LE2 36 C2
Dobney Av RLEINE/SYS LE7 5 F4
Doctor Cookes Cl
RLEIW/BAR LE9 50 A5
Doctors Flds RLEIW/BAR LE9 50 D4
Doddridge Rd
MKTHBORO LE16 78 C5
Dog & Gun La RLEIS/BBY LE8 65 H1
Dogwood Ct LEIS LE2 47 E1
Dominion Rd LEIW LE3 24 A2
Dominus Wy END/NAR LE19 33 H5
Donald Cl LEIN LE4 20 D3
Donaldson Rd LEIN LE4 26 C2
Doncaster Rd LEIN LE4 26 D1
Donnett Cl LEIE LE5 28 B4
Donnington St LEIS LE2 27 E5
Dorchester Cl RLEIS/BBY LE8 56 C5
WGSTN LE18 58 A3
Dorchester Rd LEIW LE3 34 D1
Dore Rd LEIE LE5 36 C1
Dorothy Av LEIN LE4 20 B1
LEIS LE2 44 B5
Dorothy Rd LEIE LE5 27 F5
Dorset Av LEIW LE3 24 A1
WGSTN LE18 45 F5
Dorset St LEIN LE4 26 C2
Double Rail Cl WGSTN LE18 57 G2
Doudney Cl RLEIW/BAR LE9 62 B5
Douglas Bader Dr LUTT LE17 85 G1
Douglass Dr
MKTHBORO LE16 78 D4
Dovecote Cl RLEIW/BAR LE9 72 B2
Dovecote La RLEIW/BAR LE9 63 G1
Dovecote Rd
RLEIW/BAR LE9 63 G1
Dovecote Wy
RLEIW/BAR LE9 50 B5
Dovedale Av RLEIS/BBY LE8 56 B4
Dovedale Rd LEIN LE4 12 C5
LEIS LE2 37 E4
Dove Ri LEIS LE2 47 G2
Dover St LEI LE1 3 G5
RLEIS/BBY LE8 69 H3
Downham Av LEIN LE4 19 E5
Downing Dr LEIE LE5 38 A2
Down St LEIN LE4 26 D1
Draper St LEIS LE2 36 C2
Drayton Rd LEIW LE3 24 C3
Dribdale RLEIS/BBY LE8 68 C4
Drinkstone Rd LEIE LE5 37 E1
The Drive LEIN LE4 19 G1
RLEINE/SYS LE7 29 F2
RLEIS/BBY LE8 66 B2
RLEIS/BBY LE8 70 B3
RLEIW/BAR LE9 50 B3
Dronfield St LEIE LE5 27 E5
Drovers Ct RLEIW/BAR LE9 30 B2
Drovers Wy END/NAR LE19 54 D4
RLEIW/BAR LE9 30 B2
Drumcliff Rd LEIE LE5 29 E4
Drummond Rd
END/NAR LE19 42 C5
LEIN LE4 19 F4
Drury La LEIS LE2 46 D2
Dryden St LEI LE1 3 G2
Dudleston Cl LEIE LE5 28 A5
Dudley Av LEIE LE5 28 C4
Dudley Cl LEIE LE5 28 C4
Duffield Av WGSTN LE18 45 H4
Duffield St LEIS LE2 27 E5
Dukes Cl LEIN LE4 12 D5
WGSTN LE18 45 H5
Dukes Dr LEIS LE2 36 C3
Duke St LEIS LE2 3 F6
Dulverton Cl WGSTN LE18 58 B3
Dulverton Rd LEIW LE3 25 G5
Dumbleton Av LEIW LE3 35 E4
Dunbar Rd LEIN LE4 20 C5
Dunblane Av LEIN LE4 20 B3
Duncan Av RLEIW/BAR LE9 53 H4
Duncan Rd LEIS LE2 44 D1
Duncombe Rd LEIW LE3 18 A5
Dundee Rd RLEIS/BBY LE8 56 B5
Dundonald Rd LEIN LE4 26 C1
Dunholme Rd LEIN LE4 27 G1
Dunire Cl LEIN LE4 18 C4
Dunkirk St LEI LE1 3 G6
Dunley Wy LUTT LE17 85 G2
Dunlin Rd LEIE LE5 27 E3
Dunmore Rd
MKTHBORO LE16 82 A3
Dunslade Cl
MKTHBORO LE16 82 C2
Dunslade Gv
MKTHBORO LE16 82 B2
Dunslade Rd
MKTHBORO LE16 82 B2
Duns La LEIW LE3 2 C5
Dunstall Av LEIW LE3 33 H3
Dunster St LEIW LE3 25 F5
Dunton Rd LUTT LE17 76 B4
RLEIW/BAR LE9 74 D5
Dunton St LEIW LE3 2 B1
WGSTN LE18 57 F2
Dupont Gdns LEIW LE3 24 B3
Durban Rd LEIN LE4 10 C5
Durham Dr WGSTN LE18 45 G4
Durnford Rd WGSTN LE18 58 A3
Durston Cl LEIE LE5 38 B1
Duxbury Rd LEIE LE5 27 G3
Dwyer Cl RLEINE/SYS LE7 12 D2
Dysart Wy LEI LE1 26 C3
Dyson Cl LUTT LE17 85 G2

E

Eagle Cl RLEIW/BAR LE9 74 A2
Ealing Rd LEIS LE2 35 H4
Eamont Cl LEIS LE2 44 D5
Earle Smith Cl
RLEIS/BBY LE8 55 H4
Earl Howe St LEIS LE2 3 K6
Earl Howe Ter LEIW LE3 2 B5
Earl Russell St LEIS LE2 44 C2
Earls Cl LEIN LE4 12 D5
Earl Shilton Rd
RLEIW/BAR LE9 52 A2
Earl St LEI LE1 3 G2
RLEIW/BAR LE9 51 G2
Earls Wy LEIN LE4 12 D5
Earlswood Rd LEIE LE5 38 B2
East Av LEIS LE2 36 C3
RLEINE/SYS LE7 5 F5
RLEIS/BBY LE8 55 H3
East Bond St LEI LE1 2 E2
Eastcourt Rd LEIS LE2 46 A2
Eastern Bvd LEIS LE2 35 G2
Eastfield Rd LEIN LE4 12 D4
LEIW LE3 25 F5
East Gn RLEIW/BAR LE9 50 A5
Eastleigh Rd LEIW LE3 35 E2
East Link END/NAR LE19 43 F1
Eastmere Rd WGSTN LE18 46 D5
East Park Rd LEIE LE5 36 C1
East Rd LEIN LE4 19 G3
East St LEI LE1 3 G5
LEIS LE2 47 E2
MKTHBORO LE16 81 G1
Eastway Rd WGSTN LE18 46 B4
Eastwood Rd LEIS LE2 44 D3
Ebchester Cl LEIS LE2 44 C5
Ebchester Rd LEIS LE2 44 C5
Edale Cl LEIW LE3 34 A2
Eddystone Rd LEIE LE5 29 E3
Eden Cl LEIS LE2 47 G2
Eden Gdns LEIN LE4 10 C5
Edenhall Cl LEIN LE4 20 B4
LEIS LE2 47 H4
Edenhurst Av LEIW LE3 43 H1
Eden Rd LEIS LE2 47 G2
Edensor St LEIN LE4 20 A4
Eden Wy LEIS LE2 56 D1
Edgbaston Cl LEIN LE4 10 D5
Edgcote Ct LEIE LE5 27 G2
Edgefield Cl LEIE LE5 21 F4
Edgehill Cl RLEIS/BBY LE8 60 D3
Edgehill Rd LEIN LE4 27 G1
Edgeley Cl LEIW LE3 25 E1
Edgeley Rd RLEIS/BBY LE8 67 F2
Edinburgh Cl
MKTHBORO LE16 78 D5
Edinburgh Rd
RLEIW/BAR LE9 50 D4
Edith Av LEIW LE3 44 A1
Edith Murphy Cl LEIN LE4 19 F1
Edmonton Rd LEI LE1 3 H1
Edward Av LEIW LE3 34 B5
Edward Cl LEIS LE2 47 G3
Edward Dr LEIS LE2 57 E2
Edward Rd LEIS LE2 36 B3
MKTHBORO LE16 78 B4
RLEIS/BBY LE8 68 B4
Edward St RLEINE/SYS LE7 17 G1
Egerton Av LEIN LE4 19 E5
Egginton St LEIE LE5 36 C1
Eglantine Cl LEIS LE2 47 E1
Eider Cl RLEIS/BBY LE8 65 G2
Eileen Av LEIN LE4 19 E5
Elbow La LEI LE1 2 D2
Elder Cl LEIW LE3 17 H4
Eldon St LEI LE1 3 G2
Elfin Gv LUTT LE17 77 G2
Elgin Av LEIW LE3 24 D2
Elizabethan Wy LUTT LE17 85 H2
Elizabeth Cl RLEIS/BBY LE8 68 B5
Elizabeth Ct WGSTN LE18 58 A1
Elizabeth Crs WGSTN LE18 45 H4
Elizabeth Dr LEIN LE4 12 C4
LEIS LE2 47 G4
Elizabeth Gdns
RLEIS/BBY LE8 55 H4
Elizabeth Rd RLEIS/BBY LE8 68 B4
Elizabeth St LEIE LE5 27 G5
Elland Rd LEIW LE3 23 H5
Ellesmere Pl LEIW LE3 34 D3
Ellesmere Rd LEIW LE3 34 D3
Elliot Cl LEIS LE2 48 A4
RLEIS/BBY LE8 66 A2
RLEIS/BBY LE8 70 A3
Elliots Yd RLEIS/BBY LE8 67 F3
Elliott Dr LEIN LE4 21 E1
LEIW LE3 33 F2
Elliott Rd LEIN LE4 18 D3
Ellis Av LEIN LE4 26 C1
Ellis Cl LEIW LE3 23 H2
Ellis Dr RLEIW/BAR LE9 32 D2
Ellis Flds LEIS LE2 48 A5
Ellison Cl RLEIW/BAR LE9 62 B3
WGSTN LE18 57 F3
Ellis St RLEINE/SYS LE7 17 F1
Ellwood Cl LEIE LE5 37 H1
Elm Av LUTT LE17 85 F3
Elm Cl GBY/RBY LE6 16 B5
Elmcroft Av LEIE LE5 28 B3
Elmdale Rd RLEIW/BAR LE9 50 D5
Elmdale St LEIN LE4 19 G5
Elm Dr MKTHBORO LE16 81 F2
Elmesthorpe La
RLEIW/BAR LE9 50 C4
Elmfield Av LEIN LE4 11 F5
LEIS LE2 36 C2
Elmhirst Rd LUTT LE17 85 F4
Elmhurst Cl END/NAR LE19 54 C4
Elms Cl LEIS LE2 47 E4
Elms La RLEIS/BBY LE8 61 H2
Elmsleigh Av LEIS LE2 36 D4
Elms Rd LEIS LE2 36 C5
The Elms RLEIS/BBY LE8 56 B3
RLEIS/BBY LE8 67 E2
Elmsthorpe Ri LEIW LE3 34 C2
Elm Tree Av LEIW LE3 23 G2
Elmtree Cl LEIE LE5 21 G5
Elm Tree Rd RLEIW/BAR LE9 65 E4
Elmwood Rw LEIS LE2 45 G4
Elsadene Av LEIN LE4 19 H4
Elsalene Dr GBY/RBY LE6 15 G2
Elsham Cl LEIW LE3 24 B5
Elston Flds LEIS LE2 45 F2
Elstree Av LEIE LE5 29 E2
Elsworthy Wk LEIW LE3 24 B4
Elwell Av RLEIW/BAR LE9 50 B2
Elwells Av LUTT LE17 77 F2
Elwin Av WGSTN LE18 46 B4
Emberton Cl WGSTN LE18 46 D5
Emerson Cl LEIN LE4 18 A4
Emperor Wy RLEIS/BBY LE8 65 H2
Empire Rd LEIW LE3 2 A1
Enderby Rd END/NAR LE19 55 G2
RLEIS/BBY LE8 56 A3
RLEIW/BAR LE9 41 E5
Englefield Rd LEIE LE5 28 D5
Englewood Cl LEIN LE4 25 H1
Ennerdale Cl LEIS LE2 47 H4
Ensbury Gdns LEIE LE5 37 H2
Epping Wy LEIS LE2 44 C5
Epsom Rd LEIN LE4 19 H5
Equity Rd END/NAR LE19 42 C5
LEIW LE3 2 A7
RLEIW/BAR LE9 51 E4
Equity Rd East
RLEIW/BAR LE9 51 F4
Erdyngton Rd LEIW LE3 34 B1
Erith Rd LEIS LE2 35 F4
Ernee Cl LEIW LE3 24 B3
Erringtons Cl LEIS LE2 60 A1
Erskine St LEI LE1 3 H2
Ervins Lock WGSTN LE18 57 G3
Ervin Wy RLEINE/SYS LE7 5 H3
Eskdale Cl LEIS LE2 47 H4
Eskdale Rd LEIN LE4 18 D4
Essex Cl RLEIW/BAR LE9 30 B2
Essex Gdns
MKTHBORO LE16 81 G3
Essex Rd LEIN LE4 20 C5
WGSTN LE18 45 F5
Estima Cl LEIS LE2 36 C5
Estley Rd RLEIW/BAR LE9 74 A2
Estoril Av WGSTN LE18 46 D5
Ethel Rd LEIE LE5 37 E1
Eton Cl LEIS LE2 36 B5
Eunice Av RLEIW/BAR LE9 53 H4
Euston St LEIS LE2 35 H4
Evelyn Dr LEIW LE3 35 E3
Evelyn Rd LEIW LE3 34 A3
Everard Wy END/NAR LE19 43 G3
Everest Ct LEI LE1 3 J1
Everett Cl LEIN LE4 21 E1
Every St LEI LE1 3 F4
Evesham Rd LEIW LE3 35 E3
Evington Cl LEIE LE5 37 E1
Evington Dr LEIE LE5 37 E2
Evington La LEIE LE5 37 E2
Evington Lane LEIE LE5 37 F2
Evington Ms LEIE LE5 37 H2
Evington Parks Rd LEIS LE2 36 D2
Evington Rd LEIS LE2 3 K7
Evington St LEIS LE2 3 K6
Evington Valley Gdns
LEIE LE5 36 D1
Evington Valley Rd LEIE LE5 36 D2
Excalibur Cl LEIW LE3 33 E3
Exeter Rd WGSTN LE18 45 H5
Exmoor Av LEIN LE4 17 H2
Exmoor Cl WGSTN LE18 58 B2
Exploration Dr LEIN LE4 19 F5
Exton Rd LEIE LE5 27 G3
Eyebrook Cl LEIE LE5 21 G4
Eynsford Cl LEIS LE2 37 F5

F

Factory La MKTHBORO LE16 81 H1
Fair Acre Rd RLEIW/BAR LE9 50 A5
Fairbourne Rd LEIW LE3 34 C4
Fairefield Crs LEIW LE3 17 F5
Faire Rd LEIW LE3 24 B1
Fairestone Av LEIW LE3 24 A2
Fairfax Cl LEIN LE4 20 C5
Fairfax Rd LEIN LE4 20 C5
MKTHBORO LE16 81 H2
Fairfield Rd LEIS LE2 47 F2
MKTHBORO LE16 78 B5
Fairfield St LEIE LE5 27 E5
WGSTN LE18 57 F1
Fairford Av LEIE LE5 37 H2
Fairhaven Rd
RLEINE/SYS LE7 9 G4
Fairholme Rd LEIS LE2 45 G2
Fairisle Wy RLEIS/BBY LE8 67 F3
Fairstone Hl LEIS LE2 47 F4
Fairview Av RLEIS/BBY LE8 55 H4
Fairway MKTHBORO LE16 78 B5
RLEIS/BBY LE8 70 B3
The Fairway LEIS LE2 37 F5
LEIS LE2 45 F2
RLEIS/BBY LE8 56 A4
RLEIW/BAR LE9 32 D1
Falcon Cl LEIW LE3 32 C3
RLEIW/BAR LE9 74 A2
Falconer Crs LEIW LE3 24 C2
Falcon Rd RLEINE/SYS LE7 17 F1
Faldo Cl LEIN LE4 20 C2
Fallow Cl RLEIS/BBY LE8 65 H1
RLEIW/BAR LE9 74 B5
Fallowfield Rd LEIE LE5 38 B1
Falmouth Dr WGSTN LE18 58 A2
Falmouth Rd LEIE LE5 37 F1
Faringdon Av LUTT LE17 85 H3
Farleigh Av WGSTN LE18 46 A5
Farleigh Cl RLEIW/BAR LE9 74 A2
Farley Rd LEIS LE2 36 D5
Farley Wy RLEIW/BAR LE9 23 F4
Farm Cl END/NAR LE19 55 E5
LEIN LE4 11 H5
LEIS LE2 45 F3
Farmers Cl LEIW LE3 23 G2
Farm Rd RLEIW/BAR LE9 50 C3
Farmway LEIW LE3 43 G1
Farndale WGSTN LE18 58 D1
Farndale Vw
MKTHBORO LE16 81 E2
Farndon Dr RLEIW/BAR LE9 62 A4
Farndon Rd
MKTHBORO LE16 80 C2
Farnham St LEIE LE5 27 E4
Farnworth Cl LEIN LE4 20 B4
Farrier La LEIN LE4 18 B3
Farriers' Wy RLEINE/SYS LE7 5 G2
Farringdon St LEIE LE5 27 E3
Farr Wood Cl GBY/RBY LE6 16 A4
Farthingdale Cl
RLEIW/BAR LE9 65 G3
Fastnet Rd LEIE LE5 29 E3
Faversham Cl LEIW LE3 24 A4
Fayrhurst Rd LEIS LE2 45 E2
Featherbed La
RLEIS/BBY LE8 71 E5
Featherby Dr LEIS LE2 44 A5
Featherstone Dr LEIS LE2 56 C1
Feature Rd LEIN LE4 12 C3
Federation St END/NAR LE19 54 C1
Feildingway LUTT LE17 85 G2
Feldspar Cl END/NAR LE19 42 C3
Felley Wy LEIW LE3 25 G2
Felstead Rd LEIN LE4 18 D3
Fencote Rd LEIE LE5 21 G4
Fenners Cl LEIN LE4 10 C5
Fenton Cl LEIS LE2 47 E5
Fenwick Rd LEIS LE2 48 A4
Fermain Cl LEIE LE5 28 D5
Fern Bank LEIE LE5 * 27 E4
Fern Cl RLEINE/SYS LE7 29 E5
Fern Crs GBY/RBY LE6 15 H3
Ferndale Dr GBY/RBY LE6 22 D2
Ferndale Rd LEIN LE4 20 C1
LEIS LE2 45 H2
Ferndown Cl LEIW LE3 24 A4
Fernhurst Rd LEIW LE3 34 B5
Fernie Cl LEIS LE2 47 G4
Fernie Dene RLEIS/BBY LE8 61 E2
Fernie Rd LEIE LE5 27 F3
MKTHBORO LE16 82 A1
Fernlea END/NAR LE19 54 B2
Fern Ley Cl MKTHBORO LE16 82 C2
Fernleys Cl LEIN LE4 18 B4
Fern Ri LEIE LE5 28 C1
Ferrars Ct LEIW LE3 33 H4
Ferrers Ri GBY/RBY LE6 16 A4
Ferrers Rd LUTT LE17 85 F4
Ferrers St LEIS LE2 45 F3
Ferrous Cl LEIN LE4 27 E2
Festival Av LEIN LE4 20 B1
Field Cl END/NAR LE19 55 E4
Field Court Rd GBY/RBY LE6 16 B4
Fieldfare Wk LEIE LE5 * 27 E3
Fieldgate Crs LEIN LE4 11 E4
Fieldhead Cl
MKTHBORO LE16 81 F1
Fieldhouse Rd LEIN LE4 19 G4
Fieldhurst Av LEIW LE3 34 A5
Fielding Rd LEIN LE4 11 F5
Field Vw LEIN LE4 13 E5
Field Wy RLEIW/BAR LE9 50 D3
Fieldway Crs RLEIS/BBY LE8 60 D2
The Fieldway
RLEIW/BAR LE9 74 B4
Filbert St LEIS LE2 35 G2
Filbert St East LEIS LE2 35 H2
Fillingate RLEINE/SYS LE7 11 H1
Finch Cl LEIW LE3 24 C5
The Finches RLEIW/BAR LE9 30 B3
Finch Wy END/NAR LE19 54 B4
Fineshade Av LEIW LE3 25 G2
Finsbury Rd LEIN LE4 27 E1
Finson Cl WGSTN LE18 46 B5
Fiona Dr RLEINE/SYS LE7 29 F5
Firestone Cl LEIW LE3 24 A4
Firfield Av LEIN LE4 11 G5
The Firs RLEINE/SYS LE7 13 E2
Firtree Av LUTT LE17 85 F3
Fir Tree Av RLEIS/BBY LE8 67 E2
Firtree Cl RLEIW/BAR LE9 50 B3
Fir Tree Cl WGSTN LE18 46 A3
Fir Tree La GBY/RBY LE6 16 A3
Fisher Cl RLEINE/SYS LE7 4 A1
RLEIW/BAR LE9 62 A4
Fishley Cl LEIW LE3 23 H3
Fishponds Cl LEIW LE3 23 H2
Fishpools LEIW LE3 43 G1
Fitzroy St LEIW LE3 2 A4
Fitzwilliam Cl LEIS LE2 47 H4
Flamborough Rd LEIE LE5 28 D3
Flamingo Dr RLEIS/BBY LE8 65 H2
Flatholme Rd LEIE LE5 29 E2
Flaxfield Cl GBY/RBY LE6 16 A4
Flaxland Cl MKTHBORO LE16 82 C2
Flax Rd LEIN LE4 19 H5
Fleckney Rd RLEIS/BBY LE8 68 C5
The Fleet RLEIW/BAR LE9 62 C3
Fleetwood Cl
MKTHBORO LE16 81 G3
Fleetwood Gdns
MKTHBORO LE16 81 G3
Fleetwood Rd LEIS LE2 36 A4
Fletcher Rd RLEIW/BAR LE9 62 C3
Fletchers Cl END/NAR LE19 54 D4
Fletchers' Wy RLEINE/SYS LE7 5 G2
Flora St LEIW LE3 2 A4
Florence Av WGSTN LE18 57 G2
Florence Rd LEIE LE5 27 E4
Florence St LEIS LE2 45 E1
Florence Wragg Wy LEIS LE2 48 A4
Floyd Cl LEIN LE4 20 C2
Fludes Ct LEIS LE2 47 G3
Foley Rd RLEIS/BBY LE8 69 G3
Folville Ri LEIW LE3 34 C3
Fontwell Dr LEIS LE2 44 B3
Forbes Cl LEIW LE3 24 A3
Ford Cl LEIS LE2 44 C5
Ford Ri LEIS LE2 44 C5
The Ford RLEIS/BBY LE8 56 C3
Fordview Cl RLEIS/BBY LE8 60 C2
Forest Av LEIN LE4 12 B4
Forest Cl GBY/RBY LE6 15 H4
Forest Dr RLEIW/BAR LE9 32 C1
Foresters Cl LEIW LE3 23 H2
Forest Ga RLEINE/SYS LE7 17 F1
Forest House La LEIW LE3 32 D4
Forest Ri GBY/RBY LE6 15 H4
LEIS LE2 47 G2
RLEINE/SYS LE7 29 F5
RLEIW/BAR LE9 30 C2
RLEIW/BAR LE9 32 D2
Forest Rd COAL LE67 6 A4
END/NAR LE19 54 C2
LEIE LE5 27 E3
RLEIW/BAR LE9 53 H3
Forest Vw GBY/RBY LE6 15 H3
Forest View Rd
RLEIW/BAR LE9 50 C4
Forge Cl LEIW LE3 23 G2
RLEIS/BBY LE8 68 B3
Forrester Cl RLEIW/BAR LE9 65 F3
Forryan Cl RLEIW/BAR LE9 65 F4
Forryans Cl WGSTN LE18 58 C3
Forsythia Cl LUTT LE17 85 E3
Fosse Cl END/NAR LE19 55 F1
Fosse La LEIW LE3 25 F3
Fosse Park Av
END/NAR LE19 43 H2
Fosse Pk South
END/NAR LE19 43 H3
Fosse Road Central
LEIW LE3 25 G5
Fosse Rd North LEIW LE3 25 G4
Fosse Rd South LEIW LE3 34 D3
Fosse Wy RLEINE/SYS LE7 4 D4
RLEINE/SYS LE7 12 D1
Foston Ga WGSTN LE18 58 C3
Foston La RLEIS/BBY LE8 67 F2
Fothergill Cl
MKTHBORO LE16 82 C1
Foulds La RLEIS/BBY LE8 56 A2
Foundry La LEI LE1 26 B3
RLEINE/SYS LE7 12 D1
Foundry Sq LEI LE1 * 26 C3
Fountains Av LEIS LE2 44 D5
Fowler Cl LEIN LE4 18 C3
Fox Covert RLEIS/BBY LE8 65 H1
Foxcroft Cl LEIW LE3 35 E5
Foxfield Cl LUTT LE17 85 H4
Foxglove Cl END/NAR LE19 54 C3
RLEINE/SYS LE7 5 H2
RLEIW/BAR LE9 74 C5
Foxglove Dr GBY/RBY LE6 16 C4
Foxglove Rd LEIE LE5 21 G5
Foxhill Dr LEIS LE2 44 A5
Foxholes Rd LEIW LE3 33 G1
Fox Hollow LEIS LE2 47 H4
RLEINE/SYS LE7 5 G1
RLEINE/SYS LE7 9 H2
Foxhunter Dr LEIS LE2 46 D2
Fox La RLEIW/BAR LE9 22 D4
Foxon St LEIW LE3 2 B5
Foxon Wy LEIW LE3 33 H4
Foxpond La LEIS LE2 60 A2
Fox St LEI LE1 3 H4
Foxton Lock Cl WGSTN LE18 57 G3
Fox Yd MKTHBORO LE16 * 82 A1
Frampton Av LEIW LE3 25 F5
Franche Rd LEIW LE3 25 G4
Francis Av LEIW LE3 43 H1
Francis St LEIS LE2 36 D4
Francis Wy END/NAR LE19 43 F3
Frank Booton Cl
RLEIW/BAR LE9 51 H3
Franklin Wy RLEIS/BBY LE8 65 H1
Franklyn Rd LEIS LE2 44 B3
Frankson Av LEIW LE3 34 C4
Fraser Cl LEI LE1 3 H1
Frederick Cl RLEINE/SYS LE7 5 H3
Frederick Rd LEIE LE5 27 E4
Frederick St WGSTN LE18 46 B5
Fredscott Cl LEIE LE5 29 E3
Freeboard Rd LEIW LE3 43 H1
Freehold Rd LEIN LE4 19 G2
Freehold St LEI LE1 3 K1
Freeman Rd North LEIE LE5 27 H3
Freeman's Holt LEIS LE2 44 C1
Freeman's Wy
RLEINE/SYS LE7 5 G1

Freemantle Rd LEIS LE2....... 37 E4
Freemens Common Rd
  LEIS LE2.......... 35 H3
Freer Cl RLEIS/BBY LE8....... 56 B3
  WGSTN LE18............. 58 C3
Freeschool La LEI LE1....... 2 D3
French Rd LEI LE1............. 27 G5
Frensham Cl LEIS LE2........ 47 E4
Freshwater Cl WGSTN LE18.. 58 A3
Frewen Dr RLEIW/BAR LE9.... 72 B1
Frewin St LEI LE1............ 27 G3
Friar La LEI LE1............... 2 D1
Friars Cswy LEI LE1........... 2 C5
Friday St LEI LE1............. 2 D1
Frinton Av LEIE LE5........... 38 B1
Frisby Rd LEIE LE5............ 27 E2
Friswell La RLEIW/BAR LE9... 50 A4
Fritchley Cl RLEIW/BAR LE9.. 54 A4
Frith Cl LEIW LE3............. 34 A2
Froanes Cl END/NAR LE19..... 42 C4
Frog Island LEIN LE4.......... 25 H5
Frolesworth Rd LEIW LE3..... 24 C4
  RLEIW/BAR LE9............ 74 A4
Frolesworth Wy LEIW LE3.... 24 C4
Frome Av LEIS LE2............ 47 H2
Front St LEIN LE4............. 11 H5
Fulbeck Av LEIS LE2........... 38 B1
Fulford Rd LEIE LE5........... 28 A2
Fuller Cl RLEIW/BAR LE9...... 30 C1
Fullhurst Av LEIW LE3........ 34 D2
Fulmar Rd RLEINE/SYS LE7 *. 13 G1
Furlong Cl RLEINE/SYS LE7 *. 13 G1
Furlongs Cl RLEINE/SYS LE7 . 13 G1
The Furlongs
  MKTHBORO LE16.......... 82 C1
Furnival St LEIN LE4.......... 25 H5
Furrows Cl END/NAR LE19..... 55 E5

G

Gaddesby Av LEIS LE2........ 35 E2
Gainsborough Rd LEIS LE2... 36 B5
  RLEIS/BBY LE8............ 70 A2
Galahad Cl LEIW LE3.......... 33 G3
Galby St LEIE LE5............. 27 F3
Gale Cl LUTT LE17............ 85 G1
Gallards Hl LEIW LE3.......... 33 H1
Galleywood Dr LEIN LE4...... 18 D5
Gallimore Cl LEIW LE3........ 24 C1
Galsworthy Ct LEIW LE3...... 25 E5
Galway Rd LEIN LE4........... 19 E2
Gamekeepers Ct LEIE LE5.... 21 G4
Gamel Rd LEIE LE5............ 28 A5
Gamton Rd LEIW LE3.......... 24 A3
Garden Cl LEIS LE2............ 47 E3
Gardenfield Rd LEIN LE4..... 20 D3
Garden St LEI LE1............. 3 F1
  LEIN LE4................... 12 C5
  WGSTN LE18............... 57 F2
Gardiner St MKTHBORO LE16.. 81 F1
Garendon St LEIS LE2......... 3 K3
Garendon Wy GBY/RBY LE6... 16 A5
Garfield Pk RLEIS/BBY LE8.... 60 D2
Garfield St LEIW LE3.......... 26 C2
Garfit Rd RLEIW/BAR LE9..... 73 G2
Garland Crs LEIW LE3......... 25 F2
Garnett Crs LEIS LE2.......... 44 C4
Garsdale WGSTN LE18........ 58 D1
Garth Av LEIN LE4............ 19 E5
Gartree Crs RLEIW/BAR LE9.. 52 C4
Gartree Rd LEIS LE2.......... 37 F4
Gascoigne Av RLEINE/SYS LE7 . 5 H4
Gas La WGSTN LE18........... 58 A2
Gas St LEI LE1................ 26 B3
Gateway St LEI LE1........... 2 D6
Gaulby La LEIS LE2........... 38 B5
Gaul St LEIW LE3............. 2 A7
Gavin Cl LEIW LE3............ 33 G3
Gayhurst Cl LEIW LE3........ 43 H1
  WGSTN LE18............... 58 C1
Gayton Av LEIN LE4........... 27 E1
Gayton Hts END/NAR LE19.... 42 C4
Geary Cl END/NAR LE19....... 54 D4
  GBY/RBY LE6.............. 23 E2
Gedding Rd LEIE LE5.......... 27 G5
Geddington Cl WGSTN LE18... 58 C1
Gedge Wy LEIS LE2........... 45 E2
Gees Lock Cl LEIN LE4........ 44 B4
Geileart Av LEIE LE5.......... 28 D4
George Foster Cl
  RLEIW/BAR LE9........... 51 F2
George Geary Cl
  RLEIW/BAR LE9........... 50 C4
Georgeham Cl WGSTN LE18... 50 C4
George Hill Cl
  RLEIW/BAR LE9........... 62 B3
George Marriott Cl
  RLEIW/BAR LE9........... 62 A5
George St END/NAR LE19...... 42 C5
  LEI LE1................... 85 G5
  LUTT LE17................. 17 F1
  RLEINE/SYS LE7........... 5 H5
  RLEIW/BAR LE9........... 50 B4
George Toon Ct
  RLEINE/SYS LE7 *......... 4 D3
George Ward Ct
  RLEIW/BAR LE9........... 50 B4
Gerrard Gdns
  MKTHBORO LE16.......... 81 G4
Gervas Rd LEIE LE5........... 28 C3
Geveze Wy RLEIW/BAR LE9... 50 A4
Gibbons Cl LEIN LE4.......... 26 C2
Gibson Cl WGSTN LE18........ 46 B5
Gibson Wy LUTT LE17......... 85 E4
Gifford Cl LEIE LE5........... 37 H2
Gilbert Cl LEIN LE4........... 20 C3
  MKTHBORO LE16.......... 82 C2
Gillam Butts RLEIS/BBY LE8... 67 E3

Gillbank Dr GBY/RBY LE6..... 22 C2
Gilliver St LEIS LE2........... 36 B5
Gillman Rd LEIE LE5.......... 25 E2
Gilmorton Av LEIS LE2........ 44 B5
Gilmorton Cl LEIS LE2........ 44 B5
Gilmour Cl LEIN LE4.......... 20 C3
Gilstead Cl RLEIW/BAR LE9... 58 D1
Gimson Av RLEIW/BAR LE9... 65 F3
Gimson Cl LEIE LE5........... 28 A1
Gimson Rd LEIW LE3.......... 25 F5
Gipsy La LEIE LE5............ 27 H1
Gipsy Rd LEIN LE4............ 19 H5
The Glade LEIW LE3.......... 43 H1
Gladstone Ms
  RLEIW/BAR LE9 *......... 74 A2
Gladstone St LEI LE1......... 3 G2
  LUTT LE17................. 85 H5
  MKTHBORO LE16.......... 82 A2
  RLEINE/SYS LE7........... 17 G1
  RLEIS/BBY LE8............ 68 B4
  WGSTN LE18............... 46 B5
Glaisdale Cl LEIW LE3........ 24 A1
Glaisdale Rd WGSTN LE18.... 58 C1
Glamorgan Av WGSTN LE18... 57 F1
Glazebrook Cl LEIW LE3...... 24 D1
Glazebrook Sq LEIW LE3...... 25 E2
Glean Cl RLEIW/BAR LE9...... 74 B5
Glebe Cl LEIS LE2............. 46 C1
  LEIW LE3.................. 23 H2
  RLEIS/BBY LE8............ 66 D3
Glebelands Rd LEIN LE4...... 10 D4
The Glebelands
  LEIS LE2................... 60 C3
Glebe Rd GBY/RBY LE6........ 16 A4
  LEIS LE2................... 46 D1
  MKTHBORO LE16.......... 82 B2
  RLEINE/SYS LE7........... 5 H4
  RLEIW/BAR LE9........... 74 A3
Glebe Wy RLEINE/SYS LE7 *... 3 H5
Glenbarr Av LEIN LE4......... 25 H2
Glenborne Rd LEIS LE2....... 45 G4
Glencoe Av LEIN LE4......... 20 A3
Glendale Av LEIW LE3........ 34 B3
Glendon St LEIN LE4......... 26 D1
Glendower Cl LEIE LE5........ 28 B4
Gleneagles Av LEIW LE3...... 20 B3
Glenfield Crs LEIW LE3....... 24 A2
Glenfield Frith Dr LEIW LE3.. 24 A1
Glenfield La RLEIW/BAR LE9.. 23 E4
Glenfield Rd LEIW LE3........ 24 D5
Glenfield Rd East LEIW LE3.. 25 E5
Glenfirth Cl LEIW LE3........ 17 H4
Glenfrith Wy LEIW LE3....... 17 H5
Glengarry Cl LEIW LE3........ 25 E3
Glengarry Wy LEIW LE3...... 24 D2
Glen Ga WGSTN LE18......... 57 F1
Glenhills Bvd LEIS LE2........ 44 C3
Glenhills Wy LEIS LE2........ 44 D3
Glenmere Rd LEIN LE4....... 20 B4
Glen Park Av LEIW LE3....... 17 H4
Glen Rd LEIS LE2............. 46 B5
  LEIS LE2................... 60 B2
Glen Rd LEIS LE2............. 47 G4
  RLEIS/BBY LE8............ 59 H4
Glenrothes Cl LEIW LE3...... 24 A5
Glen St LEIN LE4............. 26 B1
Glenville Av LEIW LE3........ 17 E5
Glen Wy LEIS LE2............ 47 G4
Glossop St LEIE LE5.......... 36 C2
Gloucester Av
  RLEINE/SYS LE7........... 5 F5
Gloucester Cl
  RLEIW/BAR LE9........... 30 B3
Gloucester Crs WGSTN LE18.. 45 F5
Glover Ct LEIS LE2............ 44 C2
Glyn Cl RLEIW/BAR LE9....... 50 A4
Goddards Cl LEIW LE3........ 29 C5
Goddards Cl LEIW LE3........ 18 A1
Goddards Slang LEIS LE2..... 46 D3
Godfrey Cl LEIW LE3......... 18 A1
Godwin Av WGSTN LE18...... 58 C1
Godwin Cl WGSTN LE18 *..... 58 B1
Goldhill Cl LEIS LE2.......... 45 F4
Goldhill Gdns LEIS LE2....... 46 B1
Goldsmith Rd LEIW LE3...... 34 C1
Golf Course La LEIW LE3...... 24 A5
Goode's Av RLEINE/SYS LE7.. 13 F2
Goode's La RLEINE/SYS LE7.. 13 E1
Goodheart Wy LEIW LE3..... 33 C3
Gooding Av LEIW LE3........ 34 B1
Gooding Cl LEIW LE3......... 34 D2
Goodwood Cl
  MKTHBORO LE16.......... 82 C1
Goodwood Crs LEIE LE5...... 37 H1
Goodwood Rd LEIE LE5....... 37 H2
Gopsall St LEI LE1............ 3 K1
Gordon Av LEIS LE2.......... 3 K7
Gores La MKTHBORO LE16.... 82 B1
Gorham Rd RLEIW/BAR LE9... 73 H2
Gorse Hl RLEINE/SYS LE7..... 17 G2
Gorse La LEIE LE5............ 47 H5
  RLEINE/SYS LE7........... 13 F2
Gorsty Cl LEIN LE4........... 18 A4
Goscote Dr LUTT LE17........ 85 G3
Goscote Hall Rd LEIN LE4.... 19 F1
Goshawk Cl RLEIW/BAR LE9.. 74 A2
Gosling St LEIS LE2.......... 2 D6
Gotham St LEIE LE5.......... 3 K4
Gough Rd LEIE LE5........... 27 G4
Goward St MKTHBORO LE16.. 81 H1
Gower St LEIN LE4........... 3 G1
Grace Gdns LEIS LE2 *....... 45 E1
Grace Rd LEIS LE2............ 36 B5
Grafton Dr WGSTN LE18...... 58 D1
Grafton Pl LEI LE1............ 2 D1
Graham St LEIE LE5.......... 3 J2
Grampian Cl LEIS LE2........ 45 F1

Granary Cl LEIW LE3......... 23 H3
  RLEIS/BBY LE8............ 70 A4
Granby Av LEIE LE5 *........ 27 F4
Granby Rd LEIS LE2.......... 44 D1
Granby St LEI LE1............ 3 H3
Grange Av LEIW LE3.......... 33 E2
Grange Ct GBY/RBY LE6...... 22 D2
  LEIS LE2................... 44 C5
  LEIW LE3.................. 23 H2
Grange Dr LEIS LE2.......... 60 D2
Grange Dr LEIE LE5.......... 44 B5
  RLEIS/BBY LE8............ 55 H3
Grange La LEIS LE2........... 2 E6
  RLEINE/SYS LE7........... 38 C1
Grange Rd RLEIW/BAR LE9... 74 A3
  WGSTN LE18............... 46 B4
The Grange RLEIW/BAR LE9.. 51 E4
Grangeway Rd WGSTN LE18.. 46 A4
Granite Cl END/NAR LE19..... 42 C4
Grantham Av
  RLEIW/BAR LE9........... 73 H1
Grantham Rd LEIE LE5....... 28 C2
Granville Av LEIS LE2........ 46 D2
Granville Crs WGSTN LE18.... 45 H3
Granville Rd LEIS LE2........ 36 B2
  LEIE LE5.................. 46 A3
Granville St MKTHBORO LE16. 81 H3
Grape St LEI LE1............. 2 C3
Grasmere Rd WGSTN LE18.... 46 D5
Grasmere Cl LEIS LE2........ 2 C7
Grass Acres LEIS LE2......... 43 G1
Grassington Cl LEIW LE3..... 18 C3
Grassington Dr WGSTN LE18. 58 C2
Gravel St LEI LE1............ 2 D2
The Gravel RLEIS/BBY LE8.... 61 H3
Grays Ct END/NAR LE19....... 42 C5
Grayswood Dr LEIW LE3...... 10 A5
Great Arler Rd LEIS LE2...... 36 A5
Great Bowden Rd
  MKTHBORO LE16.......... 79 E5
Great Central St LEI LE1..... 2 C2
Great Central Wy LEIW LE3... 35 F3
Great Meadow Rd LEIN LE4... 18 B5
Grebe Wy RLEIS/BBY LE8..... 70 A4
Greenacre Dr LEIE LE5........ 37 H1
Greenacres Dr LUTT LE17.... 85 F5
Greenbank Dr LEIS LE2....... 47 F5
Greenbank Rd LEIE LE5...... 28 D1
Greencoat Rd LEIW LE3...... 24 C3
Greendale Rd LEIE LE5....... 28 B4
Greenfields RLEIS/BBY LE8... 55 H4
Greengate La LEIN LE4....... 11 E5
Greenhill Cl END/NAR LE19... 54 B4
Greenhill Rd LEIS LE2........ 36 B5
Greenhithe Rd LEIE LE5...... 35 F4
Greenland Av LEIE LE5....... 28 A2
Greenland Dr LEIE LE5....... 28 A2
Green La MKTHBORO LE16.... 81 H3
  RLEIS/BBY LE8............ 67 F2
  RLEIW/BAR LE9........... 51 E2
Green Lane Ct LEIE LE5....... 28 A2
Green Lane Rd LEIE LE5...... 27 F3
Green Rd LEIW LE3........... 74 A2
Greenside Pl LEIE LE5........ 45 F5
Greensward RLEINE/SYS LE7.. 5 H1
The Green COAL LE67......... 6 B3
  LUTT LE17................. 85 H4
  MKTHBORO LE16.......... 80 B1
  RLEIW/BAR LE9........... 63 G1
Green Wk LEIW LE3.......... 24 C5
Greenway RLEIS/BBY LE8..... 70 A3
The Greenway LEIN LE4...... 19 G5
Greenwich Cl END/NAR LE19.. 54 D4
  LEIE LE5.................. 25 F1
Greenwood Cl LEIN LE4...... 20 D1
Greenwood Rd LEIE LE5...... 27 H4
Gregory Cl LEIN LE4.......... 13 C5
Gregorys Cl LEIW LE3........ 33 H4
Gregson Cl LEIN LE4......... 20 D2
Grendon Cl WGSTN LE18...... 58 C1
Grenfell Rd LEIS LE2......... 46 C5
Grenville Gdns
  MKTHBORO LE16.......... 81 G3
Gresley Cl LEIS LE2.......... 59 F1
Greta St LEIE LE5............ 29 F4
Gretna Wy LEIE LE5.......... 29 E5
Grey Cl GBY/RBY LE6......... 16 B4
Grey Crs GBY/RBY LE6........ 7 H3
Grey Friars LEI LE1.......... 2 E4
Greylag Wy RLEIS/BBY LE8... 65 H2
Greyland Paddock
  GBY/RBY LE6.............. 16 B4
Greys Dr GBY/RBY LE6........ 16 A5
Greystoke Rd LEIN LE4....... 19 E4
Greystone Av LEIE LE5....... 28 B4
Griffin Cl LEIN LE4........... 20 D1
Griffydam Cl LEIW LE3....... 21 E3
Grisedale Cl LEIS LE2......... 35 G2
Grittar Cl WGSTN LE18....... 46 C5
Grizedale Gv RLEIW/BAR LE9. 54 B2
Groby La GBY/RBY LE6........ 7 H4
Groby Rd GBY/RBY LE6....... 22 C1
  LEIW LE3.................. 18 C4
  LEIW LE3.................. 24 C1
Grocott Rd LEIE LE5.......... 17 F2
Grosvenor Cl LEIS LE2........ 37 G2
Grosvenor Crs LEIS LE2...... 56 D2
Grosvenor St LEIE LE5....... 3 G1
Grovebury Rd LEIN LE4...... 19 F4
Grove Ct END/NAR LE19...... 43 F3
Grove Rd LEIE LE5........... 27 E4
  RLEIS/BBY LE8............ 55 H5
The Grove RLEIW/BAR LE9.... 30 A2
Grove Wy END/NAR LE19..... 43 F3
Guestwick Gn LEIE LE5....... 21 H5
Guild Cl RLEINE/SYS LE7..... 9 H1
Guildford Rd LEIE LE5........ 37 E4
Guildhall La LEI LE1......... 2 D3
Guilford Dr WGSTN LE18..... 45 H3
Guinevere Wy LEIW LE3...... 33 E5

Gullet La RLEIW/BAR LE9..... 22 C5
Gumley Sq END/NAR LE19.... 42 D5
Gunnsbrook Cl
  MKTHBORO LE16.......... 79 E3
Gunthorpe Rd LEIW LE3...... 33 F1
Gurnall Rd LEIE LE5.......... 18 A3
Gurney Crs END/NAR LE19.... 55 E5
Guthlaxton Av LEIS LE2...... 3 J3
  LUTT LE17................. 85 G3
Guthlaxton Gap
  LEIS LE2................... 64 A2
Guthlaxton St LEIS LE2...... 3 K5
Guthlaxton Wy WGSTN LE18. 58 C3
Guthridge Crs LEIE LE5....... 34 D2
Gwencole Av LEIW LE3....... 34 C4
Gwencole Crs LEIW LE3...... 44 A1
Gwendolen Rd LEIE LE5...... 27 F5
Gwendolin Av LEIW LE3...... 11 H5
Gwendoline Dr
  RLEIS/BBY LE8............ 66 D2
Gynsill Cl RLEINE/SYS LE7.... 17 G2
Gynsill La RLEINE/SYS LE7... 17 F4

H

Hackett Rd LEIW LE3......... 24 D2
Haddenham Rd LEIW LE3..... 35 E3
Haddon Cl RLEINE/SYS LE7... 12 C1
Haddonian Rd
  MKTHBORO LE16.......... 81 H3
Haddon St LEIS LE2.......... 27 E4
Hadrian Cl RLEIW/BAR LE9... 12 C2
Hadrian Rd LEIN LE4......... 19 E2
Hagley Cl MKTHBORO LE16... 82 C1
Haig Pl LEIW LE3 *........... 34 C3
Halcroft Ri WGSTN LE18...... 58 C3
The Half Crft RLEINE/SYS LE7. 4 C5
Half Moon Crs LEIS LE2...... 47 G2
Halford Cl RLEIS/BBY LE8..... 58 B5
  RLEIS/BBY LE8............ 60 D3
Halford Rd RLEIS/BBY LE8.... 69 H3
Halford St LEI LE1........... 3 G4
  RLEINE/SYS LE7........... 9 H2
Halifax Dr LEIE LE5.......... 19 E4
Halkin St LEIN LE4........... 26 D1
Hallam Av LEIN LE4.......... 11 F5
Hallam Cl RLEIW/BAR LE9.... 51 C3
Hallam Crs East LEIW LE3.... 34 B1
Hallaton Rd LEIW LE3........ 27 H2
Hallaton St LEIS LE2.......... 45 E1
Hallbrook Rd RLEINE/SYS LE7. 74 B5
Hall Cl LEIS LE2.............. 44 B5
  RLEINE/SYS LE7........... 5 F2
  RLEIS/BBY LE8............ 69 H2
Hallcroft Av RLEIS/BBY LE8... 67 E3
Hall Dr LEIS LE2............. 47 F2
Halley Cl RLEIW/BAR LE9..... 18 A1
Hall Farm Crs
  RLEINE/SYS LE7........... 74 C4
Hall Farm Rd
  RLEINE/SYS LE7........... 10 B2
Hall Gdns RLEIS/BBY LE8..... 60 D3
Hall La LEIS LE2.............. 44 C1
Hall Rd RLEINE/SYS LE7...... 29 F2
Halls Crs HINC LE10.......... 72 D4
Hall Wk END/NAR LE19....... 42 D4
Halsbury St LEIE LE5......... 36 D2
Halstead St LEIE LE5......... 27 F4
Halter Slade WGSTN LE18.... 58 C2
Hamble Rd RLEIW/BAR LE9... 30 B2
Hamble Rd LEIS LE2.......... 32 D3
Hamelin Rd LEIW LE3........ 34 B1
Hamiford Cl RLEINE/SYS LE7.. 29 E1
Hamilton La LEIE LE5......... 29 E1
Hamilton St LEIS LE2......... 3 K7
Hamilton Wy LEIE LE5........ 21 F5
Hammond Wy
  MKTHBORO LE16.......... 78 C5
Hampden Rd LEIS LE2........ 20 C5
Hampshire Rd LEIS LE2....... 44 D1
Hampstead Cl
  END/NAR LE19............ 54 D3
Hampton Cl LEIS LE2......... 59 E1
  WGSTN LE18............... 58 C1
Hanbury Rd LEIE LE5......... 38 B1
Hand Av LEIW LE3........... 34 A2
Hand Cl LEIW LE3............ 34 A1
Handley St LEIE LE5.......... 3 J3
Hardie Crs LEIW LE3......... 33 H3
Hardwick Cl LEIE LE5........ 2 C1
Hardwick Ct LEIW LE3........ 35 E2
Hardwick Crs
  RLEINE/SYS LE7........... 12 D1
Hardwicke Rd
  RLEIW/BAR LE9........... 54 B3
Hardy's Av LEIN LE4......... 38 B1
Hardy's Av LEIN LE4......... 20 A3
Harebell Cl LEIE LE5.......... 21 F5
Harecroft Crs
  RLEIW/BAR LE9........... 72 C5
Harefield Av LEIW LE3........ 33 G5
Harewood Cl RLEIW/BAR LE9. 32 C5
Harewood St LEIE LE5........ 27 F5
Harland Cl RLEIW/BAR LE9... 30 B4
Harlaxton St LEIE LE5........ 34 D3
Harlequin Wy RLEIS/BBY LE8. 65 H2
Harolds La END/NAR LE19.... 42 D3
Harold St LEIS LE2........... 35 G5

Harrier Cl RLEIW/BAR LE9.... 74 A2
Harrier Pkwy LUTT LE17...... 84 B2
Harrington St WGSTN LE18... 46 C5
Harrington St LEI LE1........ 27 E2
Harringworth Rd LEIE LE5.... 37 H1
Harris Cl RLEIW/BAR LE9..... 74 C4
Harrison Cl GBY/RBY LE6..... 22 D2
  LEIW LE3.................. 24 A2
  MKTHBORO LE16.......... 81 G4
  RLEIS/BBY LE8............ 66 A1
  RLEIW/BAR LE9........... 51 F3
  WGSTN LE18............... 57 H2
Harrison Rd LEIN LE4........ 26 D1
Harrison St LEIN LE4......... 12 C4
Harris Rd LEIE LE5........... 18 B4
Harrod Dr MKTHBORO LE16... 79 E2
Harrogate Rd LEIN LE4....... 27 E1
Harrogate Wy RLEIW/BAR LE9. 58 C2
Harrop Cl LEIS LE2........... 56 A3
Harrow Cl LEIW LE3.......... 24 A2
Harrowden Ri LEIE LE5....... 28 A4
Harrowgate Dr LEIN LE4..... 11 F5
Harrow Wy LEIE LE5.......... 35 E1
Harrop Cl RLEINE/SYS LE7 *.. 65 H1
Hart Cl RLEIW/BAR LE9....... 28 D2
Hartfield Rd LEIE LE5......... 28 D2
Hartington Rd LEIS LE2...... 27 E4
Hartland Dr
  MKTHBORO LE16.......... 82 B1
Hartopp Cl RLEINE/SYS LE7.. 29 G5
Hartopp Rd LEIS LE2......... 36 B3
Hart Rd LEIE LE5............. 27 H1
Hartshorn Cl END/NAR LE19.. 20 D1
Harvard Cl LEIS LE2.......... 47 F2
Harvest Cl END/NAR LE19.... 37 H1
  LEIN LE4................... 18 B4
Harvester Cl LEIW LE3....... 32 D4
Harvest Wy RLEIW/BAR LE9.. 37 H1
Harvey Cl RLEIW/BAR LE9.... 56 B2
  RLEIW/BAR LE9........... 24 A2
Harwin Rd LEIS LE2.......... 37 H1
Haskell Cl LEIW LE3.......... 33 H3
Hassal Rd LEIW LE3.......... 24 C2
Hastings Cl RLEIS/BBY LE8... 68 C3
Hastings Dr RLEIW/BAR LE9.. 50 B4
Hastings Meadow Cl
  RLEIW/BAR LE9........... 22 C5
Hastings Rd LEIS LE2......... 27 F2
  RLEIW/BAR LE9........... 32 C1
The Hastings LEIS LE2....... 33 H4
Hathaway Av LEIW LE3....... 34 B4
Hatherleigh Rd LEIE LE5..... 37 H1
Hat Rd LEIW LE3............. 24 A2
Hattern Av LEIN LE4......... 18 D3
Havelock St LEIS LE2......... 2 D7
Haven Cl LEIW LE3........... 32 D5
Havencrest Dr LEIE LE5....... 28 B1
Hawarden Av LEIE LE5....... 27 H5
Hawk Cl RLEIW/BAR LE9...... 74 A2
Hawker Rd LEIE LE5.......... 45 E1
Hawkesbury Rd LEIS LE2..... 45 E1
Hawkes Hl LEIW LE3 *........ 45 F5
Hawke Wy LUTT LE17......... 84 A1
Hawthorn Av LEIN LE4....... 11 H4
Hawthorn Cl RLEIW/BAR LE9. 32 C3
Hawthorn Dr RLEIS/BBY LE8.. 56 B5
Hawthorne Dr LEIE LE5...... 37 G2
Hawthorne St LEIW LE3...... 48 C5
Hawthorne Wy
  RLEIW/BAR LE9........... 50 B5
Hawthorn Gv LEIE LE5....... 47 F1
Hawthorn Ri GBY/RBY LE6... 16 B4
The Hawthorns COAL LE67.... 6 B3
  LUTT LE17................. 85 F5
  RLEIS/BBY LE8............ 67 F2
Haybarn Cl END/NAR LE19.... 55 F5
Hayden Av LEIS LE2.......... 47 H4
Hayden Cl LEIN LE4.......... 19 E2
Hayes End RLEIW/BAR LE9... 30 B3
Hayes Rd WGSTN LE18....... 58 B2
Hayfield Cl LEIW LE3......... 25 H2
Hayling Crs LEIE LE5......... 28 A2
Haymarket LEI LE1........... 3 F5
Haynes Rd LEIE LE5.......... 27 G3
Haywood Cl LEIE LE5......... 37 H1
Hazelbank Ct LUTT LE17..... 85 G3
Hazelbank Rd
  RLEIW/BAR LE9........... 67 F2
Hazel Cl END/NAR LE19....... 55 E5
  LEIN LE4................... 11 H4
Hazeldene Rd LEIN LE4....... 21 H5
Hazel St LEIS LE2............ 35 H2
Hazel Wy RLEIW/BAR LE9.... 50 A2
Hazelwood Rd LEIS LE2...... 36 D2
  WGSTN LE18............... 57 F1
Heacham Dr LEIN LE4........ 18 B4
Headingly Cl LEIN LE4....... 10 C5
Headland Rd LEIE LE5........ 37 G2
The Headlands
  MKTHBORO LE16.......... 78 D5
  LEIE LE5.................. 38 B1
Headley Rd LEIW LE3......... 43 H1
Healey St WGSTN LE18....... 57 F2
Heanor St LEI LE1............ 2 D1
Heards Cl WGSTN LE18....... 58 C3
Hearth St MKTHBORO LE16... 81 G1
Heath Av END/NAR LE19...... 55 G1
  RLEINE/SYS LE7........... 12 D1
Heatherbrook Dr GBY/RBY LE6. 22 C1
Heathcott Rd LEIS LE2....... 45 F1
Heatherbrook Rd LEIN LE4... 17 H2
Heather Rd LEIS LE2......... 36 A5
Heather Wy RLEIS/BBY LE8... 67 F3
Heathfield Rd WGSTN LE18... 46 B3
Heathgate Cl LEIN LE4....... 11 F4
Heath La RLEIW/BAR LE9..... 50 C3

Heath La South
  RLEIW/BAR LE9.............. 50 D3
Heathley Cl *LEIN* LE4.............. 32 D3
Heathley Park Dr *LEIW* LE3... 25 E1
Heawood Wy *LEIW* LE5.......... 33 H4
Heays Cl *LEIN* LE3................ 62 C3
Hebden Cl *LEIS* LE2.............. 56 C1
Heddington Cl *LEIW* LE3....... 45 G3
Heddington Wy *LEIS* LE2....... 45 G3
Hedgerow La
  RLEIW/BAR LE9.............. 22 C5
Hedgerow Wy *LEIW* LE3........ 54 C1
Hefford Gdns *LEIN* LE4......... 18 D5
Heighton Crs *END/NAR* LE19... 55 E1
The Heights
  MKTHBORO LE16............. 82 C2
Helena Crs *LEIN* LE4............ 19 E3
Helmsley Rd *LEIS* LE2.......... 55 E4
Helston Cl *WGSTN* LE18........ 58 A2
Hemington Rd *LEIW* LE3........ 38 B2
Hemlock Cl *END/NAR* LE19..... 54 B2
Henley Crs *LEIW* LE3............ 34 B4
Henley Rd *LEIW* LE3............. 34 B4
Henray Av *LEIS* LE2.............. 56 C1
Henry Cl *LEIW* LE3............... 32 D3
Henshaw St *LEIS* LE2............ 2 E6
Hensman Cl *RLEIS/BBY* LE8.... 68 C5
Henson Cl *LEIN* LE4.............. 19 F1
Henton Rd *LEIW* LE3............. 25 G5
Herbert Av *LEIN* LE4............. 19 H5
Herbert Cl *RLEIS/BBY* LE8...... 55 H4
Herdsmans Cl *END/NAR* LE19... 55 E4
Hereford Rd *LEIS* LE2........... 44 D1
Hereward Dr
  RLEINE/SYS LE7.............. 29 F5
Heritage Wy *LEIE* LE5........... 21 H4
Herle Av *LEIW* LE3............... 34 B3
Hermitage Cl *LEIS* LE2.......... 47 E3
Hermitage Rd *LEIN* LE4......... 19 G2
Heron Cl *RLEIS/BBY* LE8........ 60 D2
Herongate Rd *LEIE* LE5......... 37 H2
Heron Rd *LEIE* LE5............... 21 H5
Heron Wy *END/NAR* LE19....... 55 F1
  RLEINE/SYS LE7............... 4 C5
Herrick Cl *END/NAR* LE19....... 42 C5
Herrick Dr *RLEINE/SYS* LE7.... 29 F5
Herrick Rd *LEIS* LE2............. 36 A5
Herricks Av *LEIN* LE4............ 32 A3
Herrick Wy *WGSTN* LE18........ 58 C2
Herschell St *LEIS* LE2........... 36 C2
Hesketh Av *LEIS* LE2............ 44 C5
Hesketh Cl *LEIS* LE2............. 44 C5
Hewes Cl *LEIS* LE2............... 44 B5
Hewett Cl *RLEIW/BAR* LE9...... 60 C5
Hewitt Dr *RLEIW/BAR* LE9...... 32 D1
Hextall Rd *LEIE* LE5............. 37 G2
Hexter Cl *RLEIS/BBY* LE8....... 55 H3
Heybridge Rd *LEIE* LE5.......... 27 H2
Heybrook Av *LEIW* LE4.......... 56 A4
Heycock Cl *RLEIS/BBY* LE8..... 68 C5
Heyford Rd *LEIN* LE4............. 33 H1
Heygate St *MKTHBORO* LE16... 78 C5
Heyrose Cl *LEIW* LE3............ 47 H4
Heyworth Rd *LEIW* LE3.......... 35 E3
Hidcote Rd *LEIS* LE2............. 47 E4
Higgs Cl *LEIS* LE2................ 28 A5
Highbury Rd *LEIN* LE4........... 27 E2
Highcliffe Rd *LEIE* LE5........... 21 E4
Highcroft Av *LEIS* LE2........... 47 H5
Highcroft Rd *LEIS* LE2.......... 47 H5
Highcross St *LEI* LE1............. 2 C2
  MKTHBORO LE16............. 81 F1
Higher Gn *RLEIS/BBY* LE8....... 60 B3
Highfield Crs *WGSTN* LE18..... 46 B4
Highfield Dr *WGSTN* LE18....... 46 B3
Highfield Rd *RLEIW/BAR* LE6... 16 A5
Highfield St *LEI* LE1.............. 3 J7
  MKTHBORO LE16............. 81 G1
  RLEIS/SYS LE7................ 17 G1
  RLEIS/BBY LE8................ 68 A3
  RLEIW/BAR LE9.............. 50 D4
  RLEIW/BAR LE9.............. 58 D5
Highgate Cl *LEIS* LE2............ 45 G4
Highgate Av *LEIN* LE4........... 11 E4
Highgate Dr *LEIS* LE2............ 45 H3
Highgrove Crs *LEIS* LE2......... 44 B3
Highland Av *RLEIW/BAR* LE3... 32 C3
Highmeres Rd *LEIN* LE4......... 20 D4
High St *END/NAR* LE19........... 42 D5
  LEI LE1........................ 2 D3
  LEIE LE5....................... 37 H3
  LEIE LE2....................... 47 E2
  LUTT LE17..................... 85 H1
  MKTHBORO LE16............. 81 H1
  RLEINE/SYS LE7.............. 8 B4
  RLEIS/BBY LE8................ 55 H4
  RLEIS/BBY LE8................ 60 C5
  RLEIS/BBY LE8................ 68 B3
  RLEIW/BAR LE9.............. 30 B2
  RLEIW/BAR LE9.............. 51 F3
High Tor East
  RLEIS/SYS LE7................ 13 E1
High Tor West
High View Cl *LEIN* LE4........... 51 E2
Highway Rd *LEIE* LE5............ 21 E5
  LEIN LE4....................... 12 D4
Hilary Crs *GBY/RBY* LE6......... 15 H4
Hilcot Gn *LEIW* LE3.............. 33 G3
Hilders Rd *LEIW* LE3............ 25 E4
Hildyard Rd *LEIN* LE4........... 26 C1
Hilary Pl *LEIW* LE3............... 33 G3
Hillberry Cl *END/NAR* LE19...... 54 C3
Hillcrest Av
  MKTHBORO LE16............. 78 B5
Hillcrest Rd *RLEIS/BBY* LE8.... 69 H2
Hillcrest Rd *LEIN* LE4............ 18 C5
Hillcroft Cl *LEIW* LE3............ 12 C4
Hillcroft Rd *LEIE* LE5............ 27 G5
Hill Dr *LUTT* LE17................. 85 C4
Hill Fld *LEIS* LE2................... 48 A4
Hill Gdns *MKTHBORO* LE16..... 81 H1
Hillier Rd *LEIE* LE5............... 21 G4

Hill La *COAL* LE67................. 6 A3
  RLEIS/BBY LE8................ 66 A3
Hill Lane Cl *COAL* LE67.......... 6 A2
Hill Ri *LEIN* LE4................... 11 G4
Hillrise Av *LEIW* LE3............. 34 C5
Hillsborough Cl *LEIS* LE2........ 56 C1
Hillsborough Rd *LEIS* LE2....... 56 C1
Hillsborough Rd *LEIS* LE2....... 56 C1
Hillside *COAL* LE67............... 6 B3
Hillside Av *WGSTN* LE18........ 58 B2
Hillside Rd *MKTHBORO* LE16... 78 D5
Hill St *LEI* LE1.................... 3 G2
  RLEIW/BAR LE9.............. 50 B5
  RLEIW/BAR LE9.............. 63 G2
Hill Top *RLEIW/BAR* LE9......... 51 F2
Hilltop Av *RLEIS/BBY* LE8....... 61 E3
Hilltop Rd *LEIW* LE3.............. 21 F4
Hill Vw End/NAR LE19............. 43 G5
Hill View Dr *RLEIW/BAR* LE9... 65 F3
Hill Wy *LEIS* LE2.................. 47 F2
Hinckley Rd *LEIW* LE3............ 32 N4
  RLEIW/BAR LE9.............. 40 C3
  RLEIW/BAR LE9.............. 50 B5
  RLEIW/BAR LE9.............. 72 A1
Hind Cl *RLEIS/BBY* LE8.......... 56 A5
Hindoostan Av *WGSTN* LE18... 45 E5
Hinks Av *WGSTN* LE18........... 57 H1
Hipwell Crs *LEIN* LE4............. 19 E4
Hoball Cl *LEIW* LE3............... 24 C2
Hobart St *LEIS* LE2............... 3 J5
Hobby Cl *RLEIW/BAR* LE9........ 74 A2
Hobill Cl *LEIW* LE3............... 33 F3
  RLEIW/BAR LE9.............. 54 A3
Hobrook Rd *RLEIS/BBY* LE8.... 68 C5
Hobson Rd *LEIN* LE4.............. 19 G4
Hoby St *LEIW* LE3................ 2 A2
Hockley Farm Rd *LEIW* LE3.... 33 G1
Hodgson Rd *LEIS* LE2............ 25 G1
Hodson Cl *RLEIS/BBY* LE8....... 55 H5
Hogarth Rd *LEIN* LE4............. 10 C3
Holbeck Dr *RLEIW/BAR* LE9.... 74 C5
Holbrook Cl *LEIE* LE5............. 48 A4
Holbrook Rd *LEIS* LE2........... 46 C1
Holdenby Cl
  MKTHBORO LE16............. 82 C1
Holden Cl *RLEIS/BBY* LE8........ 66 A1
Holden St *LEIN* LE4.............. 19 G5
Holderness Rd *LEIN* LE4........ 18 D2
Holgate Cl *RLEINE/SYS* LE7..... 9 F4
Holkham Av *LEIW* LE4............ 27 F1
Holland Rd *LEIS* LE2.............. 3 K2
Holland Wy *END/NAR* LE19...... 54 D3
Holliers Wy *RLEIW/BAR* LE9.... 63 G2
Hollies Cl *RLEIW/BAR* LE9....... 41 E5
Hollies Wy *RLEINE/SYS* LE7.... 38 D1
Hollington Rd *LEIE* LE5........... 36 D1
Hollins Rd *LEIW* LE3.............. 34 A1
Hollinwell Cl *LEIW* LE3........... 24 A5
Hollow Rd *RLEINE/SYS* LE7...... 17 F1
Hollow Station
  RLEIS/BBY LE8................ 70 A3
The Hollow *RLEIW/BAR* LE9.... 37 H3
Hollow Way *LEIE* LE5............. 51 F3
Hollowtree Rd *LEIN* LE4......... 21 G5
Holly Bank Cl *LEIE* LE5.......... 21 G5
Hollybrook Cl *LEIN* LE4.......... 21 E1
Hollybush Cl *LEIE* LE5........... 28 D3
Holly Cl *MKTHBORO* LE16....... 78 C5
Holly Ct *LEIE* LE5................. 47 E1
Hollylene Crs
  RLEIW/BAR LE9.............. 50 D4
Holly Dr *LUTT* LE17............... 85 F3
Holly Gv *RLEIS/BBY* LE8......... 56 B5
Holly La *RLEIW/BAR* LE9......... 50 B4
Holly Tree Av *LEIN* LE4.......... 11 G4
Holman Rw *LEIE* LE5............. 28 A4
Holmdale Rd
  RLEINE/SYS LE7.............. 13 E1
Holmden Av *WGSTN* LE18....... 57 H1
Holme Dr *LEIS* LE2............... 47 F1
Holmes Cl *GBY/RBY* LE6......... 16 A4
Holmewood Dr
  RLEIW/BAR LE9.............. 32 D1
Holmfield Av *LEIS* LE2........... 36 D3
Holmfield Av East *LEIW* LE3.... 33 G2
Holmfield Av West *LEIW* LE3... 33 G2
Holmfield Cl *LUTT* LE17.......... 85 G3
Holmfield Rd *LEIS* LE2........... 36 C5
Holmleigh Gdns
  RLEINE/SYS LE7.............. 38 D1
Holmwood Dr *RLEIW/BAR* LE5... 24 C1
Holt Crs *RLEIW/BAR* LE9......... 50 C4
Holt Dr *RLEIW/BAR* LE9.......... 32 D1
Holt La *LUTT* LE17................. 77 H2
  RLEIW/BAR LE9.............. 75 H3
Holt Rd *LEIN* LE4.................. 19 G2
Holts Cl *LEI* LE2................... 47 F4
Holyoake St *END/NAR* LE19..... 54 C1
Holyrood Dr *RLEIW/BAR* LE9.... 66 D2
Holywell Rd *LEIS* LE2............ 44 C2
Home Cl *LEIW* LE3................ 33 G4
Home Cl *MKTHBORO* LE16...... 83 H1
  RLEIS/BBY LE8................ 56 B5
  RLEIS/BBY LE8................ 68 A3
Home Farm Cl *LEIN* LE4......... 18 C4
  MKTHBORO LE16............. 81 H1
Homemead Av *LEIN* LE4......... 18 D5
Homer Dr *END/NAR* LE19........ 54 C3
Homestead Cl
  RLEIS/SYS LE7................ 4 A1
Homestead Dr *WGSTN* LE18... 58 B2
Homestead Houses
  RLEIW/BAR LE9 *.............. 72 C2
Homestone Gdns *LEIE* LE5..... 29 E4
Homestone Ri *LEIE* LE5.......... 29 E4
Homeway Rd *LEIE* LE5........... 37 E2
Honeybourne Cl *LEIS* LE2....... 47 E3
Honeycomb Cl
  END/NAR LE19................ 54 C1
Honeysuckle Cl *LUTT* LE17..... 85 E3
Honeysuckle Rd *LEIE* LE5....... 21 G5

Honeywell Cl *LEIS* LE2.......... 47 E3
Honiton Cl *WGSTN* LE18........ 58 A2
Hooper Cl *LEIN* LE4.............. 18 D1
Hopefield Rd *LEIW* LE3.......... 35 E3
Hoppner Cl *LEIN* LE4............. 10 C3
Hopton Flds
  MKTHBORO LE16............. 81 G4
Hopton Cl *LEIN* LE4.............. 18 B4
Hopyard Cl *LEIN* LE4............. 44 B4
Hornbeam Cl *END/NAR* LE19... 54 C2
  LEIS LE2....................... 47 E1
Hornby Rd *LEIN* LE4.............. 21 G4
Horndean Av *WGSTN* LE18...... 46 A5
Horsefair Cl
  RLEIS/BBY LE8................ 78 B5
Horsefair St *LEI* LE1............. 2 E4
Horseshoe Cl *RLEIW/BAR* LE9... 65 F2
Horse Shoe La
  MKTHBORO LE16............. 79 E3
Horsewell La *WGSTN* LE18...... 58 B5
Horston Rd *LEIE* LE5............. 37 E2
Horton Ct *RLEIS/BBY* LE8........ 56 A5
Horwood Cl *WGSTN* LE18....... 46 C4
Hoskins Cl *WGSTN* LE18........ 58 C3
Hospital Cl *LEIE* LE5............. 37 F1
Hospital La *RLEIS/BBY* LE8..... 56 C4
Hotel St *LEI* LE1.................. 2 D4
Hotoft Rd *LEIE* LE5............... 28 B2
Houghton La *LEIE* LE5........... 39 E4
Houghton St *LEIE* LE5........... 37 E5
HouldItch Rd *LEIN* LE4.......... 36 B5
Housman Wk *LEIN* LE4.......... 26 D2
Howard Cl *RLEIW/BAR* LE9...... 50 A4
Howard Rd *LEIS* LE2............. 36 A4
  LEIS LE2....................... 56 B1
Howard Wy
  MKTHBORO LE16............. 81 G3
Howden Rd *LEIN* LE4............. 44 C4
Howden Rd *LEIS* LE2............. 47 F5
Howe Cl *RLEIW/BAR* LE9......... 62 A5
Hoylake Cl *LEIE* LE5.............. 37 E3
Hubbard Cl *RLEIS/BBY* LE8..... 66 A1
Hudson Cl *LEIW* LE3.............. 25 E2
Huggett Cl *LEIN* LE4.............. 20 C3
Hughenden Dr *LEIS* LE2......... 35 G4
Humber Cl *LEIE* LE5.............. 28 B1
Humberstone Ct *LEIE* LE5 *..... 28 A3
Humberstone Dr *LEIE* LE5....... 27 H2
Humberstone Ga *LEI* LE1........ 2 F4
Humberstone La *LEIN* LE4....... 20 C1
Humble La *RLEINE/SYS* LE7..... 3 G1
Humble Cl *RLEIS/BBY* LE8........ 60 A1
Jessop Cl *LEIW* LE3.............. 25 E1
Huncote Rd *END/NAR* LE19..... 54 C4
  RLEIW/BAR LE9.............. 54 A4
  RLEIW/BAR LE9.............. 62 B2
Hungarton Bvd *LEIE* LE5......... 28 B2
Hungarton Dr
  RLEINE/SYS LE7.............. 13 G1
Hunter Bvd *LUTT* LE17........... 84 A4
Hunter Rd *LEIN* LE4.............. 26 C1
Hunter Dr *LUTT* LE17............. 85 F4
Hunters Rw
  RLEIW/BAR LE9 *.............. 65 F3
Hunters Wy *LEIS* LE2............ 47 H3
  LEIS LE2....................... 32 D3
Huntingdon Gdns
  MKTHBORO LE16............. 81 G3
Huntingdon Rd *LEIN* LE4........ 20 B5
The Huntings
  LEIE LE5....................... 22 C5
Huntsmans Cl *COAL* LE67....... 6 C4
Huntsman's Dl
  RLEINE/SYS LE7.............. 5 G1
Huntsmans Wy *LEIN* LE4....... 20 B4
Hurds Cl *RLEINE/SYS* LE7........ 17 F1
Hurlingham Rd
  MKTHBORO LE16............. 81 H3
Hursley Cl *LEIS* LE2.............. 47 G3
Hurst Ri *LEIE* LE5................. 28 A5
Hurst Rd *RLEIW/BAR* LE9........ 51 E4
Hutchinson St *LEIE* LE5......... 3 J4
Hyde Cl *END/NAR* LE19.......... 54 D3
  LEIS LE2....................... 47 G5
  LEIS LE2....................... 25 F1
Hydra Wk *LEIS* LE2.............. 3 K4
Hylion Rd *LEIS* LE2............... 45 G2

I

Ibbetson Av *LEIW* LE3........... 24 A3
Ibsley Wy *LEIS* LE2.............. 44 D5
Ickworth Cl *LEIE* LE5............. 27 G2
Iffley Cl *LEIE* LE5................. 27 H5
Iliffe Av *LEIE* LE5................. 46 D3
Iliffe Rd *WGSTN* LE18............ 46 D3
Illingworth Rd *LEIE* LE5.......... 28 A4
Ilmington Cl *LEIW* LE3........... 24 A1
Imperial Av *LEIW* LE3............ 34 D2
Imperial Rd *RLEIS/BBY* LE8..... 69 H3
Impey Cl *LEIW* LE3............... 33 H4
Infirmary Cl *LEI* LE2.............. 2 E6
Infirmary Rd *LEI* LE1............. 2 E6
Infirmary Sq *LEIS* LE2........... 2 E6
Ingarsby Dr *LEIE* LE5............ 38 A2
Ingleby Rd *WGSTN* LE18........ 46 A5
Ingle Dr *RLEIW/BAR* LE9......... 22 C2
Ingold Av *LEIN* LE4............... 18 D4
Ingrams Wy *WGSTN* LE18....... 58 C3
Invergary Cl *LEIN* LE4............ 20 B3
Iona Cl *LEIE* LE5.................. 18 B4
Iona Rd *RLEINE/SYS* LE7........ 4 C5
Ipswich Cl *LEIN* LE4.............. 18 A1
Ireton Av *LEIE* LE5............... 20 D5
Ireton Rd *LEIN* LE4............... 27 E1
  MKTHBORO LE16............. 81 G3
Iris Av *LEIN* LE4................... 11 H4

  LEIS LE2....................... 44 B5
Irlam St *WGSTN* LE18............ 57 F3
Ironworks Rd *LEIN* LE4.......... 27 E2
Isabel Cl *RLEIS/BBY* LE8......... 70 A3
Isis Cl *LEIE* LE5................... 47 H2
Islington St *LEIS* LE2............. 35 H3
Ismabella Rd *LEIW* LE3.......... 33 G4
Ivanhoe Cl *LEIW* LE3............. 33 G3
Ivanhoe Rd *WGSTN* LE18....... 57 F1
Ivanhoe St *LEIW* LE3............. 25 G4
Ivatt Cl *RLEINE/SYS* LE7......... 29 G5
Ivychurch Crs *LEIE* LE5......... 29 E1
Ivydale Rd *LEIN* LE4.............. 20 D1
Ivydene Cl *RLEIW/BAR* LE9...... 51 F5
Ivy Rd *LEIW* LE3................... 35 E2

J

Jack Hardy Cl *RLEINE/SYS* LE7... 5 F5
Jacklin Dr *LEIN* LE4.............. 20 B2
Jackson Cl *LEIE* LE5............. 22 A1
  MKTHBORO LE16............. 81 H4
Jackson St *LEIN* LE4............. 19 H4
Jacob Cl *END/NAR* LE19.......... 42 C5
Jacqueline Rd *LEIN* LE4......... 19 F4
Jacques Cl *END/NAR* LE19...... 42 C5
James Gavin Wy *LEIS* LE2...... 48 A4
James St *RLEINE/SYS* LE7....... 8 C5
  RLEIS/BBY LE8................ 56 A3
  RLEIW/BAR LE9.............. 51 E4
Jamesway *RLEIW/BAR* LE9...... 65 F2
Janes Wy *COAL* LE67............ 6 C4
Jarrett Cl *END/NAR* LE19........ 42 C5
Jarrom St *LEI* LE2................ 2 A6
Jarvis St *LEIS* LE3................ 2 C3
Jasmine Cl *LEIN* LE4............. 21 F4
  LUTT LE17..................... 85 E3
Jasmine Ct *END/NAR* LE19...... 54 B2
  WGSTN LE18.................. 46 B5
Jean Dr *LEIN* LE4................. 25 H1
Jellicoe Rd *LEIE* LE5............. 27 G4
Jennett Cl *LEIE* LE5.............. 28 A3
Jeremy Cl *LEIN* LE4.............. 19 H5
Jermyn St *LEIN* LE4.............. 19 H5
Jersey Rd *LEIN* LE4.............. 18 D3
Jersey Wy *RLEIW/BAR* LE9...... 50 A5
Jerwood Wy
  MKTHBORO LE16............. 82 A2
Jessons Cl *LEIN* LE4............. 20 B4
Jessop Cl *LEIW* LE3.............. 25 E1
Jewsbury Wy *LEIS* LE3........... 33 G5
John Bold Av *RLEIW/BAR* LE9... 62 C3
Johnnie Johnson Dr
  LUTT LE17..................... 85 G1
Johnscliffe Cl *GBY/RBY* LE6..... 7 H3
Johnson Cl *RLEIS/BBY* LE8..... 68 B4
Johnson Ri *RLEIW/BAR* LE9..... 62 C4
Johnson Rd *LEIN* LE4............ 11 F5
Johnson St *LEI* LE1.............. 2 C1
John St *END/NAR* LE19.......... 54 D3
Jonathan Ct *GBY/RBY* LE6...... 16 C4
Jordan Av *WGSTN* LE18......... 57 G2
Jordan Cl *LEIS* LE2............... 24 A2
Journeyman's Gn
  GBY/RBY LE6.................. 22 D2
Jowett Cl *LEIW* LE3............... 25 E1
Joyce Rd *LEIN* LE4................ 25 F2
Jubilee Cl *RLEINE/SYS* LE7....... 5 E4
Jubilee Ct *END/NAR* LE19........ 55 E4
  RLEIW/BAR LE9.............. 51 E4
Jubilee Gdns *LEIN* LE4.......... 27 F2
Jubilee Houses
  RLEIW/BAR LE9 *.............. 22 D4
Jubilee Rd *LEI* LE1............... 3 F1
  RLEIW/BAR LE9.............. 74 A3
Judith Dr *LEIE* LE5............... 37 H1
  RLEIS/BBY LE8................ 56 A4
Julian Rd *LEIE* LE5............... 56 C1
Junction Rd *LEIS* LE2............ 26 C3
  WGSTN LE18.................. 46 B5
June Av *LEIN* LE4................. 21 E2
Juniper St *LEIE* LE5.............. 3 G2
Juniper Cl *LEIS* LE2.............. 32 D5
  LUTT LE17..................... 85 F2
Juno Cl *LEIW* LE3................. 24 A3
Jupiter Cl *LEIS* LE2............... 3 K3

K

Kamloops Crs *LEI* LE1........... 3 G1
Kashmir Rd *LEIN* LE4............ 26 D3
Kate St *LEIW* LE3................. 2 A4
Kay Rd *LEIN* LE4.................. 24 D2
Keats Cl *END/NAR* LE19.......... 42 C5
  RLEIW/BAR LE9.............. 51 F2
Keats La *RLEIW/BAR* LE9......... 51 E2
Keats Wk *LEIN* LE4............... 26 D2
Keays Wy *END/NAR* LE19........ 54 B2
Keble Dr *RLEINE/SYS* LE7........ 15 F1
Keble Rd *LEIS* LE2................ 36 A4
Kedleston Av *LEIN* LE4.......... 19 G5
Kedleston Rd *LEIE* LE5........... 36 D1
Keenan Cl *LEIS* LE2.............. 44 B5
Keepers' Cft *RLEINE/SYS* LE7... 5 H2
The Keep *RLEIW/BAR* LE9....... 22 D5
Kegworth Av *LEIS* LE2........... 27 H5
Keightley Rd *LEIW* LE3.......... 24 C1
Kelbrook Cl *LEIS* LE2............. 18 C3
Kelmarsh Av *WGSTN* LE18...... 58 B1
Kelso Gn *LEIS* LE2................ 44 D5
Kelvon Cl *LEIW* LE3.............. 34 D4
Kemble Sq *LEI* LE1............... 3 F3
Kemp Rd *LEIN* LE4................ 24 C1
Kempson Rd *LEIS* LE2........... 35 G5

Kendall's Av *RLEIW/BAR* LE9... 63 G2
Kendal Rd *LEIN* LE4.............. 20 B4
Kendrick Dr *LEIS* LE2............ 47 F3
Kenilworth Cl
  WGSTN LE18.................. 74 A1
Kenilworth Dr *LEIS* LE2.......... 46 D5
Kenilworth Rd *WGSTN* LE18.... 45 H5
Kenmackenzie Cl *LUTT* LE17... 85 G1
Kennedy Wy *LEIW* LE3........... 33 E3
Kenneth Gamble Ct
  WGSTN LE18.................. 45 H4
Kenny Cl *RLEIS/BBY* LE8......... 56 A5
Kensington Cl *LEIS* LE2.......... 47 E2
  LEIS LE2....................... 55 D2
Kensington Dr *WGSTN* LE18.... 46 B3
Kensington St *LEIN* LE4......... 26 C1
Kent Crs *WGSTN* LE18........... 45 F5
Kent Dr *LEIS* LE2................. 47 G3
Kenton Av *WGSTN* LE18......... 58 A2
Kent St *LEIE* LE5................. 3 J2
Kenwood Rd *LEIS* LE2........... 46 A1
Kepston Cl *LEIS* LE2............. 44 D4
Kerrial Rd *LEIW* LE3............. 24 C3
Kerrysdale Av *LEIN* LE4......... 20 B5
Kertley *RLEIS/BBY* LE8........... 68 B4
Kestian Cl *MKTHBORO* LE16.... 78 B4
Kestral La *LEIS* LE2.............. 21 G5
Kestrel Cl *LEIE* LE5.............. 27 E3
  LEIW LE3....................... 32 C3
Kestrel Dr *RLEIS/BBY* LE8....... 68 C5
  RLEIW/BAR LE9.............. 74 A2
Keswick Cl *LEIN* LE4............. 11 H4
  LEIS LE2....................... 44 C5
Keswick Rd *RLEIS/BBY* LE8..... 56 A4
Kettering Rd
  MKTHBORO LE16............. 82 C2
Kevern Cl *WGSTN* LE18.......... 58 A2
Kew Dr *LEIS* LE2.................. 47 G5
  WGSTN LE18.................. 45 H3
Keyham Cl *LEIS* LE2............. 28 B1
Keyham La *LEIE* LE5.............. 28 B1
Keyham La West *LEIE* LE5...... 28 D1
Keythorpe St *LEIS* LE2........... 3 K3
Kibworth Br *RLEIS/BBY* LE8..... 69 E1
Kibworth Rd *RLEIS/BBY* LE8.... 68 B4
Kielder Cl *END/NAR* LE19........ 55 E4
Kilburn Av *LEIE* LE5.............. 46 D2
Kilby Av *LEIN* LE4................ 19 G2
Kilby Dr *WGSTN* LE18............ 58 C2
Kilby Rd *RLEIS/BBY* LE8.......... 68 B5
Kildare St *LEI* LE1................ 3 H3
Kilmeford Cl *LEIE* LE5............ 20 B3
Kiln Av *LEIN* LE4.................. 20 D1
Kiln Cl *RLEIW/BAR* LE9........... 74 C4
Kilverstone Av *LEIE* LE5......... 38 B2
Kilworth Dr *LEIE* LE5............. 37 E2
Kimberley Rd *LEIS* LE2.......... 3 J1
Kimberley St *RLEIS/BBY* LE8... 69 H3
Kincaple Rd *LEIN* LE4............ 20 B3
Kinchley Cl *LEIW* LE3............ 17 H4
Kincraig Rd *LEIN* LE4............. 20 B3
Kinder Cl *RLEIS/BBY* LE8........ 66 A1
Kingcup Cl *LEIW* LE3............. 32 D3
King Edward Av
  END/NAR LE19................ 55 E3
King Edward Rd *LEIW* LE3....... 27 H3
Kingfisher Av *LEIE* LE5.......... 27 E3
Kingfisher Cl *LEIW* LE3.......... 32 C3
  RLEIW/BAR LE9.............. 4 C5
  RLEIS/BBY LE8................ 60 D2
Kingfisher Wk *LEIE* LE5 *........ 27 E3
King Richard's Hl
  RLEIW/BAR LE9.............. 51 H2
King Richards Dr *LEIS* LE2...... 25 C5
Kingsbridge Cl
  END/NAR LE19................ 54 C3
Kingsbridge Crs *LEIN* LE4....... 10 B5
Kingsbury Av *LEIN* LE4.......... 38 A1
Kingscliffe Crs *LEIS* LE2......... 38 B1
Kings Ct *RLEIW/BAR* LE9 *........ 50 B4
Kingsdale Rd *WGSTN* LE18..... 58 C3
Kingsfield Rd
  RLEIW/BAR LE9.............. 50 B4
  RLEIW/BAR LE9.............. 65 E4
Kingsgate Av *LEIN* LE4.......... 11 F4
King's Head Pl
  MKTHBORO LE16............. 81 H1
Kingsley Cl *END/NAR* LE19...... 54 C2
Kingsley St *LEIS* LE2............. 36 A5
Kingsmead Rd *LEIS* LE2......... 46 A2
Kings Newton St *LEIS* LE2...... 3 H6
King's Rd *MKTHBORO* LE16..... 81 H1
Kingsthorpe Cl *LEIN* LE4......... 19 F4
Kingston Av *WGSTN* LE18....... 58 A1
Kingston Rd *LEIS* LE2............ 36 C2
Kingston Wy
  MKTHBORO LE16............. 78 B3
King St *END/NAR* LE19........... 54 D3
  LEI LE1........................ 3 F6
  LEIS LE2....................... 47 F3
  RLEINE/SYS LE7.............. 21 H1
  RLEIS/BBY LE8................ 55 H4
Kings Wk *LEIS* LE2............... 33 E2
King's Wk *RLEIW/BAR* LE9...... 51 E3
King's Wy *LUTT* LE17............. 85 F4
Kingsway *LEIN* LE4............... 38 A1
  LEIS LE2....................... 43 H1
Kingsway North *LEIS* LE2........ 34 A3
Kingsway Rd *LEIE* LE5........... 37 E3
Kingswood Av *LEIS* LE2......... 34 D1
King Williams Wy
  RLEINE/SYS LE7.............. 9 G5
Kinley Rd *LEIN* LE4............... 18 E5
Kinross Av *LEIE* LE5.............. 28 C1
Kinsdale Dr *LEIE* LE5............. 29 F4
Kintyre Dr *LEIN* LE4.............. 20 A3
Kiplin Dr *END/NAR* LE19......... 54 C1
Kipling Gv *LEIS* LE2.............. 18 A5

Kirby Cl *RLEIW/BAR* LE9 .... 72 B1
Kirby La *RLEIW/BAR* LE9 .... 32 D2
Kirby Rd *LEIW* LE5 .... 23 G2
   LEIW LE3 .... 25 G5
Kirkby Rd *RLEIW/BAR* LE9 .... 50 B4
Kirkdale Rd *WGSTN* LE18 .... 58 C3
Kirkfield Rd *RLEIS/BBY* LE8 ..... 67 F2
Kirkland Rd *LEIW* LE5 .... 34 B5
Kirk La *END/NAR* LE19 .... 43 E5
Kirkstone Cl *LEIH* LE3 .... 24 B1
Kirkwall Crs *LEIE* LE5 .... 29 E3
Kirobe Av *LEIW* LE3 .... 32 D2
Kirminton Gdns *LEIE* LE5 .... 28 C4
Kirtley Wy *RLEIW/BAR* LE9 ..... 74 C3
Kitchener Rd *LEIE* LE5 .... 27 G5
   RLEINE/SYS LE7 .... 9 C5
Kite Cl *RLEIW/BAR* LE9 .... 74 A1
Knight Cl *LEIH* LE4 .... 12 D5
Knighton Church Rd
   LEIS LE2 .... 46 A1
Knighton Cl *RLEIW/BAR* LE9 ... 74 C5
Knighton Dr *LEIS* LE2 .... 36 C5
Knighton Fields Rd East
   LEIS LE2 .... 35 H5
Knighton Fields Rd West
   LEIS LE2 * 35 H5
Knighton Grange Rd
   LEIS LE2 .... 37 E3
Knighton Junction La
   LEIS LE2 .... 36 A4
Knighton La *LEIS* LE2 .... 35 G5
Knighton La East *LEIS* LE2 ...... 36 A5
Knighton Park Rd *LEIS* LE2 ..... 36 C3
Knighton Ri *LEIE* LE2 .... 37 E4
Knighton Rd *LEIS* LE2 .... 36 B5
Knighton St *LEIS* LE2 .... 2 E7
Knightsbridge Rd *LEIS* LE2 ..... 36 C3
Knights End Rd
   MKTHBORO LE16 .... 79 F3
Knights Link *LEIH* LE3 .... 51 H2
Knights Rd *LEIH* LE4 .... 18 C1
Knollgate Cl *LEIN* LE4 .... 11 E4
Knoll St *MKTHBORO* LE16 ...... 81 F1
Knowles Rd *LEIW* LE5 .... 24 C3
Krefeld Wy *LEIN* LE4 .... 18 A4

L

Labrador Cl *LEI* LE1 .... 3 H1
Laburnum Av *LUTT* LE17 .... 85 F3
Laburnum Dr
   RLEIW/BAR LE9 .... 50 D4
Ladbroke Rd *RLEIW/BAR* LE9 .. 28 C1
Lacey Cl *LUTT* LE17 .... 85 G1
Ladbroke Gv *RLEIS/BBY* LE8 ... 67 F2
Lady Hey Rd *LEIH* LE3 .... 17 H4
Lady Jane Wk
   RLEINE/SYS LE7 .... 29 G2
Lady Leys *RLEIW/BAR* LE9 ...... 65 F3
Ladysmith Rd
   RLEIW/BAR LE9 .... 22 D4
   WGSTN LE18 .... 45 E5
Ladywood Ct *LUTT* LE17 .... 85 G2
Laithwaite Cl *LEIW* LE3 .... 18 B1
Lakeside Ct *RLEINE/SYS* LE7 ... 38 C1
Lakeview Cha *LEIH* LE3 .... 21 G4
Lakin Dr *LEIW* LE3 .... 33 G5
Lambert Rd *LEIW* LE3 .... 35 E3
Lamborne Rd *LEIH* LE4 .... 11 H4
Lambourne Rd *LEIN* LE4 .... 11 H4
Lamen Rd *LEIH* LE4 .... 24 C1
Lamplighters *RLEIS/BBY* LE8 .. 68 D4
Lamport Cl *WGSTN* LE18 .... 58 D1
Lancashire St *LEIW* LE4 .... 45 E3
Lancaster Cl *RLEIW/BAR* LE9 .. 30 B5
Lancaster Ct *GBY/RBY* LE6 ...... 16 A1
Lancaster St *LEIS* LE2 .... 3 F7
Lancaster Wy *LEIS* LE2 .... 57 C2
Lancelot Cl *LEIW* LE3 .... 33 E5
Lancing Av *LEIW* LE3 .... 32 D2
Landscape Dr *LEIE* LE5 .... 38 A1
Landsdowne Rd *LEIS* LE2 .... 35 G5
Landseer Rd *LEIH* LE4 .... 36 B4
Land Society La
   RLEIW/BAR LE9 .... 51 E3
Lane Cl *LEIW* LE3 .... 24 A2
Lanesborough Cl
   RLEIW/BAR LE9 .... 10 B1
Lanesborough Dr
   RLEIW/BAR LE9 .... 10 B1
Lanesborough Rd *LEIN* LE4 .... 19 H3
Lanes Hill Gv *RLEIS/BBY* LE8 .. 62 C5
Langdale *RLEIS/BBY* LE8 .... 68 B5
Langdale Rd *LEIH* LE3 .... 18 B1
Langham Dr *END/NAR* LE19 ... 54 D5
Langham Rd *LEIH* LE4 .... 20 D4
The Langhill *LEIE* LE5 .... 27 H4
Langholme Rd *LEIH* LE3 .... 29 E4
Langley Av *LEIW* LE4 .... 19 F4
Langton Rd *MKTHBORO* LE16 . 79 E1
   RLEIS/BBY LE8 .... 70 B2
   WGSTN LE18 .... 58 B2
Langton St *LEIW* LE4 .... 45 E3
Lansdowne Gv *WGSTN* LE18 ... 57 G3
Lapwing Cl *LEIN* LE4 .... 18 B1
Lapwing Ct *END/NAR* LE19 .... 54 C4
Larch Dr *LUTT* LE17 .... 85 F3
Larch Gv *LEIW* LE3 .... 35 G1
Larchmont Rd *LEIN* LE4 .... 25 H1
Larch St *LEIW* LE4 .... 45 E3
Larchwood Rd *LEIS* LE2 .... 67 E2
Larchwood Av *GBY/RBY* LE6 .. 16 B4
Larchwood Cl *LEIS* LE2 .... 67 E3
Lark Cl *LEIW* LE3 .... 32 D3
Larkspur Cl *RLEIW/BAR* LE9 ... 50 D4
Larkswood *RLEIS/BBY* LE8 ..... 70 B3
Lastingham Cl *LEIS* LE2 .... 45 G2

Lathkill St *MKTHBORO* LE16 .... 82 A3
Latimer Cl *RLEIS/BBY* LE8 .... 56 A5
Latimer Ct *RLEINE/SYS* LE7 .... 17 F2
Latimer Crs *MKTHBORO* LE16 . 82 A2
Latimer Rd *LEIW* LE4 * 26 C2
Latimer Rd *RLEINE/SYS* LE7 .... 9 H1
Latimer St *LUTT* LE17 .... 2 A6
   RLEINE/SYS LE7 .... 17 G2
Laughton Rd
   MKTHBORO LE16 .... 80 B1
Launceston Rd *WGSTN* LE18 ... 58 A3
Launde Pk *MKTHBORO* LE16 ... 82 B2
Launde Rd *COAL* LE67 .... 6 C4
   LEIS LE2 .... 47 G1
Laundon Cl *GBY/RBY* LE6 .... 16 B5
Laundon Wy *GBY/RBY* LE6 ..... 23 E1
   RLEIS/BBY LE8 .... 66 A1
Laundry La *LEIH* LE4 .... 19 H5
Laurel Bank Cl
   RLEINE/SYS LE7 .... 5 H3
Laurel Cl *LEIW* LE3 .... 24 C2
Laurel Dr *RLEINE/SYS* LE7 ...... 17 H5
   RLEIS/BBY LE8 .... 67 E2
Laurel Rd *LEIS* LE2 .... 36 C1
   RLEIS/BBY LE8 .... 56 B4
The Laurels *COAL* LE67 .... 14 C1
Laureston Dr *LEIS* LE2 .... 36 D5
Lavender Cl *LUTT* LE17 .... 85 E5
Lavender Rd *LEIW* LE3 .... 35 E3
   RLEINE/SYS LE7 .... 56 A5
Lavender Rd *LEIW* LE3 .... 35 E3
Laverstock Rd *WGSTN* LE18 .... 58 A3
Lawford Rd *LEIS* LE2 .... 44 D4
Lawn Av *LEIN* LE4 .... 11 H4
Lawn Cl *LEIH* LE4 .... 12 D5
The Lawns *LEIS* LE2 .... 36 D5
Lawnwood Rd *GBY/RBY* LE6 .. 15 H4
Lawrence Cl *LEIH* LE4 .... 10 C3
Law St *LEIW* LE4 .... 26 C1
Lawyers La *LEIH* LE4 .... 18 C5
Laxford Cl *LEIW* LE3 .... 18 C5
Laxton Cl *LEIH* LE4 .... 11 H4
   LEIS LE2 .... 58 D1
Layton Rd *LEIS* LE2 .... 27 C5
Lea Cl *LEIN* LE4 .... 12 B5
   RLEIW/BAR LE9 .... 74 C4
The Lealand
   MKTHBORO LE16 .... 81 E4
Leamington Dr
   RLEIS/BBY LE8 .... 56 B5
Leas Cl *RLEINE/SYS* LE7 .... 29 F4
The Lea *RLEIS/BBY* LE8 .... 70 B3
Ledbury Cl *LEIS* LE2 .... 47 H4
Ledbury Gn *LEIN* LE4 .... 18 D2
Ledwell Dr *LEIW* LE3 .... 24 A1
Lee Cir *LEI* LE1 .... 3 C2
Lee Ni *LEIW* LE3 .... 62 C3
   RLEIW/BAR LE9 .... 51 F3
Lee Ri *GBY/RBY* LE6 .... 22 D2
Leeson St *LEIS* LE2 .... 45 E1
   LEI LE2 .... 3 G2
Legion Wy *LEIW* LE3 .... 33 H5
Leicester La *END/NAR* LE19 .... 42 C5
   MKTHBORO LE16 .... 78 A2
   RLEIW/BAR LE9 .... 30 D2
Leicester Rd *COAL* LE67 .... 6 C4
   END/NAR LE19 .... 55 E3
   GBY/RBY LE6 .... 16 B4
   LEIH LE4 .... 10 C4
   LEIS LE2 .... 47 E2
   LEIS LE2 .... 36 B5
   LEIW LE3 .... 17 F5
   MKTHBORO LE16 .... 78 B5
   RLEINE/SYS LE7 .... 17 G1
   RLEIS/BBY LE8 .... 56 B5
   RLEIS/BBY LE8 .... 68 B2
   RLEIW/BAR LE9 .... 40 A4
   RLEIW/BAR LE9 .... 50 C4
   RLEIW/BAR LE9 .... 72 C2
   RLEIW/BAR LE9 .... 46 A3
Leicestershire Round
   COAL LE67 .... 6 A4
Leicester St *LEIS* LE5 .... 27 F4
Leire La *LUTT* LE17 .... 76 A4
Leire Rd *RLEIW/BAR* LE9 .... 73 H5
Leire St *LEIN* LE4 .... 19 H5
Lema Cl *LEIH* LE4 .... 20 C2
Lena Dr *GBY/RBY* LE6 .... 15 G2
Lenthall Sq *MKTHBORO* LE16 . 81 H3
Leopold Cl *RLEIS/BBY* LE8 ...... 66 C1
Leopold Rd *LEIS* LE2 .... 36 A4
Leopold St *WGSTN* LE18 .... 59 F4
Lethworth Rd *LEIH* LE3 .... 25 E4
   LEIS LE2 .... 32 C5
Lethbridge Cl *LEI* LE1 .... 3 C1
Leveret Dr *RLEIS/BBY* LE8 ...... 65 H1
Leveric Rd *LEIE* LE5 .... 27 G2
Lewett Cl *LEIH* LE4 .... 11 E4
Lewin Br *RLEINE/SYS* LE7 .... 4 D3
Lewis Cl *LEIN* LE4 .... 18 B5
Lewis Ct *END/NAR* LE19 .... 43 F5
Lewisher Rd *LEIN* LE4 .... 11 H5
Lewis Wy *RLEIS/BBY* LE8 .... 67 F3
Lexham St *LEIH* LE4 .... 19 H5
Leybury Wy *RLEINE/SYS* LE7 .. 9 F1
Leycroft Rd *LEIH* LE4 .... 18 B1
Leyland Rd *LEIW* LE3 .... 43 H1
Leys Cl *LEIS* LE2 .... 47 E4
Leysdale Cl *LEIH* LE4 .... 18 B4
Leys Dr *LEIE* LE5 .... 27 F2
Leysland Av *RLEIS/BBY* LE8 ... 66 C3
The Leys *RLEIS/BBY* LE8 .... 70 A2
   RLEIS/BBY LE8 .... 55 H4
Leyton Cl *LUTT* LE17 .... 85 F4
Liberty Rd *LEIW* LE3 .... 24 B4
Lichfield Av *RLEIW/BAR* LE9 .. 73 H1
Lichfield Dr *RLEIS/BBY* LE8 .... 56 A5
Lichfield St *LEI* LE1 .... 2 E1
Lidster Cl *LEIW* LE3 .... 28 B2
Lilac Av *LEIH* LE3 .... 18 B2
Lilac Dr *LUTT* LE17 .... 85 E3
Lilac Wy *RLEINE/SYS* LE7 .... 5 H3
Lillingstone Cl *COAL* LE67 .... 6 C3
Limber Crs *LEIW* LE3 .... 34 D3

Lime Av *GBY/RBY* LE6 .... 23 E1
Lime Cl *RLEINE/SYS* LE7 .... 13 F1
Lime Ct *RLEINE/SYS* LE7 .... 13 F2
Lime Gv *RLEIS/BBY* LE8 .... 56 B5
   RLEINE/SYS LE7 .... 13 F2
Limegrove Cl *LEIN* LE4 .... 18 C3
Limehurst Rd *LEIE* LE5 .... 28 D1
Lime Kilns *WGSTN* LE18 .... 58 C3
Lime Tree Av *LEIW* LE3 .... 14 C4
Lime Tree Rd *END/NAR* LE19 .. 55 F1
Linacres Rd *LEIH* LE4 .... 34 A2
Lincoln Cl *MKTHBORO* LE16 ... 78 D4
Lincoln Dr *RLEINE/SYS* LE7 .... 13 C2
   RLEIS/BBY LE8 .... 56 B5
   WGSTN LE18 .... 57 F1
Lincoln Rd *RLEIW/BAR* LE9 .... 66 C2
Lincoln St *LEIS* LE2 .... 3 J5
Linden Av *RLEIW/BAR* LE9 ..... 66 C2
Linden Dr *LEIS* LE2 .... 37 F2
   LUTT LE17 .... 85 F3
Linden Farm Dr
   RLEIS/BBY LE8 .... 66 D2
Linden La *RLEIW/BAR* LE9 ..... 32 D1
Linden St *LEIE* LE5 .... 27 G5
Lindfield Rd *LEIH* LE3 .... 25 E4
Lindisfarne Rd
   LEIH LE4 .... 12 D1
Lindrick Dr *LEIE* LE5 .... 37 E3
Lindridge La *RLEIW/BAR* LE9 . 30 B1
Linford Cl *WGSTN* LE18 .... 58 C1
Linford Crs *COAL* LE67 .... 6 C4
Linford St *LEIW* LE4 .... 19 G4
   RLEINE/SYS LE7 .... 9 F5
Ling Di *RLEIW/BAR* LE9 .... 65 F3
Link Ri *COAL* LE67 .... 6 D4
Link Rd *LEIS* LE2 .... 46 C1
   RLEINE/SYS LE7 .... 5 G4
   RLEINE/SYS LE7 .... 9 F5
Links Rd *RLEIS/BBY* LE8 .... 70 B3
   RLEIW/BAR LE9 .... 32 A1
Linkway Gdns *LEIW* LE3 .... 25 G5
Linley Gn *RLEIW/BAR* LE9 ...... 65 F3
Linnett Cl *END/NAR* LE19 .... 54 C4
Linney Rd *LEIH* LE4 .... 18 C4
Lintlaw Cl *LEIW* LE5 .... 29 E3
Linton St *LEIE* LE5 .... 36 C2
Linwood La *LEIS* LE2 .... 45 F2
Lipton Rd *LEIW* LE5 .... 18 A1
Litelmede *LEIE* LE5 .... 27 G5
Little Av *LEIW* LE4 .... 19 G4
Little Barley Cl *LEIH* LE4 .... 9 F1
Little Dl *WGSTN* LE18 .... 58 C2
Little Dunmow Rd *LEIE* LE5 ... 27 H2
Little Easton Cl *LEIE* LE5 .... 27 H2
The Littlefare *LEIW* LE3 .... 33 H5
Littlefield La *RLEIW/BAR* LE9 . 30 B2
Littlegarth *LEIS* LE2 .... 37 F4
Little Glen Rd *LEIS* LE2 .... 56 C2
Little Hill *WGSTN* LE18 .... 58 B1
Little Holme St *LEIW* LE3 .... 2 B5
Littlejohn Rd *LEIS* LE2 .... 44 D4
Little Lunnon *LUTT* LE17 .... 76 A4
Little Masons Cl *LEIW* LE4 ...... 33 H4
Littlemeer Cl *LEIW* LE4 .... 33 H4
Littlemore Cl *LEIE* LE5 .... 27 H4
Littleton St *LEIW* LE4 .... 25 H3
The Littleway *LEIE* LE5 .... 27 H4
Little Wood Cl *LEIH* LE4 .... 11 G5
Livesey Dr *RLEIS/BBY* LE8 ...... 72 A2
Livingstone St *LEIW* LE3 .... 25 G5
Lobbs Wood Ct *LEIE* LE5 .... 28 B2
Lobelia Cl *END/NAR* LE19 .... 54 B3
Locke Av *LEIH* LE4 .... 11 G4
Lockerbie Av *LEIH* LE4 .... 20 A5
Lock Gate Cl *WGSTN* LE18 ...... 57 C3
Locke Av *LEIH* LE4 .... 44 B4
Lock Keeper Cl *WGSTN* LE18 .. 57 G5
Lockley Cl *GBY/RBY* LE6 .... 22 D2
Lockside Cl *LEIS* LE2 .... 44 A3
Lock Cl *LEIH* LE4 .... 20 D1
   RLEINE/SYS LE7 .... 9 C5
   RLEIS/BBY LE8 .... 69 H1
Lodge Farm Rd *LEIE* LE5 .... 28 C5
Lodge La *RLEIW/BAR* LE9 ...... 9 F1
Lodge Rd *RLEIS/BBY* LE8 .... 68 B2
Lodgewood Av *LEIH* LE4 .... 11 F5
Logan Av *LEIS* LE2 .... 32 C5
Logan Ct *MKTHBORO* LE16 .... 78 A5
Logan Crs *MKTHBORO* LE16 .. 78 A5
Logan St *MKTHBORO* LE16 ..... 81 G1
Lombardy Rd *LEIE* LE5 .... 28 C5
Lomond Crs *LEIH* LE4 .... 18 C5
London Rd *COAL* LE67 .... 6 C4
   LEIS LE2 .... 3 H6
   LEIS LE2 .... 47 F3
   RLEIS/BBY LE8 .... 68 B2
London St *LEIE* LE5 .... 27 F4
Long Brimley Cl
   MKTHBORO LE16 .... 82 C1
Longcliffe Rd *LEIE* LE5 .... 27 E3
Long Cl *RLEINE/SYS* LE7 .... 9 E5
Longfellow Rd *LEIS* LE2 .... 36 A5
Longford Ct *WGSTN* LE18 .... 58 A3
Long Furrow *RLEINE/SYS* LE7 . 5 H3
Longgrey *RLEIS/BBY* LE8 .... 68 A2
Longhade Furlong
   RLEINE/SYS LE7 .... 9 H4
Longhurst Cl *LEIH* LE4 .... 20 C2
The Longlands
   MKTHBORO LE16 .... 82 C1
Long La *LEI* LE1 .... 3 J3
Longleat Cl *LEIE* LE5 .... 27 F2
Long Meadow *WGSTN* LE18 ... 58 C3
Longstone Gn *LEIE* LE5 .... 29 E3

Long St *RLEIW/BAR* LE9 .... 62 C3
   WGSTN LE18 .... 58 A1
Lonsdale Rd *LEIH* LE4 .... 20 C1
Lonsdale St *LEIS* LE2 .... 36 C1
Lord Byron St *LEIS* LE2 .... 47 E1
Lord Cl *END/NAR* LE19 .... 54 D4
Lords Av *LEIH* LE4 .... 10 C5
Lorne Rd *LEIS* LE2 .... 36 A4
Lorraine Rd *LEIS* LE2 .... 44 D1
Loseby Ct *LEIE* LE5 .... 35 C5
Loseby La *LEI* LE1 .... 3 F4
Lothair Rd *LEIS* LE2 .... 35 G4
Loughborough Rd *LEIW* LE4 .. 19 C5
   RLEINE/SYS LE7 .... 11 C2
Loughland Cl *RLEIS/BBY* LE8 .. 56 A3
Louise Av *RLEIW/BAR* LE9 .... 40 A3
Lovelace Wy *RLEIS/BBY* LE8 .. 68 B4
Loves La *LUTT* LE17 .... 77 E3
Lowcroft Dr *LEIS* LE2 .... 47 G4
Lower Brown St *LEI* LE1 .... 2 E6
Lower Church St
   RLEINE/SYS LE7 .... 5 E5
Lower Hastings St *LEI* LE1 ...... 3 G7
Lower Hill St *LEI* LE1 .... 3 F2
Lower Keyham La *LEIE* LE5 ..... 28 B1
Lower Lee St *LEI* LE1 .... 3 F2
Lower Leicester Rd
   LUTT LE17 .... 85 H2
Lower Willow St *LEI* LE1 .... 26 C5
Lowick Dr *WGSTN* LE18 .... 58 C1
Lowland Av *RLEIW/BAR* LE9 .. 33 E3
Loxley Rd *LEIW* LE5 .... 24 A1
Lubbesthorpe Bridle Rd
   END/NAR LE19 .... 33 C5
Lubbesthorpe Rd *LEIS* LE2 ..... 43 C1
Lubbesthorpe Wy
   END/NAR LE19 .... 33 H5
Lubenham Hl
   MKTHBORO LE16 .... 81 E1
Lubenham Rd
   MKTHBORO LE16 .... 81 E3
Lucas Wy *RLEIW/BAR* LE9 ..... 51 E4
Ludgate Cl *LEIH* LE4 .... 11 E4
Ludlam Cl *RLEIS/BBY* LE8 .... 67 C3
Ludlow Cl *LEIS* LE2 .... 47 G3
Lulworth Cl *LEIS* LE2 .... 57 G1
   WGSTN LE18 .... 58 B4
Lunsford Rd *LEIE* LE5 .... 27 F2
Luther St *LEIW* LE3 .... 35 E1
Lutterworth Rd *LEIH* LE4 .... 44 C4
   LUTT LE17 .... 85 H2
   RLEIS/BBY LE8 .... 56 A5
   RLEIW/BAR LE9 .... 75 H1
   RLEINE/SYS LE7 .... 9 C2
Lychgate Cl *RLEINE/SYS* LE7 .. 9 C2
Lydall Rd *LEIS* LE2 .... 44 D4
Lydford Rd *LEIH* LE4 .... 20 C2
Lyle Cl *LEIH* LE4 .... 20 C2
Lymington Rd *LEIS* LE2 .... 28 D2
Lyn Cl *RLEIW/BAR* LE9 .... 17 H4
Lyncote Rd *LEIW* LE3 .... 34 D5
Lyncroft Leys
   RLEINE/SYS LE7 .... 29 F3
Lyndale Av *RLEIW/BAR* LE9 ... 20 C1
Lyndale Rd *LEIE* LE5 .... 34 B5
Lyndene Cl *RLEIW/BAR* LE9 ... 51 E4
Lyndhurst Rd *LEIS* LE2 * 47 E2
Lyndon Dr *LEIS* LE2 .... 47 E2
Lyngate Av *LEIW* LE4 .... 11 G4
Lynholme Rd *LEIS* LE2 .... 45 H2
Lynmouth Cl *RLEIE* LE5 .... 24 A3
Lynmouth Dr *WGSTN* LE18 ... 45 C5
Lynroyd Cl *RLEIW/BAR* LE9 ... 28 D2
Lynwood Cl *RLEIW/BAR* LE9 . 30 B2
Lyon Cl *WGSTN* LE18 .... 45 C5
Lytham Rd *LEIS* LE2 .... 36 A4
Lytton Rd *LEIS* LE2 .... 36 B4

M

Mablowe Fld *WGSTN* LE18 ..... 58 C5
Macaulay Rd *LUTT* LE17 .... 85 H4
Macdonald Rd *LEIN* LE4 .... 26 C1
Machin Dr *RLEIW/BAR* LE9 .... 74 C5
Mackenzie Wy *LEI* LE1 .... 3 H1
Madeline Cl *MKTHBORO* LE16 79 F4
Madeline Rd *LEIH* LE4 .... 18 C1
Madras Rd *LEIE* LE5 .... 9 F1
Magna Rd *WGSTN* LE18 .... 57 C2
Magnolia Cl *LEIS* LE2 .... 44 C3
   LEIE LE5 .... 32 C5
Magnolia Dr *LUTT* LE17 .... 85 F2
Magnus Rd *LEIH* LE4 .... 20 A5
Maidenhead Av *LEIE* LE5 .... 21 H5
Maiden St *RLEINE/SYS* LE7 .... 17 D1
Maidstone Av *LEIE* LE5 .... 21 G5
Maidstone Rd *LEIS* LE2 .... 3 J5
Maidwell Cl *WGSTN* LE18 .... 58 D1
Maino Cl *LUTT* LE17 .... 85 E4
Mains Rd *RLEINE/SYS* LE7 ...... 83 C1
Main St *COAL* LE67 .... 6 B5
   GBY/RBY LE6 .... 7 H5
   GBY/RBY LE6 .... 22 D1
   LEIE LE5 .... 28 A2
   LEIH LE3 .... 23 H1
   LUTT LE17 .... 76 A3
   MKTHBORO LE16 .... 79 E5
   MKTHBORO LE16 .... 80 B1
   RLEINE/SYS LE7 .... 13 G4
   RLEINE/SYS LE7 .... 58 D5
   RLEIS/BBY LE8 .... 60 D5
   RLEIW/BAR LE9 .... 9 B3
   RLEIW/BAR LE9 .... 22 D5
   RLEIW/BAR LE9 .... 30 B1
   RLEIW/BAR LE9 .... 74 A2
Malabar Rd *LEI* LE1 .... 3 J2
Malcolm Ar *LEI* LE1 * 2 E5
Malham Cl *RLEIW/BAR* LE9 .... 18 B4

Malham Wy *LEIS* LE2 .... 47 H1
Mallard Av *GBY/RBY* LE6 .... 16 A4
Mallard Dr *RLEINE/SYS* LE7 ... 4 C5
Mallard Wy *LEIW* LE3 .... 73 H2
Malling Cl *LEIH* LE4 .... 11 H3
Mallory Pl *LEIS* LE2 .... 27 G2
Mallory St *RLEIW/BAR* LE9 .... 50 C5
Mallow Cl *LEIE* LE5 .... 21 G4
Malsbury Av *RLEINE/SYS* LE7 . 23 H1
The Maltings *LEIH* LE4 .... 11 E3
Malton Dr *LEIS* LE2 .... 47 G2
Malvern Crs *RLEIW/BAR* LE9 . 65 F3
Malvern Rd *LEIS* LE2 .... 36 D3
Mandarin Wy *RLEIW/BAR* LE9 65 F3
Manderveil Rd *LEIS* LE2 .... 66 D5
Mandora La *LEI* LE1 .... 3 J7
Manitoba Rd *LEI* LE1 .... 3 G1
Mann Cl *LEIW* LE4 .... 33 H3
Manners Rd *LEIS* LE2 .... 45 E1
Manor Brook Cl
   RLEIW/BAR LE9 .... 62 C3
Manor Cl *LEIS* LE2 .... 37 H5
Manor Ct *RLEIS/BBY* LE8 .... 56 C3
Manor Dr *LEIH* LE4 .... 18 A2
Manor Farm Cl
   RLEIW/BAR LE9 .... 74 B3
Manor Farm Wy *LEIE* LE5 ...... 23 H3
Manor Gdns *LEIE* LE5 .... 24 A2
   RLEIW/BAR LE9 .... 30 A2
Manor House Gdns *LEIE* LE5 .. 28 B2
Manor Rd *LEIH* LE4 .... 20 B1
   LEIS LE2 .... 37 F5
   LUTT LE17 .... 85 F1
   MKTHBORO LE16 .... 79 E5
   RLEIW/BAR LE9 .... 68 C4
   RLEIW/BAR LE9 .... 30 A2
   RLEIW/BAR LE9 .... 65 F2
   RLEIW/BAR LE9 .... 72 B1
Manor Road Extension
   LEIS LE2 .... 47 F1
Manor St *WGSTN* LE18 .... 57 H1
Mansfield St *LEI* LE1 .... 2 E2
Manston Cl *LEIW* LE4 .... 21 E2
Mantle Rd *LEI* LE3 .... 2 A2
Manton Cl *RLEIW/BAR* LE9 .... 74 D3
Maple Av *LEIW* LE3 .... 33 G2
   RLEIS/BBY LE8 .... 56 B5
Maple Dr *LUTT* LE17 .... 85 F3
Maple Rd *RLEIW/BAR* LE9 ...... 50 B1
Mapleton Rd *WGSTN* LE18 ..... 46 A5
Maple Tree Wk
   END/NAR LE19 .... 55 E4
Maple Wy *RLEIW/BAR* LE9 .... 30 A2
Maplewell Dr *LEIE* LE5 .... 18 A1
Maplin Rd *LEIS* LE3 .... 29 E1
Marble St *LEI* LE1 .... 2 E5
Marcus Cl *RLEINE/SYS* LE7 .... 12 C2
Marefield Cl *RLEINE/SYS* LE7 . 29 C5
Marfitt St *LEIN* LE4 .... 19 H5
Margam Cl *LEIW* LE3 .... 33 E5
Margaret Anne Rd *LEIS* LE2 ... 47 F4
Margaret La *LEIW* LE4 .... 12 C4
Margaret Crs *WGSTN* LE18 ..... 45 H5
Margaret Rd *LEIE* LE5 .... 27 G5
Marigold Wy *END/NAR* LE19 .. 54 B3
Marina Dr *GBY/RBY* LE6 .... 16 C1
Marina Rd *LEIE* LE5 .... 36 D1
Marion Cl *LEIW* LE5 .... 17 H5
Marion's Wy *RLEIW/BAR* LE9 . 63 H2
Marjorie St *LEIW* LE4 .... 26 C1
Market Pl *LEI* LE1 .... 2 E4
Market Pl South *LEI* LE1 .... 2 E4
Market St *LEI* LE1 .... 2 E5
   LUTT LE17 .... 85 H3
Markfield La *COAL* LE67 .... 6 D3
   GBY/RBY LE6 .... 7 G3
Markfield Rd *GBY/RBY* LE6 .... 14 C3
Markland Cl *LEIW* LE3 .... 44 C4
Marlborough Dr
   RLEIS/BBY LE8 .... 68 C3
Marlborough St *LEI* LE2 .... 3 F5
Marlborough Wy
   MKTHBORO LE16 .... 78 C4
Marlow Rd *LEIW* LE3 .... 35 F3
Marmion Cl *RLEIS/BBY* LE8 .... 68 C5
Maromme Sq *WGSTN* LE18 ... 46 B5
Marquis St *LEI* LE1 .... 3 F6
Marriott Cl *LEIW* LE3 .... 33 F2
Marriott Dr *RLEIS/BBY* LE8 .... 70 B3
Marriott Rd *LEIS* LE2 .... 36 C2
Marsden Av *RLEINE/SYS* LE7 .. 5 G4
Marsden La *RLEIW/BAR* LE9 .. 44 B2
Marshall Cl *LEIW* LE3 .... 33 C3
Marsham Cl *LEIN* LE4 .... 21 F5
Marsh Av *RLEIS/BBY* LE8 .... 70 B2
Marsh Cl *LEIN* LE4 .... 21 G5
Marsh Dr *RLEIS/BBY* LE8 .... 70 A2
Marston Cl *LEIS* LE2 .... 47 E5
Marston Crs *RLEIS/BBY* LE8 ... 67 G3
Marston Dr *GBY/RBY* LE6 ...... 16 B4
Marston Rd *LEIH* LE4 .... 20 C5
   MKTHBORO LE16 .... 80 A3
Marston Trussell Rd
   MKTHBORO LE16 .... 80 B5
Marstowe Av *WGSTN* LE18 .... 57 F1
Martel Rd *LEIS* LE2 .... 47 F3
Martin *RLEIW/BAR* LE9 .... 30 D2
Martin Dr *LEIH* LE3 .... 62 B5
Martindale Cl *LEIS* LE2 .... 35 H2
Martin Dr *RLEINE/SYS* LE7 ..... 4 B5
Martinshaw La *GBY/RBY* LE6 . 16 A4
Martin St *LEIH* LE4 .... 25 G5
Martival *LEIE* LE5 .... 27 G2
Marvel Cl *RLEIW/BAR* LE9 ...... 50 A5
Marvin Cl *LEIW* LE4 .... 19 F5
Marwell Cl *LEIN* LE4 .... 18 B4
Marwood Rd *LEIN* LE4 .... 18 B5
Marydene Ct *LEIE* LE5 .... 38 A2
Marylebone Dr *LEIE* LE5 .... 38 A2
Marylebone Dr *LUTT* LE17 ...... 85 H1

Mary Rd *LEIS* LE3 .... 25 F2
Mary St *RLEIW/BAR* LE9 .... 51 F3
Masefield Cl *RLEIW/BAR* LE9 .... 50 B3
Masefield Rd *RLEIW/BAR* LE9 .... 51 F3
Mason Rw *LEIE* LE5 .... 21 H4
Masons Cl *END/NAR* LE19 .... 54 D4
Matlock Av *WGSTN* LE18 .... 57 G2
Matlock St *LEIS* LE2 .... 27 E4
Matts Cl *LEIS* LE2 .... 44 D3
Maughan St *RLEIW/BAR* LE9 .... 51 F2
Maurice Cl *RLEIW/BAR* LE9 .... 65 H1
Maurice Dr *RLEIS/BBY* LE8 .... 66 D3
Maurice Rd *MKTHBORO* LE16 .... 81 G4
Mavis Av *LEIW* LE3 .... 35 E3
Mawby Cl *RLEIS/BBY* LE8 .... 66 A1
Maxwell Wy *LUTT* LE17 .... 85 G1
May Cl *LEIW* LE3 .... 34 C1
Mayfield Dr *MKTHBORO* LE16 .... 62 B4
Mayfield Rd *LEIS* LE2 .... 36 C2
Mayfield Wy *RLEIW/BAR* LE9 .... 51 E2
Mayflower Cl *COAL* LE67 .... 6 C4
Mayflower Rd *LEIE* LE5 .... 37 E2
Maynard Rd *LEIS* LE2 .... 3 K3
Mayrs La *RLEIS/BBY* LE8 .... 61 F5
Mayor's Wk *LEI* LE1 .... 36 A2
Mayre Cl *RLEIW/BAR* LE9 .... 74 D4
Mays Farm Dr
  RLEIW/BAR LE9 .... 62 B3
Maytree Cl *RLEIW/BAR* LE9 .... 32 C2
Maytree Dr *RLEIW/BAR* LE9 .... 32 C2
McDowell Wy *END/NAR* LE19 .... 54 D4
McVicker Cl *LEIE* LE5 .... 28 A4
Meadhurst Rd *LEIS* LE2 .... 25 E5
Meadowbrook Rd
  RLEIS/BBY LE8 .... 69 H3
Meadow Cl *GBY/RBY* LE6 .... 22 D2
Meadow Ct *END/NAR* LE19 .... 54 C2
  WGSTN LE18 * 58 B1
Meadowcourt Rd *LEIS* LE2 .... 46 D1
Meadow Court Rd
  GBY/RBY LE6 .... 16 B4
  RLEIW/BAR LE9 .... 51 F4
Meadowcroft Cl *LEIW* LE3 .... 23 H3
Meadow Edge
  LEIN LE4 .... 11 H4
Meadow Gdns *LEIS* LE2 .... 45 F3
Meadow Hl *RLEIS/BBY* LE8 .... 60 C5
Meadow La *COAL* LE67 .... 6 C3
  LEIN LE4 .... 11 H4
  RLEIS/SYS LE7 .... 4 A4
Meadow Rd *RLEIW/BAR* LE9 .... 50 C4
The Meadows
  END/NAR LE19 .... 55 F4
  RLEIS/SYS LE7 .... 5 H1
Meadowsweet Rd *LEIE* LE5 .... 28 C5
Meadowsweet Rd *LEIE* LE5 .... 28 C5
The Meadow Vw *RLEIW/BAR* LE9 .... 74 C4
Meadow Vw *LEIE* LE5 .... 47 F3
Meadow Wy *GBY/RBY* LE6 .... 16 B4
  RLEIW/BAR LE9 .... 30 B3
  WGSTN LE18 * 58 B1
The Meads *LEIW* LE3 .... 46 C5
Meadvale Rd *LEIS* LE2 .... 46 A1
Meadway *LEIW* LE3 .... 25 E4
The Meadway *LEIN* LE4 .... 11 G4
  RLEIS/SYS LE7 .... 12 D2
Meadwell Rd *LEIW* LE3 .... 33 H1
Medhurst Cl *RLEIS/BBY* LE8 .... 66 A1
Medina Rd *LEIW* LE3 .... 25 H2
Medway Cl *MKTHBORO* LE16 .... 82 B1
Medway St *LEIS* LE2 .... 36 C1
The Meer *RLEIS/BBY* LE8 .... 68 C5
Melba Wy *LEIN* LE4 .... 11 H1
Melbourne Cl *RLEIS/BBY* LE8 .... 69 H3
Melbourne Rd *LEIS* LE2 .... 27 E5
Melbourne St *LEIS* LE2 .... 3 K3
Melcroft Av *LEIW* LE3 .... 25 F5
Melford St *LEIE* LE5 .... 27 H3
Melland Pl *LEIS* LE2 .... 45 E5
Mellier Cl *END/NAR* LE19 .... 54 C1
Mellor Rd *LEIW* LE3 .... 25 E5
Melody Av *RLEINE/SYS* LE7 .... 17 G1
Melrose St *LEIN* LE4 .... 26 D1
Melton Av *LEIN* LE4 .... 20 A2
Melton Rd *LEIW* LE3 .... 74 A1
Melton Rd *LEIN* LE4 .... 20 A4
  LEIN LE4 .... 20 B2
  RLEINE/SYS LE7 .... 13 E1
  RLEIS/SYS LE7 .... 71 H1
Melton St *LEI* LE1 .... 26 C3
Melville St *LEIS* LE2 .... 51 E3
Memory La *LEI* LE1 .... 26 C5
Mendip Av *LEIN* LE4 .... 19 E1
Mennecy Cl *RLEIS/BBY* LE8 .... 66 D3
Mensa Cl *LEIS* LE2 .... 27 E5
Menzies Rd *LEIN* LE4 .... 19 E5
Mercia Dr *LEIS* LE2 .... 44 D2
Mercury Cl *LEIS* LE2 .... 3 K5
Mere Cl *LEIE* LE5 .... 27 E4
Meredith Rd *LEIW* LE3 .... 34 D4
Mere La *LEIS* LE2 .... 59 H1
Mere Rd *LEIE* LE5 .... 27 E5
  LEIE LE5 .... 49 E2
  WGSTN LE18 .... 57 F2
The Mere *RLEIS/BBY* LE8 .... 60 C5
Mereworth Cl *LEIE* LE5 .... 27 F2
Meridian East *END/NAR* LE19 .... 33 H5
Meridian North
  END/NAR LE19 .... 43 F1
Meridian South
  END/NAR LE19 .... 43 F2
Meridian Wy *LEIW* LE3 .... 33 H4
Meridian West
  END/NAR LE19 .... 43 F1
Merton Rd *LUTT* LE17 .... 85 H4
Merlin Cl *RLEIW/BAR* LE9 .... 50 C4
  RLEIW/BAR LE9 .... 74 A2
Merthuil Rd *LEIE* LE5 .... 28 C4
Merton Av *LEIE* LE5 .... 25 C5
  RLEIS/SYS LE7 .... 13 F1
Merton Rd *RLEIW/BAR* LE9 .... 73 H2
Merton Wy *RLEIS/BBY* LE8 .... 69 H2

Merus Ct *END/NAR* LE19 .... 33 H4
Mervyn Rd *LEIE* LE5 .... 36 D1
Metcalf Cl *RLEIW/BAR* LE9 .... 62 B4
Metcalfe St *RLEIW/BAR* LE9 .... 51 E4
Methuen Av *LEIN* LE4 .... 12 C4
Meynell Cl *LEIS* LE2 .... 47 E5
Meynell Rd *LEIE* LE5 .... 27 F5
Michael Cl *RLEINE/SYS* LE7 .... 5 H3
Michael Ramsey Ct *LEIS* LE2 .... 44 C5
Mickleton St *LEIE* LE5 .... 37 H2
Middlebrook Cl *GBY/RBY* LE6 .... 22 D2
Middlebrook Gn
  MKTHBORO LE16 .... 78 D5
Middledale Rd
  MKTHBORO LE16 .... 82 B1
Middlefield Rd
  RLEIS/SYS LE7 .... 4 A2
Middlesex Rd *LEIS* LE2 .... 44 D1
Middleton Cl *RLEIW/BAR* LE9 .... 62 C4
  WGSTN LE18 .... 46 D5
Middletons Cl *RLEIS/BBY* LE8 .... 68 B3
Middleton St *LEIS* LE2 .... 44 C1
Midhurst Av *LEIW* LE3 .... 34 B3
Midland St *LEI* LE1 .... 3 H5
Midway Rd *LEIE* LE5 .... 37 H2
Milestone Cl *RLEIS/BBY* LE8 .... 70 C3
Milford Cl *END/NAR* LE19 .... 54 C3
Milford Rd *LEIS* LE2 .... 36 B5
Millbrook Cl *LEIN* LE4 .... 19 F4
Millbrook Dr *RLEIW/BAR* LE9 .... 74 B4
Mill Cl *LEIN* LE4 .... 19 H1
  RLEIS/BBY LE8 .... 69 H5
  RLEIW/BAR LE9 .... 72 C1
  WGSTN LE18 .... 57 F3
Mill Dr *GBY/RBY* LE6 .... 22 D5
Miller Cl *LEIN* LE4 .... 20 C2
Millers Cl *LEIS* LE2 .... 23 G2
  RLEINE/SYS LE7 .... 13 E2
Millersdale Av *LEIE* LE5 .... 28 D5
Millers Gdns
  MKTHBORO LE16 .... 81 E2
Millers Gra *RLEIW/BAR* LE9 .... 74 B4
Millfield Cl *LEIE* LE5 .... 17 F2
Millfield Crs *LEIE* LE5 .... 43 H2
Mill Gv *LUTT* LE17 .... 85 H4
Mill Hill *RLEIW/BAR* LE9 .... 42 B1
  MKTHBORO LE16 .... 80 B1
Mill Hill Cl *RLEIS/BBY* LE8 .... 55 H4
Mill Hill La *COAL* LE67 .... 6 B3
  LEIS LE2 .... 3 J7
Mill Hill Rd *MKTHBORO* LE16 .... 82 A1
Milligan Rd *LEIS* LE2 .... 45 E2
Mill La *END/NAR* LE19 .... 42 D5
  HINC LE10 .... 72 A4
  LEIN LE4 .... 12 B4
  LEIS LE2 .... 2 C6
  RLEIS/BBY LE8 .... 56 D3
  RLEIS/BBY LE8 .... 58 B4
  RLEIW/BAR LE9 .... 51 G2
The Mill La *LEIS* LE3 .... 23 G2
Mill Rd *RLEINE/SYS* LE7 .... 10 B1
Millstone La *LEI* LE1 .... 2 E5
  RLEINE/SYS LE7 .... 5 F4
Mill St *LEIS* LE2 .... 3 F6
Mill Vw *RLEIW/BAR* LE9 .... 53 H4
Millwood Cl *LEIN* LE4 .... 19 E2
Milnroy Rd *LEIE* LE5 .... 29 E4
Milton Cl *WGSTN* LE18 .... 58 C1
Milton Crs *LEIN* LE4 .... 18 C5
Milton Gdns *LEIS* LE2 .... 47 E5
Milton St *END/NAR* LE19 .... 54 C2
Milverton Av *LEIN* LE4 .... 25 H1
Milverton Cl *WGSTN* LE18 .... 46 A4
Milverton Dr *WGSTN* LE18 .... 46 A4
Minehead St *LEIW* LE3 .... 35 F5
Minster Crs *LEIN* LE4 .... 25 H1
Mint Rd *LEIS* LE2 .... 2 B7
Misterton Wy *LUTT* LE17 .... 85 H4
Mitchell Gv *RLEINE/SYS* LE7 .... 29 G2
Mitchell Rd *END/NAR* LE19 .... 42 C5
Moat Cl *RLEIW/BAR* LE9 .... 40 D5
Moat Ct *LEIE* LE5 .... 27 F5
Moat Gdns *LEIE* LE5 .... 72 B2
Moat St *WGSTN* LE18 .... 58 A1
Modbury Av *LEIN* LE4 .... 19 E3
Moira St *LEIN* LE4 .... 26 D1
Monal Cl *RLEIS/BBY* LE8 .... 65 H2
Monar Cl *LEIN* LE4 .... 20 B3
Mona St *RLEIW/BAR* LE9 .... 51 E4
Monica Rd *LEIN* LE4 .... 43 H1
Monks Crs *LEIN* LE4 .... 10 C4
Monroe Cl *LEIS* LE2 .... 56 B1
Monroe Cl *MKTHBORO* LE16 .... 78 B4
Monsell Dr *LEIS* LE2 .... 44 C3
Montague Av
  RLEINE/SYS LE7 .... 13 F2
Montague Rd *LEIS* LE2 .... 36 B4
  RLEIW/BAR LE9 .... 74 B2
Montgomery Cl *LUTT* LE17 .... 85 E5
Montgomery Rd
  RLEIW/BAR LE9 .... 51 G3
Montreal Cl *LEI* LE1 .... 3 H1
Montreal Rd *LEI* LE1 .... 26 C3
Montrose Cl
  MKTHBORO LE16 .... 81 G3
Montrose Rd *LEIS* LE2 .... 44 C3
Montrose Rd South *LEIS* LE2 .... 44 C3
Montvale Gdns *LEIN* LE4 .... 25 H1
Moon Cl *LEIS* LE2 .... 3 J5
Moore Rd *RLEIW/BAR* LE9 .... 50 B4
Moores Cl *WGSTN* LE18 .... 57 E1
Moores La *END/NAR* LE19 .... 42 D5
Moores Rd *LEIN* LE4 .... 19 H5
Moorfields *LEIE* LE5 .... 28 D2
Moorgate Av *LEIN* LE4 .... 11 F4
Moorland Av *LEIE* LE5 .... 26 C2
Moorland Rd
  RLEINE/SYS LE7 .... 12 C1
Morban Rd *LEIS* LE2 .... 44 B2
Morcote Rd *LEIW* LE3 .... 34 A1
Morland Av *LEIS* LE2 .... 37 E5
Morledge St *LEI* LE1 .... 3 H3

Morley Rd *LEIS* LE2 .... 27 E4
  RLEIW/BAR LE9 .... 72 C2
Morley St *MKTHBORO* LE16 .... 81 G1
Mornington St *LEIE* LE5 .... 27 F3
Morpeth Av *LEIW* LE3 .... 18 D2
Morpeth Dr *LEIS* LE2 .... 45 E2
Morris Cl *LEIW* LE3 .... 33 H3
Morrison Ct *RLEIS/BBY* LE8 .... 70 A3
Morris Rd *LEIS* LE2 .... 36 A4
Mortiboys Wy
  RLEIW/BAR LE9 .... 62 B4
Mortimer Pl *LEIW* LE3 .... 34 C4
Mortimer Rd *END/NAR* LE19 .... 54 C4
Mortimer Wy *LEIW* LE3 .... 34 C4
Mortoft Rd *LEIN* LE4 .... 19 G4
Morton Wk *LEIE* LE5 .... 27 F2
The Morwoods *LEIS* LE2 .... 47 E3
Mossdale Rd *LEIN* LE4 .... 34 A5
Mosse Wy *LEIS* LE2 .... 45 E2
Mossgate *LEIW* LE3 .... 25 E3
Mosswithy *RLEIS/BBY* LE8 .... 68 B5
Mostyn Av *RLEINE/SYS* LE7 .... 5 F5
Mostyn St *LEIW* LE3 .... 25 F5
Mottisford Rd *LEIN* LE4 .... 19 F4
Mountain Rd *LEIS* LE2 .... 21 E3
Mount Av *LEIE* LE5 .... 27 F4
Mount Av *LEIS* LE2 .... 50 C4
Mountbatten Wy *LUTT* LE17 .... 85 H4
Mountcastle Rd *LEIW* LE3 .... 35 E3
Mountfield Rd
  RLEIW/BAR LE9 .... 51 E3
Mount Mews *LEIE* LE5 .... 47 F4
Mount Pleasant *LEIS* LE2 .... 47 H4
Mount Rd *LEIN* LE4 .... 27 E4
  LEIE LE5 .... 47 F3
  RLEIS/SYS LE7 .... 29 F2
The Mount *LUTT* LE17 .... 77 E3
  RLEINE/SYS LE7 .... 29 F2
Mount Vw *RLEIS/BBY* LE8 .... 60 D2
Mowbray Dr *RLEINE/SYS* LE7 .... 5 H4
Mowmacre Hl *LEIN* LE4 .... 19 E2
Mowsley End *WGSTN* LE18 .... 58 B1
Muirfield Cl *LEIN* LE4 .... 24 A4
Mulberry Av *LEIN* LE4 .... 24 A4
Mulberry Cl *LUTT* LE17 .... 85 F2
Mull Wy *RLEIS/BBY* LE8 .... 67 F3
Muncaster Cl *RLEIW/BAR* LE9 .... 74 C5
Mundella St *LEIS* LE2 .... 46 D2
Munnings Cl *LEIN* LE4 .... 26 D2
Munnjack Rd *RLEIS/BBY* LE8 .... 65 H1
Murby Wy *LEIW* LE3 .... 33 G4
Muriel Rd *LEIW* LE3 .... 25 G5
Murrayfield Rd *RLEIW/BAR* LE9 .... 74 B5
Murrayfield Rd *LEIN* LE4 .... 24 A5
Museum Sq *LEI* LE1 .... 3 K3
Museum Sq *LEI* LE1 .... 3 J5
Musgrove Cl *LEIW* LE3 .... 2 A5
Musson Rd *LEIW* LE3 .... 24 C3
Muston Gdns *LEIS* LE2 .... 56 A4
Myrtle Av *LEIN* LE4 .... 11 H3
Myrtle Cl *RLEIW/BAR* LE9 .... 50 A4
Myrtle Rd *LEIS* LE2 .... 36 C1

N

Nagle Gv *LEIN* LE4 .... 20 B2
Namur Rd *WGSTN* LE18 .... 45 E5
Namsen Rd *LEIE* LE5 .... 37 E1
Narborough Rd
  END/NAR LE19 .... 65 E1
  LEIW LE3 .... 34 D4
  RLEIW/BAR LE9 .... 53 H4
Narborough Rd North
  LEIW LE3 .... 2 B5
Narborough Rd South
  LEIW LE3 .... 43 G3
Narborough Wood Pk
  END/NAR LE19 * 42 A1
Narrow Boat Cl *WGSTN* LE18 .... 57 G3
Narrow La *LEI* LE1 .... 2 D5
Naseby Cl *MKTHBORO* LE16 .... 81 H2
  WGSTN LE18 .... 58 C1
Naseby Rd *LEIN* LE4 .... 20 C5
Naseby Sq *MKTHBORO* LE16 .... 81 H2
Navigation Dr *LEIS* LE2 .... 45 E2
Navigation St *LEI* LE1 .... 3 F2
Naylor Rd *RLEINE/SYS* LE7 .... 5 F4
Neal Av *LEIW* LE3 .... 34 A3
Necton St *RLEINE/SYS* LE7 .... 13 E1
Nedham St *LEIS* LE2 .... 3 K2
Ned Ludd Cl *RLEINE/SYS* LE7 .... 17 G1
Needham Av *LEIN* LE4 .... 44 A5
Needham Cl *LEIS* LE2 .... 48 A4
Needwood Wy
  END/NAR LE19 .... 54 B1
Nelot Wy *LEIS* LE2 .... 28 B5
Nelson St *LEI* LE1 .... 3 H6
  MKTHBORO LE16 .... 81 G1
  RLEINE/SYS LE7 .... 13 F1
Nene Dr *LEIS* LE2 .... 47 G3
Neptune Cl *LEIS* LE2 .... 27 E5
Neston Gdns *LEIS* LE2 .... 45 F2
Neston Rd *LEIS* LE2 .... 45 F2
Netherfield Cl
  RLEIW/BAR LE9 .... 74 D3
Netherfield Rd
  RLEINE/SYS LE7 .... 9 F5
Nether Field Wy *LEIW* LE3 .... 33 H4
Netherhall La *LEIE* LE5 .... 19 H1
Netherhall Rd *LEIE* LE5 .... 28 C1
Netton Cl *WGSTN* LE18 .... 58 A3
Nevanthon Rd *LEIW* LE3 .... 24 A5
Neville Dr *COAL* LE67 .... 6 B4
Neville Rd *LEIW* LE3 .... 34 B5
Neville Smith Cl
  RLEIS/BBY LE8 .... 72 B2
Newall Cl *LUTT* LE17 .... 85 G3
Newarke Cl *LEIS* LE2 .... 2 C6
Newarke St *LEI* LE1 .... 2 D5
The Newarke *LEIS* LE2 .... 2 C5

Newark Rd *LEIN* LE4 .... 12 C5
New Bond St *LEI* LE1 .... 2 E3
New Bridge Rd *LEIS* LE2 .... 56 B1
New Bridge St *LEIS* LE2 .... 35 G2
Newbury Cl *WGSTN* LE18 .... 58 A2
Newby Cl *RLEIS/BBY* LE8 .... 55 H3
Newby Gdns *LEIE* LE5 .... 47 H4
Newby Rd *RLEIW/BAR* LE9 .... 34 D3
Newcombe St
  MKTHBORO LE16 .... 81 H2
New Fields Av *LEIW* LE3 .... 34 C3
New Fields Sq *LEIW* LE3 .... 34 C4
New Forest Cl *WGSTN* LE18 .... 58 B5
Newgate End *WGSTN* LE18 .... 58 A1
Newham Cl *LEIN* LE4 .... 21 E2
Newhaven Rd *LEIE* LE5 .... 38 B2
New Henry St *LEIW* LE3 .... 2 C1
Newington St *LEIN* LE4 .... 19 H5
New Inn Cl *RLEIW/BAR* LE9 .... 74 C4
Newlands Rd
  RLEIW/BAR LE9 .... 50 B4
Newlyn Pde *LEIE* LE5 .... 28 D1
Newmarket St *LEIS* LE2 .... 36 B5
New Park Rd *LEIS* LE2 .... 35 G5
New Parks Bvd *LEIW* LE3 .... 24 B5
New Parks Crs *LEIW* LE3 .... 25 E2
New Parks St *LEIW* LE3 .... 2 B5
New Parks Wy *LEIW* LE3 .... 24 B5
New Pingle St *LEIW* LE3 .... 2 B3
Newpool Bank *LEIS* LE2 .... 48 A4
Newport Pl *LEI* LE1 .... 3 G5
Newport St *LEIS* LE2 .... 25 G4
Newquay Dr *LEIW* LE3 .... 24 A1
New Rd *LEI* LE1 .... 2 E2
  RLEIS/BBY LE8 .... 70 B3
  RLEINE/SYS LE7 .... 29 F2
New Romney Cl *LEIE* LE5 .... 29 E2
The Newry *LEIS* LE2 .... 45 F3
New Star Rd *LEIN* LE4 .... 20 D4
Newstead Av *LEIS* LE2 .... 25 G1
  RLEINE/SYS LE7 .... 39 E1
Newstead Rd *LEIS* LE2 .... 36 C5
New St *LEI* LE1 .... 2 E4
  LEIS LE2 .... 47 E2
  LUTT LE17 .... 85 H4
  RLEINE/SYS LE7 .... 13 E2
Newton La *RLEIW/BAR* LE9 .... 60 B4
  WGSTN LE18 .... 58 D2
Newton Wy *RLEIW/BAR* LE9 .... 74 B5
Newtown Cl *RLEIS/BBY* LE8 .... 69 H3
Newtown Linford La
  GBY/RBY LE6 .... 16 A4
Newtown St *LEI* LE1 .... 3 F7
New Wk *LEI* LE1 .... 3 F6
  RLEIW/BAR LE9 .... 72 D3
New Way Rd *LEIE* LE5 .... 38 A2
New Zealand La
  RLEINE/SYS LE7 .... 5 F3
Nicholas Dr *GBY/RBY* LE6 .... 16 A5
Nichols St *LEI* LE1 .... 3 H5
Nicklaus Rd *LEIN* LE4 .... 20 B2
Nidderdale Rd *WGSTN* LE18 .... 58 B5
Nithsdale Av
  MKTHBORO LE16 .... 81 H2
Nithsdale Crs
  MKTHBORO LE16 .... 82 A2
Noble Cl *LUTT* LE17 .... 85 G5
Noble St *LEIW* LE3 .... 25 G5
Nock Verges *RLEIW/BAR* LE9 .... 51 C2
  RLEIW/BAR LE9 .... 62 B4
Noel St *LEIW* LE3 .... 35 F2
Nook Cl *GBY/RBY* LE6 .... 22 C1
Nook St *LEIW* LE3 .... 25 F5
The Nook *COAL* LE67 .... 6 B3
  END/NAR LE19 .... 42 C5
  LUTT LE17 .... 85 F1
  RLEINE/SYS LE7 .... 18 D3
  RLEIS/BBY LE8 .... 55 H4
  RLEIW/BAR LE9 .... 69 H3
Norbury Av *LEIN* LE4 .... 27 E1
Norbury Rd *MKTHBORO* LE16 .... 78 B5
Norfolk Rd *RLEIW/BAR* LE9 .... 30 B3
  WGSTN LE18 .... 45 F5
Norfolk St *LEIW* LE3 .... 35 G3
Norfolk Wk *LEIW* LE3 .... 2 A4
Norman Ct *LEIS* LE2 .... 47 H5
Norman Dagley Cl
  RLEIW/BAR LE9 .... 51 E4
Normandy Cl *LEIN* LE4 .... 24 A3
Norman Rd *LEIN* LE4 .... 12 B4
Norman St *LEIW* LE3 .... 2 A7
Normanton Cl
  RLEIW/BAR LE9 .... 51 F4
Normanton Rd *LEIE* LE5 .... 36 C1
Norris Cl *LEIN* LE4 .... 18 A4
Northampton Rd
  MKTHBORO LE16 .... 82 A2
Northampton St *LEI* LE1 .... 3 G5
North Av *LEIS* LE2 .... 36 C4
North Bridge Pl *LEIW* LE3 .... 35 H3
Northcote Rd *LEIS* LE2 .... 36 B5
Northdene Rd *LEIE* LE5 .... 47 F4
Northdown Dr *LEIN* LE4 .... 20 C1
North Dr *LEIE* LE5 .... 28 A2
North End Cl *LEIS* LE2 .... 47 F3
Northfield Av *LEIN* LE4 .... 11 G4
  WGSTN LE18 .... 46 B5
Northfield Rd *LEIS* LE2 .... 47 G1
  RLEIS/BBY LE8 .... 56 B2
Northfields *RLEINE/SYS* LE7 .... 5 E5
Northfold Rd *LEIS* LE2 .... 46 A2
Northgate St *LEIW* LE3 .... 2 B3
Northleigh Gv
  MKTHBORO LE16 .... 78 B5
Northleigh Wy
  RLEIW/BAR LE9 .... 51 F4
North Mills *LEIW* LE3 * 2 B1
North St *RLEINE/SYS* LE7 .... 4 D5
  WGSTN LE18 .... 46 B5

Northumberland Av
  LEIN LE4 .... 20 A5
Northumberland Rd
  WGSTN LE18 .... 45 F5
Northumberland St *LEI* LE1 .... 2 D1
North Rd *RLEIW/BAR* LE9 .... 50 C4
Norton St *LEI* LE1 .... 2 E6
Norwich Rd *LEIN* LE4 .... 18 D4
Norwood Rd *LEIE* LE5 .... 37 E2
Nottingham Rd *LEIS* LE2 .... 27 F4
Nowell Cl *LEIS* LE2 .... 56 D2
Nugent St *LEIW* LE3 .... 2 A2
Nunneley Wy
  MKTHBORO LE16 .... 78 D5
Nursery Cl *LEIN* LE4 .... 20 B1
  RLEINE/SYS LE7 .... 5 H4
  RLEIW/BAR LE9 .... 53 E1
Nursery Gdns
  RLEIW/BAR LE9 .... 50 C4
Nursery Hollow *LEIS* LE2 .... 44 A5
Nursery Rd *LEIE* LE5 .... 28 D3
Nutfield Rd *LEIW* LE3 .... 35 E2
Nuthall Gv *LEIS* LE2 .... 44 B4

O

Oadby Hill Dr *LEIS* LE2 .... 46 D2
Oadby Rd *WGSTN* LE18 .... 46 C5
Oakberry Rd *LUTT* LE17 .... 85 H1
Oak Cl *MKTHBORO* LE16 .... 78 D5
  RLEIW/BAR LE9 .... 41 E5
Oakcroft Av *RLEIW/BAR* LE9 .... 23 E5
Oakdale Cl *LEIW* LE3 .... 23 H3
Oakdale Rd *RLEIW/BAR* LE9 .... 50 D4
Oakdene Rd *LEIS* LE2 .... 45 G2
Oak Dr *RLEINE/SYS* LE7 .... 13 F2
Oakenshaw Cl *LEIN* LE4 .... 19 E2
Oakfield Av *COAL* LE67 .... 6 A4
  LEIN LE4 .... 11 F5
  LEIW LE3 .... 17 F5
  LUTT LE17 .... 85 F3
Oakfield Cl *RLEIS/BBY* LE8 .... 60 D2
Oakfield Crs *RLEIS/BBY* LE8 .... 56 C4
Oakfield Rd *LEIS* LE2 .... 36 C2
Oakland Av *LEIN* LE4 .... 20 A2
Oakland Rd *LEIS* LE2 .... 36 A4
Oakleigh Av *LEIS* LE2 .... 57 E2
Oakley Rd *LEIE* LE5 .... 27 F3
Oakmeadow Av
  GBY/RBY LE6 .... 23 H3
Oak Mews *LEIS* LE2 .... 16 A5
Oakridge Cl *LEIE* LE5 .... 21 G4
Oak Rd *END/NAR* LE19 .... 54 D5
Oaks Cl *END/NAR* LE19 .... 30 A2
Oaks Dr *RLEIS/BBY* LE8 .... 56 C4
Oakside Crs *LEIE* LE5 .... 28 C3
Oak Spinney Pk *LEIW* LE3 .... 33 F1
Oaks Rd *RLEIS/BBY* LE8 .... 60 D3
Oak St *LEIE* LE5 .... 37 F3
Oaks Wy *LEIS* LE2 .... 57 E5
  RLEIW/BAR LE9 .... 51 E3
Oakthorpe Av *LEIW* LE3 .... 34 D1
Oaktree Cl *GBY/RBY* LE6 .... 16 A5
  LEIS LE2 .... 21 G5
  RLEIS/BBY LE8 .... 70 B2
Oakwood Av *WGSTN* LE18 .... 46 B4
Oakwood Cl *LEIW* LE3 .... 32 D3
Oakwood Rd *LEIN* LE4 .... 25 H1
The Oasis *LEIW* LE3 .... 23 H2
Oban St *LEIW* LE3 .... 25 G5
Ocean St *LEIE* LE5 .... 28 C3
Ocean Rd *LEIE* LE5 .... 28 C4
Odam Cl *LEIW* LE3 .... 34 B3
Odeon Ar *LEI* LE1 .... 2 E4
Offranville Cl *LEIN* LE4 .... 20 D1
Ogwen Cl *LEIN* LE4 .... 20 B3
Okehampton Av *LEIE* LE5 .... 37 G2
Old Charity Farm *LEIS* LE2 .... 38 C4
Old Church St *LEIS* LE2 .... 44 C5
The Old Coach Rd
  LUTT LE17 .... 77 F2
Old Field Cl *RLEIS/BBY* LE8 .... 66 C2
Old Garden Cl
  RLEIS/BBY LE8 .... 56 A4
Old Hall Cl *GBY/RBY* LE6 .... 16 B5
  LEIN LE4 .... 12 C4
Old Hall La *MKTHBORO* LE16 .... 80 C1
Old Mill Cl *RLEIW/BAR* LE9 .... 74 B4
Old Mill La *LEI* LE1 .... 2 C2
Old Mill Rd *RLEIW/BAR* LE9 .... 74 B4
Old Milton St *LEI* LE1 .... 3 G1
Old Rectory Cl
  RLEIW/BAR LE9 .... 74 A3
Old School Ms
  MKTHBORO LE16 .... 81 H1
Oliver Cl *RLEIS/BBY* LE8 .... 12 D2
Oliver Rd *LEIN* LE4 .... 20 B5
Oliver St *LEIS* LE2 .... 35 G5
Olphin St *LEIW* LE3 .... 24 B2
Olympic Cl *LEIW* LE3 .... 36 C1
Ontario Cl *LEI* LE1 .... 3 G1
Orange Hl *LUTT* LE17 .... 85 H4
Orange St *WGSTN* LE18 .... 58 B1
Orchard Av *LEIS* LE2 .... 56 B1
Orchard Cl *LEIS* LE2 .... 47 E4
Orchard La *RLEIW/BAR* LE9 .... 20 D1
Orchard La *RLEIS/BBY* LE8 .... 66 D4
  RLEIS/BBY LE8 .... 67 F3
Orchard Rd *LEIN* LE4 .... 11 H5
  LUTT LE17 .... 85 F4
  RLEIW/BAR LE9 .... 74 B4
Orchards Dr *WGSTN* LE18 .... 57 H1
Orchardson Av *LEIN* LE4 .... 26 D2
The Orchards *LEIE* LE5 .... 29 E3
Orchard St *LEI* LE1 .... 3 F1
  MKTHBORO LE16 .... 78 C5
  RLEIS/BBY LE8 .... 68 B4

The Orchard GBY/RBY LE6..... 16 A4
  RLEIW/BAR LE9..... 62 C4
Orchard Wy RLEINE/SYS LE7... 13 C1
Orchid Cl END/NAR LE19..... 54 C2
  LEIE LE5..... 21 G5
Orchid Pl RLEIW/BAR LE8..... 74 D5
Oriel Dr RLEIW/SYS LE7 *..... 15 F1
Orkney Wy RLEIS/BBY LE8..... 67 F3
Orlando Rd LEIS LE2..... 36 B3
Orme Cl LEIW LE3..... 18 A4
Ormen Gn LEIW LE3..... 28 B4
Ormond Cl RLEIW/BAR LE9..... 50 A4
Oronsay Rd LEIW LE4..... 18 B4
Orpine Rd LEIE LE5..... 21 F4
Orsett Cl LEIE LE5..... 27 H2
Orson Dr WGSTN LE18..... 45 H5
Orson St LEIE LE5..... 27 F5
Orton Rd LEIW LE4..... 19 E4
  RLEIW/BAR LE8..... 51 F3
Orwell Dr LEIW LE4..... 18 A3
Osborne Rd LEIE LE5..... 27 F5
The Osiers LEIW LE4..... 43 H1
Osmaston Rd LEIE LE5..... 36 C1
Osprey Cl RLEIW/BAR LE9..... 74 A2
Osprey Rd LEIE LE4..... 18 A4
Oswin Rd LEIW LE3..... 24 C5
Ottawa Rd LEI LE1..... 3 H2
Otter Wy RLEIS/BBY LE8..... 65 H1
Outfields Dr RLEINE/SYS LE7..... 9 H2
Outwood Cl LEIW LE4..... 24 B5
The Oval LEI LE1..... 3 H7
  LEIS LE2..... 46 D4
  MKTHBORO LE16..... 78 C5
Overdale Av RLEIW/BAR LE9..... 62 C4
Overdale Cl LEIW LE3..... 16 D5
  MKTHBORO LE16..... 82 B2
Overdale Rd LEIN LE4..... 20 D1
Overfield Av LEIS LE2..... 46 A1
  MKTHBORO LE16..... 78 D4
Overfield Cl END/NAR LE19..... 54 A1
  GBY/RBY LE6..... 22 D2
Overing Cl LEIW LE4..... 19 C4
Overpark Av LEIW LE3..... 34 B1
Overseal Rd LEIW LE4..... 18 A3
Overstrand LEIE LE5..... 21 F5
Overton Rd LEIE LE5..... 27 F3
Owen Cl LEID LE3..... 24 A5
  LEIW LE3..... 33 H4
Owston Dr WGSTN LE18..... 45 H5
Oxendon St LEIS LE2..... 3 K5
Oxendon Wk LEIS LE2 *..... 3 K5
Oxen Wy LEIE LE5..... 28 A4
Oxford Av LEIS LE2..... 36 B2
Oxford Ct RLEINE/SYS LE7..... 5 F5
Oxford Dr WGSTN LE18..... 45 H5
Oxford St LEIE LE5..... 36 B3
  RLEIW/BAR LE8..... 50 A4
Oxford St LEI LE1..... 2 E5
  RLEINE/SYS LE7..... 5 F5
  RLEIW/BAR LE8..... 50 B4
Oxted Ri LEIS LE2..... 47 E5

P

Packer Av LEIW LE3..... 33 F1
Packhorse Dr END/NAR LE19... 55 F1
Packhorse Rd LEIS LE2..... 44 D5
Packwood Rd LEIW LE4..... 19 E3
Paddock Cl LEIS LE2..... 46 D3
  RLEIS/BBY LE8..... 67 E2
The Paddocks
  END/NAR LE19..... 55 E4
Paddock St LEIW LE4..... 58 B1
The Paddock COAL LE67..... 6 C3
  RLEIS/BBY LE8..... 70 B3
Paddock Vw RLEINE/SYS LE7.. 12 D1
Padgate Cl RLEINE/SYS LE7.. 12 A4
Padstow Rd LEIN LE4..... 20 C5
Padwell La RLEINE/SYS LE7.. 39 E1
  RLEIS/BBY LE8..... 67 E2
Page Cl LUTT LE17..... 85 A3
Paget Av LEIN LE4..... 11 H4
Paget Ct RLEIS/BBY LE8..... 70 A3
Paget Dr MKTHBORO LE16..... 80 B1
Paget St LEIS LE2..... 44 D2
  RLEIS/BBY LE8..... 70 A3
Paigle Rd LEIS LE2..... 45 G5
Painter St LEI LE1..... 26 C2
Palfreyman La LEI LE1..... 48 A4
Pallet Cl LUTT LE17..... 85 G4
Palmerston Bvd LEIS LE2..... 46 A2
Palmerston Cl
  RLEIS/BBY LE8..... 69 H3
Palmerston Wy LEIS LE2..... 46 A2
Pamela Pl LEIW LE4..... 19 C3
Pankhurst Rd LEIW LE4..... 18 A1
Paper Mill Cl RLEINE/SYS LE7.. 17 F1
The Parade LEIS LE2..... 56 A1
  LEIS LE2 *..... 56 A1
Paranmore Cl RLEIS/BBY LE8.. 66 A1
Pares St LEI LE1..... 26 B3
Parham Cl LEIW LE3..... 25 F1
Park Av COAL LE67..... 6 C3
  LEIE LE5..... 35 G5
Park Cl RLEIW/BAR LE9..... 51 E2
  RLEIW/BAR LE9..... 65 F4
Park Crs LEIS LE2..... 47 C4
Parkdale Rd LEIN LE4..... 23 H2
Park Dr LEIW LE3..... 23 H2
  MKTHBORO LE16..... 78 D4
Parker Dr LEIN LE4..... 18 D5
Parkfield Cl GBY/RBY LE6..... 22 D2
Parkhill LEIS LE2..... 35 F5
Park Hill Av LEIS LE2..... 44 D1
Park Hill Dr LEIW LE3..... 34 A5
Parkhouse Cl LEIN LE4..... 19 G2
Parkland Dr LEIS LE2..... 47 E1

Parklands Av GBY/RBY LE6..... 15 H4
Park La LEIS LE2..... 36 D3
Park Ri LEIN LE3..... 24 C5
Park Rd END/NAR LE19..... 54 D4
  GBY/RBY LE6..... 22 C3
  LEIE LE5..... 36 C1
  RLEINE/SYS LE7..... 17 F1
  RLEIS/BBY LE8..... 56 A3
  RLEIW/BAR LE8..... 51 E3
  RLEIW/BAR LE8..... 65 F4
  RLEIW/BAR LE8..... 72 B2
  WGSTN LE18..... 57 H1
Parkside GBY/RBY LE6..... 16 B3
Parkside Cl LEIE LE4..... 18 A1
Parkstone Cl LEIS LE2..... 28 D2
  RLEIW/BAR LE8..... 5 E4
Park St LEI LE1..... 3 F5
  RLEIS/BBY LE8..... 68 B3
Park Vale Rd LEIS LE2..... 27 E5
Park Vw LEIW LE3..... 24 C4
Park View Cl RLEIW/BAR LE9.. 74 B3
The Parkway LEIE LE5..... 28 B5
Parliament St LEIS LE2..... 2 B7
Parlour Cl RLEIW/BAR LE8..... 58 A1
Parnell Ct END/NAR LE19..... 55 F5
Parry St LEIE LE5..... 27 E3
Parsons Dr LEIS LE2..... 44 A5
Partridge Cl RLEINE/SYS LE7.. 4 C5
Partridge Rd LEIN LE4..... 20 D2
Parvian Rd LEIE LE5..... 45 C4
Pasley Cl LEIS LE2..... 44 D4
Pasley Rd LEIS LE2..... 44 D4
Pasture La LEI LE1..... 2 D1
The Pastures END/NAR LE19.. 54 C2
  LEIS LE2..... 48 A4
  MKTHBORO LE16..... 81 F1
  RLEIW/BAR LE8..... 12 C1
  RLEINE/SYS LE7..... 17 G2
  RLEIW/BAR LE9..... 74 B4
Paterson Cl LEIN LE4..... 18 A1
Paton St LEI LE1..... 2 A7
Patrick St MKTHBORO LE16.. 82 A2
Patterdale Rd LEIN LE4..... 12 C5
Paul Dr LEIN LE4..... 20 D3
Pauline Av LEIW LE4..... 19 H3
Pawley Cl RLEIS/BBY LE8..... 66 A1
Pawley Gdns LEIS LE2..... 44 D4
Payne St LEIN LE4..... 19 H4
Peacock Dr RLEIW/BAR LE8.. 65 H1
Peacock La LEI LE1 *..... 2 D4
Peakdale WGSTN LE18..... 58 D2
Peake Rd LEIN LE4..... 27 F1
Peartree Cl RLEINE/SYS LE7..... 4 C5
  LEIW LE3..... 23 H3
Pear Tree Cl LUTT LE17..... 85 E3
  RLEIW/BAR LE8..... 50 B3
Pear Tree Gdns
  MKTHBORO LE16..... 81 G2
Peatling Rd RLEIS/BBY LE8.. 67 G4
Peckleton Common
  RLEIW/BAR LE9..... 40 A1
Peckleton La RLEIW/BAR LE9.. 30 B4
Peckleton Vw
  RLEIW/BAR LE9..... 30 B3
Pedlars Cl LEIN LE4..... 18 B4
Peebles Wy LEIN LE4..... 20 B4
Peel Cl RLEIS/BBY LE8..... 69 H5
Peewitt Cl LEIE LE5..... 38 C4
Pegasus Cl LEIS LE2..... 3 K4
Peggs Cl RLEIW/BAR LE8..... 51 F3
Peldon Cl LEIE LE5..... 18 D5
Pelham St LEI LE1..... 47 E2
  LEIS LE2..... 2 E6
Pelham Wy LEI LE1..... 2 E6
Pells Cl RLEIS/BBY LE8..... 68 B3
Pembroke Av
  RLEINE/SYS LE7..... 13 F2
  WGSTN LE18..... 57 F1
Pembroke St LEIE LE5..... 27 E5
Pembury Cl RLEIS/BBY LE8.. 60 D2
Pen Cl LEIS LE2..... 45 E4
Penclose Rd RLEIW/BAR LE8.. 58 C4
Pendene Rd LEIS LE2..... 36 C4
Pendlebury Dr LEIS LE2..... 45 G1
Pendragon Wy LEIW LE3..... 32 D3
Penfold Cl RLEIW/BAR LE8.. 72 B1
Penfold Rd LEIW LE4..... 66 D3
Penhale Rd LEIW LE3..... 34 A5
Penman Wy END/NAR LE19.. 43 G5
Pennant Cl LEIW LE3..... 24 B3
Penney Cl LEIE LE5..... 28 A2
Pennine Cl LEIS LE2..... 47 H5
Penny La RLEIW/BAR LE9.. 50 A5
Penny Long La LEIW LE3..... 32 D2
Penrith Rd LEIN LE4..... 20 D5
Penryn Dr WGSTN LE18..... 58 A3
Pensilva Cl WGSTN LE18..... 58 A2
Pentridge Cl WGSTN LE18.. 58 A3
Penzance Av WGSTN LE18.. 58 A2
Peppercorn Cl LEIE LE5..... 18 C4
Percival St LEIE LE5..... 27 F5
Percival Wy GBY/RBY LE6.. 16 D4
Percy Rd LEIS LE2..... 45 E1
Percy St LEIW LE3..... 18 A1
Peregrine Ri LEIE LE5..... 18 A1
Peregrine Rd
  RLEIW/BAR LE9..... 74 A2
Perkins Cl MKTHBORO LE16.. 78 D5
Perkyn Rd LEIE LE5..... 28 C1
Perseverance Rd LEIE LE5.. 19 G2
Perth Av LEIW LE3..... 24 B3
Peter's Cl RLEIW/BAR LE8.. 62 A4
Peters Dr LEIE LE5..... 28 B3
Petersfield RLEIW/BAR LE9.. 68 B3
Petunia Cl LEIN LE4..... 18 G3
Petworth Dr LEIW LE3..... 25 F1
  MKTHBORO LE16..... 82 C1
Pevensey Av LEIW LE3..... 34 C3
Peverel Cl LEIW LE3..... 34 C3
Phillip Dr LEIS LE2..... 57 E2

Phillips Crs LEIN LE4..... 18 A1
Phipps Cl RLEIS/BBY LE8..... 56 A5
Phoenix Cl LEIE LE5..... 25 F3
Piccaver Ri LEIW LE3..... 24 B4
Pickering Cl LEIN LE4..... 19 E1
Pickering Rd RLEIW/BAR LE9.. 74 B5
Pickhill Rd LEIE LE5..... 21 H4
Picks Cl MKTHBORO LE16.. 82 C1
Pickwell Cl LEIE LE5..... 24 C2
Piers Rd LEIW LE3..... 24 A1
Pilgrim Gdns LEIE LE5..... 27 H3
Pilkington Rd LEIS LE2..... 34 A2
Pimpernel Cl END/NAR LE19.. 54 B2
Pindar Rd LEIW LE3..... 25 E2
Pine Cl LUTT LE17..... 85 E3
Pine Dr RLEINE/SYS LE7..... 13 F2
Pinehurst Cl LEIW LE3..... 23 H3
Pinel Cl RLEIW/BAR LE8..... 74 C5
Pine Rd LEIW LE3..... 24 A2
The Pines MKTHBORO LE16.. 79 E3
Pine Tree Av LEIE LE5..... 16 B5
Pine Tree Cl LEIS LE2..... 28 A2
Pine Tree Rd RLEIW/BAR LE9.. 32 C3
Pinehurst Cl LEIW LE3..... 23 H3
Pinewood Av LEIN LE4..... 20 C2
Pinewood Cl LEIW LE3..... 18 A2
  RLEIS/BBY LE8..... 67 G2
Pinewood Dr COAL LE67..... 14 C1
Pinfold Cl LEIS LE2..... 44 B5
Pinfold Rd LEIN LE4..... 20 A1
The Pinfold COAL LE67..... 6 C4
  GBY/RBY LE6..... 22 C2
Pingle La RLEIW/BAR LE9.. 62 D1
Pingle St LEI LE1..... 2 B2
Pintail Cl RLEIS/BBY LE8..... 65 G2
Piper Cl LEIE LE5..... 25 E3
Piper Wy LEIW LE3..... 28 A2
Pipistrelle Wy LEIS LE2..... 48 A4
Pitchens Cl LEIN LE4..... 19 H3
Pit Hi RLEIS/BBY LE8..... 69 H5
Pits Av LEIW LE3..... 43 G1
Pitton Cl WGSTN LE18..... 58 A3
Plantation Av LEIS LE2..... 44 C2
The Plantation
  RLEIS/BBY LE8..... 67 E2
Player Cl LEIN LE4..... 20 B2
Pleasant Cl LEIS LE2..... 32 D3
Plough Cl LEIW LE3..... 32 D4
  RLEIW/BAR LE9..... 74 C5
Ploughman's Lea
  RLEINE/SYS LE7..... 5 G2
Plover Crs LEIW LE4..... 18 B1
Plowman Cl LEIW LE3..... 24 A1
Plumtree Wy
  RLEINE/SYS LE7..... 13 F2
Pluto Cl LEIS LE2..... 3 K4
Plymouth Dr LEIE LE5..... 37 F2
Plymstock Cl LEIW LE3..... 25 F4
Poachers Cl LEIW LE3..... 23 H2
Poachers Pl LEIS LE2..... 47 H4
Pochin Dr RLEIW/BAR LE9.. 78 D4
Pochin's Bridge Rd
  WGSTN LE18..... 57 C5
Pochins Cl WGSTN LE18.. 58 A2
Pochin St LEIW LE3..... 63 C2
Pocklingtons Wk LEI LE1.. 3 F4
Polaris Cl LEIS LE2..... 3 K4
Pollard Rd LEIN LE4..... 34 A2
Pomeroy Dr LEIE LE5..... 46 D3
Pool Rd LEIW LE3..... 25 F4
Pope Crs END/NAR LE19..... 42 C5
Pope St LEIS LE2..... 36 A5
Poplar Av COAL LE67..... 6 B4
  LEIN LE4..... 11 G4
  LUTT LE17..... 85 G3
  RLEIS/BBY LE8..... 67 E3
Poplar Rd END/NAR LE19..... 54 D5
Poplars Cl RLEIW/BAR LE9.. 50 A4
Poplars Ct MKTHBORO LE16.. 78 B5
The Poplars GBY/RBY LE6.. 15 F5
  LEIE LE5..... 16 B5
  RLEIW/BAR LE9..... 51 C2
The Poppins RLEIW/BAR LE9.. 74 C4
Popple Cl RLEIW/BAR LE9 *.. 74 C4
Poppy Cl GBY/RBY LE6..... 16 C4
  LEIS LE2..... 54 B2
Porlock St LEIW LE3..... 25 F5
Portcullis Rd LEIE LE5..... 29 E1
Portgate WGSTN LE18..... 58 C2
Portishead Rd LEIN LE4..... 27 C2
Portland Rd LEIS LE2..... 36 B3
  RLEIW/BAR LE8..... 23 E5
Portland Wk LEIS LE2..... 65 F3
Portloc Dr WGSTN LE18..... 58 A3
Portman St LEIN LE4..... 19 H5
Portmore Cl LEIE LE5..... 18 C5
Portsdown Rd LEIE LE5..... 46 B2
Portsmouth Rd LEIN LE4.. 26 C1
The Portway LEIE LE5..... 27 G2
Post Office La
  RLEIS/BBY LE8..... 59 H4
Post Rd LEIN LE4..... 12 C5
Potter St LEI LE1..... 3 J3
Potterton Rd LEIN LE4..... 18 D3
Pougher Cl RLEIW/BAR LE8.. 73 C2
Powys Av LEIS LE2..... 37 E4
Powys Gdns LEIS LE2..... 37 E4
Poynings Av LEIW LE4..... 25 E4
Prebend St LEIS LE2..... 3 H6
Preston Cl GBY/RBY LE6.. 22 D3
Preston Ri LEIE LE5..... 28 C1
Prestwold Rd LEIE LE5..... 27 F2
Pretoria Cl LEIN LE4..... 10 C5
Pretoria Rd RLEIW/BAR LE8.. 22 D4
Pride Pl MKTHBORO LE16.. 81 G2
Priestley Rd LEIE LE5..... 34 C1
Priestman Rd LEIW LE3..... 33 C4
Priest Meadow
  RLEIS/BBY LE8..... 68 B3
Primrose Wy
  RLEINE/SYS LE7..... 5 H3

Primrose Cl END/NAR LE19.. 54 C3
  GBY/RBY LE6..... 16 C4
Primrose Hi LEIS LE2..... 46 D2
Primrose Wy RLEIW/BAR LE9.. 23 F4
Prince Albert Dr LEIW LE3.. 16 C3
Prince Dr LEIS LE2..... 47 G5
Princes Av LEIS LE2..... 47 G4
Princess Dr RLEIW/BAR LE9.. 32 B1
Princess Road Backways
  LEI LE1..... 3 F6
Princess Rd East LEI LE1.. 3 G7
Princess Rd West LEI LE1.. 3 F6
Princess St END/NAR LE19.. 55 E5
Priory Cl RLEIW/BAR LE9.. 12 D1
Priory Crs LEIW LE4..... 25 E2
Priory La COAL LE67..... 6 B1
Priory Wk LEIS LE2..... 33 G2
Progress Wy LEIN LE4..... 21 E4
Prospect Hi LEIE LE5..... 27 E4
Prospect Rd LEIE LE5..... 27 F4
Prospect Wy RLEIW/BAR LE9.. 51 E3
Pulford Dr RLEIW/SYS LE7.. 29 F4
Pullman Rd WGSTN LE18.. 57 H1
Purbeck Cl WGSTN LE18.. 58 B3
Purcell Rd LEIN LE4..... 26 C2
Purley Rd LEIN LE4..... 11 G4
Putney Rd LEIS LE2..... 35 H3
Putney Rd West LEIS LE2.. 35 C3
Pymm Ley Cl GBY/RBY LE6.. 16 B5
Pymm Ley La GBY/RBY LE6.. 16 B5
Pytchley Cl LEIN LE4..... 19 E2

Q

The Quadrant LEIE LE4 *.. 19 F5
Quarry La END/NAR LE19.. 42 C4
Quebec Rd LEI LE1..... 3 H2
Queen Mary St LEI LE1.. 26 B3
Queens Dr END/NAR LE19.. 55 F1
  LEIW LE3..... 33 G2
  WGSTN LE18..... 57 H1
Queensferry Pde LEIS LE2.. 44 C5
Queensgate Dr LEIN LE4.. 11 F4
Queensmead Cl
  GBY/RBY LE6..... 16 A5
Queens Park Wy LEIS LE2.. 56 D1
Queens Rd RLEIS/BBY LE8.. 56 A4
Queen's Rd LEIS LE2..... 36 B4
Queen St COAL LE67..... 6 B4
  LEI LE1..... 3 G3
  MKTHBORO LE16..... 82 B2
  RLEINE/SYS LE7..... 13 C5
  RLEIW/BAR LE8..... 50 B5
Queensway RLEIW/BAR LE8.. 50 C4
Quemby Cl LEIW LE4..... 19 G5
Quenby Crs RLEINE/SYS LE7.. 13 C1
Quenby St LEIE LE5..... 27 F5
Queniborough Rd LEIE LE5.. 27 E1
  RLEINE/SYS LE7..... 13 H4
Quickthorns LEIS LE2..... 47 F1
Quiney Wy LEIS LE2..... 47 G2
Quinton Rd LEIS LE2..... 44 B3
Quorn Av LEIS LE2..... 47 E5
Quorndon Ri GBY/RBY LE6.. 16 A5
Quorn Rd LEIE LE5..... 27 F3

R

Radar Rd LEIW LE3..... 24 B3
Radcot Lawns LEIS LE2.. 44 D5
Radford Dr LEIW LE3..... 33 G2
Radiant Rd LEIE LE5..... 28 C3
Radnor Ct END/NAR LE19.. 54 B1
Radnor Rd WGSTN LE18.. 57 G1
Raeburn Rd LEIE LE5..... 36 B4
Ragdale Rd LEIN LE4..... 27 F1
Railway St WGSTN LE18.. 57 F3
Raine Wy LEIS LE2..... 47 H5
Rainsborough Gdns
  MKTHBORO LE16..... 81 G3
Rainsford Crs LEIN LE4..... 19 E4
Ralph's Cl LUTT LE17 *..... 77 F2
Ramsbury Rd LEIS LE2..... 46 C1
Ramsdean Av WGSTN LE18.. 46 A5
Ramsey Cl LUTT LE17..... 85 H3
Ramsey Gdns LEIE LE5..... 29 E1
Ramsey Cl LEIE LE5..... 29 E1
Ramson Cl LEIS LE2..... 21 G5
Rancliffe Crs LEIE LE5 *..... 27 C2
Randles Cl RLEINE/SYS LE7.. 39 F1
Ranndoch Cl LEIW LE4..... 18 A4
Ranton Wy LEIW LE3..... 25 G2
Ratby La COAL LE67..... 14 C1
  LEIS LE2..... 23 G5
  LEIS LE2..... 23 E3
Ratby Meadow La
  END/NAR LE19..... 43 G5
Ratby Rd GBY/RBY LE6..... 16 A4
Ratcliffe Cl LEIS LE2..... 36 D5
Ratcliffe Rd LEIS LE2..... 53 H4
Ratcliffe St LEIN LE4..... 19 H5
Ravenhurst Rd LEIE LE5.. 34 B5
Raven Rd LEIW LE3..... 33 H4
Ravensbridge Dr LEIN LE4.. 25 H2
Ravensthorpe Rd
  LEIE LE5..... 58 B1
Raw Dykes Rd LEIS LE2.. 35 G3
Rawlings Ct LEI LE1..... 3 F6
Rawson St END/NAR LE19.. 42 D5
Rawsthorne Wk LEIN LE4.. 26 C2
Rayleigh Gn LEIE LE5..... 29 E1

Rayleigh Wy LEIE LE5..... 29 E1
Raymond Rd LEIW LE3..... 35 E1
Rayner Rd LEIE LE5..... 20 C4
Rearsby Rd LEIN LE4..... 27 E1
  RLEINE/SYS LE7 *..... 5 H5
Rectory Gdns LEIE LE5..... 37 H3
Rectory La MKTHBORO LE16.. 82 B2
  RLEINE/SYS LE7..... 10 B2
  RLEIS/BBY LE8..... 70 A2
Rectory Rd COAL LE67..... 6 C3
  RLEIS/BBY LE8..... 11 H2
Redcar Rd LEIN LE4..... 19 H5
Red Hall Dr RLEIW/BAR LE9.. 50 B4
Red Hall Gdns LEIW LE4.. 50 C4
Red Hill Av LEIN LE4..... 19 F2
Red Hill Cl END/NAR LE19.. 54 C5
Red Hill Ct LEIW LE4..... 12 C4
Red Hill La LEIN LE4..... 12 D4
Red Hill Wy LEIN LE4..... 18 D2
Red House Cl LEIS LE2..... 44 C4
Red House Gdns LEIS LE2.. 44 C4
Red House Rd LEIS LE2.. 44 C4
Red House Wy LEIE LE5.. 44 A5
Redliech Cl MKTHBORO LE16.. 82 C2
Redmarle Rd LEIE LE5..... 34 C2
Redpath Cl LEIN LE4..... 26 D3
Redwing Wk LEIE LE5 *.. 27 E3
Redwood Av LEIE LE5 *.. 27 E3
Reedpool Cl RLEIS/BBY LE8.. 67 F2
Rees Gv LEIN LE4..... 20 B2
Reeth Cl LEIN LE4..... 18 C4
Reeves Cl RLEIS/BBY LE8.. 65 H1
Regal Ct END/NAR LE19.. 55 F1
Regency Cl LEIS LE2..... 56 D2
Regent Cl WGSTN LE18.. 45 H5
Regent Rd LEI LE1..... 3 F6
  RLEIS/BBY LE8..... 67 F2
Regent St END/NAR LE19.. 55 E3
  LEI LE1..... 47 E2
  LUTT LE17..... 85 C4
  RLEIW/BAR LE8..... 50 B4
Regents Wk LEIW LE3..... 25 F1
Rendell Rd LEIN LE4..... 26 D1
Renfrew Rd LEIE LE5..... 29 E2
Renishaw Dr LEIE LE5..... 37 E3
Repington Rw LEIS LE2.. 45 F3
Repton Rd WGSTN LE18.. 58 B3
Repton St LEIW LE3..... 2 B1
Reservoir Rd RLEIW/SYS LE7.. 9 F1
The Retreat LEIE LE5..... 27 H5
Reynolds Cha WGSTN LE18.. 46 B5
Reynolds Pl LEIW LE4..... 34 C3
Rhodes Cl MKTHBORO LE16.. 81 F2
Ribble Av LEIS LE2..... 47 H5
Richard Cl LEIW LE3..... 33 C2
Richard III Rd LEIS LE2..... 2 B3
Richardson Cl
  RLEIW/BAR LE9..... 62 B5
Richardsons Cl
  LEIW LE4..... 74 C4
Richmond Cl LEIS LE2..... 35 G5
  RLEIS/BBY LE8..... 68 B4
Richmond Dr LEIS LE2..... 57 E2
Richmond Rd LEIS LE2..... 35 G4
Richmond St LEIS LE2..... 2 D6
Richmond Wy LEIS LE2..... 47 G5
Richmore Rd LEIE LE5..... 21 H4
Riddington Rd
  END/NAR LE19..... 55 E5
  LEIE LE5..... 43 H1
Ridgemere Cl RLEINE/SYS LE7.. 5 F5
Ridgeway END/NAR LE19.. 55 E5
Ridge Wy LEIS LE2..... 47 F5
Ridgeway Dr LEIN LE4..... 20 D1
The Ridgeway LEIS LE2.. 25 E3
  MKTHBORO LE16..... 78 D4
Ridgeway West
  MKTHBORO LE16..... 78 C4
Ridgway Rd LEIS LE2..... 36 C5
The Ridings RLEINE/SYS LE7.. 5 H4
The Ridings LEIE LE5..... 18 B1
Ridley Cl RLEIW/BAR LE9.. 50 C3
  RLEIS/BBY LE8..... 56 A5
Ridley St LEIW LE3..... 2 A6
Riley Cl MKTHBORO LE16.. 81 G2
Ringers Cl LEIS LE2..... 37 G5
Ringer's Spinney LEIS LE2.. 47 F5
Ring Rd LEI LE1..... 47 E2
The Ringway RLEIW/BAR LE9.. 5 H3
Ringwood Cl RLEIW/BAR LE9.. 30 B2
  WGSTN LE18..... 58 B2
Ringwood Rd LEIE LE5..... 29 E1
Ripley Cl MKTHBORO LE16.. 82 C5
Ripon Dr RLEIS/BBY LE8.. 68 B5
Ripon St LEIS LE2..... 36 C2
Riseholme Cl LEIE LE5..... 43 H1
The Rise END/NAR LE19.. 54 C3
Riston Cl LEIS LE2..... 47 E5
Ritchie Pk MKTHBORO LE16.. 81 H4
Riversdale Cl LEIN LE4..... 11 H5
Riverside MKTHBORO LE16.. 79 E4
Riverside Cl LEIS LE2..... 44 D2
Riverside Ct END/NAR LE19 *.. 55 E4
Riverside Dr LEIS LE2..... 44 D2
Riverside Rd RLEIW/SYS LE7.. 12 A2
Riverside Wy END/NAR LE19.. 55 E5
Rivers St LEIW LE3..... 2 B3
Rivets Meadow Cl LEIW LE3.. 33 H4
Robert Hall St LEIW LE4 *.. 18 C4
Robertsbridge Av LEIN LE4.. 19 E4
Robertson Cl RLEIW/BAR LE8.. 66 C1
Roberts Rd LEIE LE5..... 26 C1
Robin Cl LEIS LE2..... 45 E1
Robinia Cl LUTT LE17..... 85 G3
Robinson Rd LEIE LE5..... 27 G4
Robinson Wy COAL LE67.. 6 D4
Roborough Gn LEIE LE5.. 29 E4

Robotham Cl END/NAR LE19... 54 D4
RLEIW/BAR LE9.............. 53 H4
Roche Cl LEIS LE2 .... 44 C4
Rochester Cl RLIES/BBY LE8 .. 69 H1
Rochester Gdns
MKTHBORO LE16.............. 81 G3
Rockbridge Rd LEIS LE2......... 47 H4
Rockery Cl LEIS LE2 .... 28 A3
Rockingham Cl LEIS LE2 .... 28 B4
RLEIS/BBY LE8................ 56 B5
Rockingham Rd
MKTHBORO LE16.............. 82 B1
Rockley Rd LEIN LE4 .... 19 G5
Roebuck Cl RLEIS/BBY LE8 ..... 65 H1
Roecliff Cl COAL LE67 .... 6 C4
Roecliffe St LEIS LE5 .... 17 H5
Roehampton Dr
WGSTN LE18.................. 45 H3
Rogerstone Rd LEIE LE2 .... 38 B1
Rolleston Cl
MKTHBORO LE16.............. 82 B1
Rolleston Rd WGSTN LE18...... 45 H5
Rolleston St LEIE LE5 .... 17 G2
Roman Cl RLEIW/BAR LE9 ...... 30 C2
RLEIW/BAR LE9 *............. 51 G2
Roman Hl WGSTN LE18.......... 58 C3
Roman Rd LEIN LE4 .... 19 G2
Roman St LEIS LE2 .... 2 A6
Roman Wy MKTHBORO LE16... 81 H1
RLEINE/SYS LE7............... 22 C7
Romulus Ct END/NAR LE19..... 33 H4
Romway Av LEIE LE5 .... 37 E3
Romway Rd LEIE LE5 .... 37 E3
Rona Gdns LEIE LE5 .... 29 E3
Ronald Toon Rd
RLEIW/BAR LE9 .... 51 G3
Rookery Cl GBY/RBY LE6........ 16 B4
Rookery Cl RLIES/BBY LE8 ..... 70 B3
Rookery La GBY/RBY LE6........ 16 A4
LEIN LE4..................... 20 B1
Rookwell Dr
MKTHBORO LE16.............. 82 A3
Rosamund Av LEIW LE3.......... 34 B5
Rose Acre Cl RLEIW/SYS LE7 .. 29 F3
Rosebank Rd RLIES/BBY LE8 ... 87 F2
Rosebarn Wy LEIE LE5 .... 28 D1
Rosebery Av RLIES/BBY LE8.... 69 H5
Rosebery Cl LEIS LE2 .... 28 A3
Rosebery Rd RLEIW/SYS LE7 ... 9 G5
Rosebery St LEIE LE5 .... 27 F4
Rose Crs LEIW LE3 .... 32 D3
Rosedale Av LEIN LE4 .... 20 D5
Rosedale Rd WGSTN LE18....... 58 D1
Rosedene Av LEIN LE4........... 20 C1
Rosedene Cl RLEIW/BAR LE9 ... 52 A3
Rosemead Dr LEIS LE2 .... 47 E4
Rosemoor Cl
MKTHBORO LE16.............. 82 C1
Roseneath Av LEIN LE4 .... 20 C5
Rose Tree Av LEIN LE4 .... 11 G4
Roseway LEIN LE4................ 20 B4
Rossendale Rd
RLEIW/BAR LE9 .... 50 D3
Rossett Dr LEIN LE4 .... 18 D5
Rossetti Rd END/NAR LE19 ..... 42 C5
Rosshill Crs LEIE LE5 .... 29 E3
Ross Wk LEIN LE4 .... 26 D1
Ross' Wk LEIN LE4 .... 26 C2
Rotherby Av LEIE LE5 .... 27 F1
Rothley St LEIN LE4.............. 26 C1
Roughton St LEIN LE4 .... 19 G5
Roundhay Rd LEIW LE3.......... 35 E3
Roundhill Av RLEIW/BAR LE9.. 23 E5
Roundhill Cl
MKTHBORO LE16.............. 82 C2
RLEINE/SYS LE7............... 12 D1
Roundhill Rd LEIE LE5 .... 36 D2
The Roundway LEIN LE4........ 20 D2
Rowan Av MKTHBORO LE16.... 81 H5
Rowanberry Av LEIW LE5....... 34 A4
Rowan Dr LUTT LE17 .... 85 F3
The Rowans RLIES/BBY LE8 .... 67 E2
Rowan St LEIW LE3 .... 25 G4
Rowlandson Cl LEIN LE4 .... 10 D5
Rowlands Wy LEIS LE2.......... 56 C1
Rowlatts Hill Rd LEIE LE5 ...... 27 H4
Rowley Cl RLIES/BBY LE8 .... 68 B5
Rowley Fields Av LEIW LE3 ..... 34 D4
Rowsley Av LEIE LE5 .... 36 D1
Rowsley St LEIE LE5 .... 36 D1
Royal Ct END/NAR LE19 *....... 55 E3
Royal East St LEI LE1 .... 3 F1
Royal Kent St LEI LE1 .... 2 C1
Royal Rd LEIN LE4............... 19 H5
Royce Cl LEIW LE3 .... 33 G3
Roy Cl END/NAR LE19 .... 55 E3
Roydene Crs LEIN LE4 .... 20 B1
Royston Cl LEIS LE2 .... 56 C1
Ruby St LEIW LE3 .... 25 G4
Ruding Rd LEIW LE3 .... 2 B6
Ruding St LEIW LE3.............. 2 C5
Rufford Cl LEIS LE5 .... 27 G4
Rugby Cl MKTHBORO LE16 ..... 81 G2
Rugby Rd LUTT LE17 .... 85 G2
Rugby St LEIW LE3 .... 25 H5
Rumsey Dr RLIES/BBY LE8 ..... 55 H3
Runcorn Cl LEIS LE2 .... 44 C5
Runcorn Rd LEIS LE2............ 44 D5
Rupert Crs RLEINE/SYS LE7.... 9 H4
Rupert Rd MKTHBORO LE16.... 81 H5
Rupert St LEI LE1 .... 2 E4
Ruperts Wy RLIES/BBY LE8 .... 60 D3
Rushes La MKTHBORO LE16.... 80 C1
The Rushes COAL LE67 .... 6 C3
Rushey Cl LEIW LE4 .... 20 A3
Rushford Cl LEIN LE4 .... 27 F1
Rushford Dr LEIN LE4 .... 27 F1
Rushmere Wk LEIW LE3......... 33 E3
Rushton Dr LEIS LE2............. 44 B4
Ruskin Av RLEINE/SYS LE7 ..... 13 G2
Ruskin Fld RLEINE/SYS LE7 .... 9 E5
Ruskington Dr WGSTN LE18.... 46 B3

Russell Cl RLEIW/BAR LE9 ...... 50 A4
Russett Cl MKTHBORO LE16.... 78 D4
Russet Wy LEIN LE4 .... 12 A3
Rutherford Rd LEIN LE4 .... 18 A3
Rutland Av LEI LE1 .... 35 G4
WGSTN LE18.................. 45 H5
Rutland Cl LEIW LE3 .... 33 E2
Rutland Dr LEIE LE5 .... 12 C5
Rutland St LEI LE1 .... 3 G4
Rydal St LEIS LE2 .... 2 C7
Ryde Av LEIS LE2 .... 46 A4
Ryder Rd LEIN LE4 .... 24 A4
Ryderway LUTT LE17 .... 85 F4
Rye Cl LEIS LE2 .... 45 E4
Ryegate Crs LEIN LE4 .... 11 F4
Rye Hill Av LUTT LE17 .... 85 H5
Rylands Cl MKTHBORO LE16... 79 F5

S

Sacheverell Wy
GBY/RBY LE6.................. 23 E1
Sacheverel Rd LEIW LE3......... 24 B4
Sackville Gdns LEIE LE5......... 36 C5
Saddington Rd
RLIES/BBY LE8 .... 68 C4
Saddlers Cl LEIW LE3 .... 23 H2
Saddlers' Cl RLEINE/SYS LE7 .. 5 G2
Saffron Cl RLEIW/BAR LE9 ..... 50 C3
Saffron Hill Rd LEIS LE2......... 35 G5
Saffron La LEIS LE2 .... 35 G4
St Columba Wy
RLEINE/SYS LE7............... 4 C5
St Crispin's Wy LEIW LE3 .... 12 C5
St Cuthbert's Av
RLIES/BBY LE8 .... 60 D3
St David's Cl LEIS LE2 .... 37 E4
St Davids Cl LEIS LE2............ 32 D3
St Davids Rd LEIW LE3.......... 24 A4
St Denys Rd LEIE LE5 .... 37 H1
St Dunstan Rd LEIW LE3 .... 25 F3
St George St LEI LE1 .... 3 H4
St Georges Wy LEI LE1 .... 3 G5
St Helen's Cl HINC LE10 .... 72 A5
St Helens Cl LEIN LE4 .... 25 G1
St Helens Dr LEIN LE4 .... 25 H1
St Hildas Cl RLEINE/SYS LE7 .. 13 G2
St Ives Rd LEIN LE4 .... 20 C5
WGSTN LE18.................. 58 A2
St James Cl LEIS LE2 .... 47 G5
RLEIW/BAR LE9................ 53 H4
St James Rd LEIS LE2 .... 36 C2
St James St LEI LE1 .... 3 G2
St Johns End/NAR LE19 .... 43 G5
St John's Av RLEINE/SYS LE7 .. 13 G2
St Johns Rd LEIS LE2 .... 36 C3
St John St LEI LE1 .... 2 E1
St Leonards Rd LEIS LE2 .... 36 B3
St Luke's Cl RLEINE/SYS LE7 .. 13 G2
St Margarets Dr LUTT LE17 .... 76 A4
St Margaret's St LEI LE1 .... 2 E1
St Margaret's Wy LEIN LE4 .... 26 A2
St Marks St LEI LE1 .... 26 C3
St Martins LEI LE1 .... 2 E4
St Martins Dr RLEIW/BAR LE9.. 30 A2
St Martins Sq LEI LE1 *......... 2 E4
St Marys Av LEIE LE5 .... 28 C2
St Mary's Av LEIW LE3 .... 33 G2
St Marys Cl RLEIW/BAR LE9 ... 74 A3
St Mary's Ct LEIW LE3 .... 33 G2
St Marys Rd LEIS LE2 .... 36 B3
St Mary's Rd LEIW LE3 .... 56 B5
St Mary's Rd LUTT LE17........ 85 F5
MKTHBORO LE16.............. 82 A1
St Matthews Wy LEI LE1........ 3 G1
St Mellion Cl LEIN LE4 .... 10 B5
St Michaels Av LEIN LE4 .... 19 H4
St Michael's Cl COAL LE67...... 6 B3
St Nicholas Cir LEI LE1 .... 2 C4
St Nicholas Cl
MKTHBORO LE16.............. 82 A2
St Nicholas Pl LEI LE1 .... 2 D4
St Nicholas Wy
MKTHBORO LE16.............. 82 A2
St Oswalds Rd LEIW LE3........ 24 D3
St Pauls Cl LEIS LE2 .... 47 H2
St Paul's Dr RLEINE/SYS LE7 .. 13 G2
St Pauls Rd LEIW LE3 .... 25 G5
St Peter's Cl LEIW LE5 .... 23 H2
RLIES/BBY LE8 .... 76 B5
St Peters Dr RLIES/BBY LE8 .... 55 H5
St Peters La LEI LE1 .... 2 D3
St Peters Rd LEIS LE2 .... 3 K6
St Peter's St RLEINE/SYS LE7 .. 13 G1
St Philips Rd LEIE LE5 .... 36 D2
St Saviour's Hl LEIE LE5 .... 27 E4
St Saviour's Rd LEIE LE5........ 27 E4
St Stephens Rd LEIS LE2 .... 36 C1
St Swithin's Rd LEIE LE5........ 28 D5
St Thomas Rd LEIS LE2......... 57 E2
St Thomas's Rd
RLIES/BBY LE8................ 61 E3

St Wilfrid's Cl RLIES/BBY LE8.. 70 A2
St Wolstan's Cl WGSTN LE18... 46 B5
Salcombe Cl WGSTN LE18 ...... 58 A2
Salcombe Dr LEIE LE5 .... 24 A1
Salisbury Av LEI LE1 .... 3 J7
RLEIW/BAR LE9................ 65 G2
Salisbury Cl RLIES/BBY LE8.... 56 B5
Salisbury Dr LEIN LE4........... 8 B4
Salkeld Rd LEIS LE2 .... 56 C1
Saltash Cl WGSTN LE18 .... 58 A2
Saltcoates Av LEIN LE4.......... 20 B5
Saltersford Rd LEIE LE5 .... 27 H3
Saltersgate Dr LEIN LE4 .... 11 C4
Salt's Cl END/NAR LE19......... 54 D1
Samphire Cl LEIS LE2 .... 21 H5
Samson Rd LEIW LE3............ 25 F3
Samuel St LEI LE1 .... 3 J3
Sandacre St LEI LE1 .... 2 E2
Sanderson Cl RLIES/BBY LE8... 56 A5
Sandfield Cl LEIS LE2 .... 20 C2
Sandford Cl LEIS LE2 .... 28 A4
Sandford Rd RLEIW/SYS LE7... 13 E1
Sandgate Av LEIN LE4 .... 11 H4
Sandham Bridge Rd
RLEINE/SYS LE7............... 9 H1
Sandhill Dr END/NAR LE19..... 55 F2
Sandhills Av LEIE LE5 .... 21 F4
Sandhurst Cl LEIW LE3.......... 35 F2
Sandhurst Gdns LEIW LE3...... 35 F2
Sandhurst Rd LEIW LE3......... 25 F3
Sandhurst St LEIE LE2 .... 47 E2
Sandiacre Dr LEIN LE4 .... 12 D4
Sandown Rd LEIE LE5 .... 36 D4
LEIW LE3..................... 46 B4
Sandpiper Cl LEIS LE2 .... 27 E3
Sandringham Av LEIN LE4 ..... 19 H4
Sandringham Rd LEIS LE2...... 50 D4
Sandringham Wy
MKTHBORO LE16.............. 82 C2
Sandy Ri WGSTN LE18 .... 46 C4
Sanvey Ga LEI LE1 .... 2 D2
Sanvey La LEIS LE2.............. 44 B2
Sapcote Rd RLEIW/BAR LE9 ... 72 C1
Saunderson Rd LEIN LE4 .... 18 D5
Savernake Rd LEIN LE4 .... 25 C1
Saville Rd RLIES/BBY LE8 ...... 56 C5
Saville St LEIE LE2 .... 27 G4
Sawbrook RLIES/BBY LE8 ...... 68 C4
Sawday St LEIS LE2 .... 35 G5
Sawley St LEIE LE2 .... 36 D2
Saxby St LEIE LE2 .... 3 J6
Saxon Cl MKTHBORO LE16..... 78 D5
Saxon Dr LEIS LE2............... 56 C1
Saxondale Rd WGSTN LE18.... 58 C3
Saxons Ri GBY/RBY LE6......... 22 C1
Saxon St LEIS LE2 .... 2 A6
Saxthorpe Rd LEIE LE5.......... 21 F5
Scalborough Cl
RLIES/BBY LE8 .... 66 C2
Scalpay Cl LEIN LE4 .... 18 B4
Scarborough Rd LEIN LE4 ...... 19 H5
School Cl RLEIW/BAR LE9....... 63 C3
School Crs RLEIW/BAR LE9 .... 74 A2
Schoolgate LEIS LE2 .... 45 F4
School House Cl
RLEINE/SYS LE7 .... 17 F2
School La END/NAR LE19 .... 54 D4
HINC LE10.................... 72 A5
LEIE LE5 .... 37 H3
LEIN LE4..................... 19 G1
MKTHBORO LE16.............. 80 C1
RLEINE/SYS LE7............... 13 H4
RLEIW/BAR LE9................ 53 H4
School Rd RLIES/BBY LE8 ...... 70 A3
School St RLEINE/SYS LE7 ..... 5 E5
RLIES/BBY LE8................ 68 B4
School Wk RLIES/BBY LE8...... 70 A3
Scotland Rd
MKTHBORO LE16.............. 82 B2
Scotland Wy RLIES/BBY LE8... 67 F3
Scotswood Crs LEIS LE2 .... 44 C5
Scott Cl MKTHBORO LE16...... 78 C4
Scott Ct LEIS LE2 .... 36 A5
Scott St LEIS LE2 .... 35 H5
Scraptoft La LEIE LE5 .... 28 A3
Scraptoft Ms LEIE LE5 .... 28 A3
RLEINE/SYS LE7............... 29 F2
Scraptoft Ri RLEINE/SYS LE7 .. 29 F2
Scrivener Cl RLEINE/SYS LE7 .. 29 F2
Scudamore Rd LEIW LE3 .... 23 C5
Seacole Cl LEIW LE3............. 33 H5
Seaford Rd LEIS LE2 .... 44 D3
Seagrave Dr LEIS LE2 .... 46 D2
Seaton Ri LEIE LE2 .... 29 E1
Seaton Rd LEIN LE4.............. 33 G4
WGSTN LE18.................. 58 A2
Seddons Cl LEIN LE4 .... 18 D3
Sedgebrook Rd LEIE LE5........ 29 E4
Sedgefield Dr
RLEINE/SYS LE7 .... 12 C1
RLEINE/SYS LE7 .... 29 F4
Segrave Rd LEIW LE3 .... 34 D5
Seine La END/NAR LE19 .... 54 D3
Selbury Dr LEIS LE2 .... 46 D3
Selby Av LEIE LE5................ 28 D1
Selby Rd MKTHBORO LE16..... 81 H5
Selkirk Rd LEIN LE4 .... 20 B4
Senator Cl RLEINE/SYS LE7 *.. 12 D2
Sence Crs RLIES/BBY LE8 ...... 60 C3
Severn Cl RLEIW/BAR LE9 ...... 65 F3
Severn Rd LEIS LE2 .... 47 H3
Severn St LEIS LE2 .... 3 K6
Sextant Rd LEIE LE5 .... 28 C3
Seymour Rd LEIS LE2 .... 35 H5
Seymour St LEIS LE2 .... 3 J6
Seymour Wy LEIN LE4........... 32 D3
Shackelton Wy LUTT LE17 ..... 84 A4
Shackerdale Rd WGSTN LE18.. 45 H5
Shackleton St LEI LE1 .... 26 C3
Shades Cl RLEIW/BAR LE9 ..... 63 C2

Shadrack Cl RLEIW/BAR LE9 ... 62 B5
Shady La LEIS LE2 .... 37 H4
Shaeffer Ct LEIE LE5 .... 18 B5
Shaftesbury Av LEIN LE4........ 19 C5
Shaftesbury Rd LEIW LE3 ...... 35 E1
Shakespeare Cl LEIW LE4....... 34 B4
Shakespeare Ct LEIW LE3 ...... 34 B4
Shakespeare St LEIS LE2 .... 35 H5
Shalford Rd LEIE LE5 .... 27 H2
Shanford Rd
RLEIW/BAR LE9 .... 72 C3
Sharpe Wy END/NAR LE19 ..... 54 D4
Sharpland LEIS LE2 .... 44 C3
Sharpley Dr LEIN LE4 .... 18 A1
Sharply Hl GBY/RBY LE6........ 7 H2
Shaw La RLEIS/BBY LE8 .... 66 C5
Shaw Wood Cl GBY/RBY LE6... 16 A4
Shearer Cl LEIN LE4 .... 20 C5
Shearsby Cl RLEIW/BAR LE9 ... 58 B1
Sheene Rd LEIN LE4 .... 18 A3
Sheffield St LEIW LE3 .... 35 F2
Shelbourne St LEIE LE5 .... 27 E4
Sheldon St LEIE LE5 .... 3 J2
Shelland Cl MKTHBORO LE16.. 82 C2
Shellduck Cl RLIES/BBY LE8.... 65 H2
Shelley Dr LUTT LE17 .... 85 G2
Shelley Rd END/NAR LE19...... 54 C1
Shelley St LEIS LE2 .... 35 H5
Shenley Rd WGSTN LE18 .... 46 C4
Shenton Av LEIN LE4............ 21 E1
RLEIS/BBY LE8................ 55 H4
WGSTN LE18.................. 46 A5
Shenton Rd RLEIW/BAR LE9 ... 50 B4
Shepherd Cl LEIE LE5 .... 28 D4
LEIW LE3..................... 32 D2
Sherborne Av WGSTN LE18 .... 58 C3
Sherford Cl WGSTN LE18 .... 58 A1
Sheridan Cl LEIN LE4 .... 54 C1
Sheringham Rd LEIN LE4 .... 18 D5
Sherloyd Cl LEIN LE4 .... 20 D3
Sherrard Rd LEIE LE5 .... 27 E4
MKTHBORO LE16.............. 78 C4
Sherrier Wy LUTT LE17 .... 85 H3
Sherwood St LEIE LE5 .... 27 C4
Shetland Av LEIN LE4 .... 20 A5
Shetland Wy RLIES/BBY LE8... 67 F3
Shield Crs LEIS LE2 .... 57 F2
Shilton Rd RLEIW/BAR LE9..... 50 B5
Shipley Rd LEIE LE5 .... 36 D1
Shipman Rd LEIW LE3 .... 43 H2
Shipston Hl LEIS LE2............ 47 E4
Shipton Cl WGSTN LE18 .... 58 D1
Shipton Rd LEIE LE5............. 21 G4
Shires Cl LEIN LE4 .... 24 C5
Shires La LEI LE1 .... 2 D5
Shires Wk LEI LE1 * 2 D5
Shirley Av LEIS LE2 .... 36 D5
Shirley Dr RLEINE/SYS LE7 ..... 5 E4
Shirley Rd LEIS LE2 .... 36 D5
Shirley St LEIN LE4 .... 26 D1
Shoesmith Cl RLEIW/BAR LE9.. 50 A5
Short Cl RLIES/BBY LE8......... 68 B4
Shortridge La END/NAR LE19.. 42 D5
Short St LEI LE1 .... 3 K6
Shottens Cl LEIN LE4 .... 18 B5
Shottery Av LEIN LE4 .... 19 G5
Shoulbard RLIES/BBY LE8 ...... 68 A3
Shrewsbury Av LEIS LE2 .... 45 G2
MKTHBORO LE16.............. 82 C2
Shrewsbury Cl
RLEIW/BAR LE9 .... 50 A4
Shropshire Pl
MKTHBORO LE16.............. 78 C5
Shropshire Rd LEIS LE2 .... 44 D1
Shuttleworth La
RLEIW/BAR LE9 .... 75 G2
Sibson Rd LEIN LE4 .... 11 G5
Sibton La LEIS LE2 .... 47 E4
Sicklehom Dr LEIE LE5 .... 37 E3
Sidmouth Av LEIE LE5 .... 37 C1
Sidwell St LEIE LE5 .... 25 C1
Silbury Rd LEIN LE4 .... 25 G1
Silsden Ri LEIS LE2 .... 44 D5
Silver Ar LEIE LE1 .... 2 E3
Silverdale Dr LEIN LE4 .... 20 D1
Silverstone Dr LEIN LE4 .... 20 B2
Silver St LEI LE1 .... 2 E3
Silverton Rd LEIS LE2 .... 47 G2
Silver Wk LEIE LE1 * 2 E3
Silverwood Ct LEIE LE5 .... 28 C5
Simborough Wy
MKTHBORO LE16.............. 82 C1
Simmins Crs LEIS LE2........... 44 D4
Simons Cl WGSTN LE18......... 58 C3
Simpson Cl RLEINE/SYS LE7 ... 12 C1
Siskin Cl LEIS LE2 .... 22 A5
Siskin Hl LEIS LE2 .... 44 A5
Sitch Cl RLEIW/BAR LE9 .... 74 C4
Sitwell Wk LEIE LE5 .... 37 E3
Six Acres Cl GBY/RBY LE6....... 16 A4
Six Acres Rd GBY/RBY LE6...... 74 A3
Skampton Rd LEIE LE5.......... 37 G2
Skeiton Dr LEIS LE2 .... 45 G2
Sketchley Cl LEIE LE5 .... 28 D4
Skippon Cl MKTHBORO LE16.. 81 C2
Skipworth St LEIE LE2 .... 36 C1
Skye Wy RLIES/BBY LE8......... 67 F3
Slade Cl LEIW LE3 .... 33 G5
The Slade Greens LEIS LE2..... 44 A5
Slate Brook Cl GBY/RBY LE6... 16 B4
Slate Cl LEIE LE2 .... 23 H2
Slate Pit La GBY/RBY LE6....... 15 F4
Slater St LEIW LE3 .... 26 A3
Slate St LEIS LE2 .... 3 H5

Sloane Cl END/NAR LE19 .... 42 C5
Smart Cl LEIW LE3 .... 33 H3
Smedmore Rd LEIE LE5 .... 27 F2
Smeeton Ct RLIES/BBY LE8 .... 70 A3
Smeeton Rd RLIES/BBY LE8 ... 69 H5
Smith Av LEIN LE4............... 20 D1
Smith Dorrien Rd LEIE LE5 ..... 27 G5
Smith Wy END/NAR LE19 ...... 43 G4
Smithy Farm Dr
RLEIW/BAR LE9 .... 62 A4
Smore Slade Hills LEIE LE5..... 38 C4
Smyth Cl MKTHBORO LE16..... 78 C4
Snowdens End WGSTN LE18 ... 58 C2
Snowdrop Cl END/NAR LE19... 54 B3
Snow Hl LEIN LE4 .... 25 G1
Soar La LEIW LE3 .... 2 B2
Soar Mill La RLEIW/BAR LE9 ... 75 H1
Soar Valley Wy
END/NAR LE19 .... 34 C5
Sockburn Cl LEIS LE5 .... 21 H4
Somerby Dr LEIS LE2 .... 47 G3
Somerby Rd RLEINE/SYS LE7 .. 29 C4
Somerfield Wy LEIS LE2......... 32 D3
Somerscales Wk LEIN LE4 ..... 26 D2
Somerset Av LEIN LE4 .... 18 D5
Somerset Dr LEIW LE3 .... 23 H3
Somers Rd LEIE LE5 .... 28 C4
Somerville Rd LEIW LE3 .... 34 C4
Sonning Wy LEIS LE2 .... 56 B1
Sopers Rd RLEIW/BAR LE9 ..... 63 C3
Sorrel Rd LEIE LE5 .... 21 G5
Sorrel Wy END/NAR LE19 ...... 54 B3
South Albion St LEI LE1......... 3 G5
Southampton St LEI LE1 .... 3 G5
South Av LEIS LE2 .... 33 F2
WGSTN LE18.................. 58 A1
South Church Ga LEI LE1 ...... 2 D1
Southdown Dr LEIN LE4 .... 24 C5
Southdown Rd LEIS LE2 .... 27 F4
South Dr LEIE LE5 .... 28 A2
RLEIW/BAR LE9 .... 62 C5
Southernhay Av LEIS LE2 ...... 36 C5
Southernhay Cl LEIS LE2 .... 36 C5
Southernhay Rd LEIS LE2....... 36 C4
Southey Ct END/NAR LE19 *... 26 D2
LEIS LE2...................... 26 D2
Southfield Av
RLEINE/SYS LE7 .... 13 F1
Southfield Cl LEIS LE2 .... 44 A5
RLEINE/SYS LE7............... 29 F3
Southfields Av LEIS LE2 .... 46 D2
Southfields Dr LEIS LE2 .... 45 E3
Southgates LEI LE1 .... 2 D4
Southgates U/P LEI LE1 * 2 D4
South Kingsmead Rd
LEIS LE2...................... 46 A2
South Knighton Rd LEIS LE2 ... 46 B1
Southland Rd LEIS LE2 .... 46 B2
Southleigh Gv
MKTHBORO LE16.............. 78 B5
Southmeads Cl LEIS LE2 .... 46 B1
Southmeads Rd LEIS LE2 ...... 37 G5
Southside Rd LEIW LE3 .... 43 H2
South St LEIS LE2 .... 47 E2
Southview Dr LEIE LE5 .... 37 F3
Southway RLIES/BBY LE8 ...... 56 B5
South Wy RLIES/BBY LE8 ...... 70 B2
Spa Dr RLEIW/BAR LE9 .... 72 B1
Spa La WGSTN LE18 .... 58 B3
Spalding St LEIE LE5 .... 27 G4
Sparkenhoe RLEIW/BAR LE9 .. 63 C3
Sparkenhoe St LEIS LE2 .... 3 J5
Sparsis Gdns END/NAR LE19 .. 55 F2
Speedwell Cl END/NAR LE19 .. 54 B2
Speedwell Dr LEIE LE5 .... 21 F4
RLEIW/BAR LE9 .... 74 C5
Speers Rd LEIE LE5 .... 37 H2
Spencefield Dr LEIE LE5......... 37 H2
Spencefield La LEIE LE5......... 37 H3
Spencer Av LEIN LE4 .... 12 C5
Spencer Rd LUTT LE17 .... 85 G5
Spencer St LEIS LE2 .... 47 E2
MKTHBORO LE16.............. 81 G1
Spence St LEIS LE2 .... 3 J5
Spendlow Gdns LEIS LE2 .... 45 E4
Spiers Cl END/NAR LE19 .... 54 D4
Spinner Cl RLEIW/BAR LE9 .... 74 D5
Spinney Av RLIES/BBY LE8 ..... 67 E2
Spinney Cl GBY/RBY LE6 .... 14 A5
LEIS LE2...................... 44 A5
LEIW LE3..................... 33 G3
MKTHBORO LE16.............. 81 F1
RLEINE/SYS LE7............... 12 C1
Spinney Halt RLIES/BBY LE8 .. 55 G4
Spinney Hill Rd LEIE LE5 .... 27 F3
Spinney Ri LEIN LE4 .... 11 F5
Spinneyside GBY/RBY LE6...... 14 A5
Spinney St LEIE LE5 .... 48 C4
RLEINE/SYS LE7............... 58 C1
Spinney Vw RLIES/BBY LE8 .... 61 F2
Sponne Ri LEIS LE2 .... 45 E4
Sports Field La
RLEIW/BAR LE9 .... 53 H3
Sports Rd LEIW LE3 .... 24 A2
Springbrook Dr
RLEINE/SYS LE7............... 29 F4
Spring Cl GBY/RBY LE6.......... 22 D2
Springclose La LEIS LE2 .... 44 D3
Spring Cl LUTT LE17 .... 85 G2
Springdale Rd LEIN LE4 .... 20 C1
Spring Field Cl LEIW LE3 .... 23 H3
Springfield Cl RLIES/BBY LE8 .. 70 A4
Springfield Ct
MKTHBORO LE16.............. 82 A2
Springfield Crs
RLIES/BBY LE8 .... 70 A4
Springfield La RLIES/BBY LE8.. 70 A4
Springfield Rd LEIE LE2 .... 36 C1
MKTHBORO LE16.............. 82 A2
Spring Gdns END/NAR LE19 *.. 55 E5
Springhill Gdns
MKTHBORO LE16.............. 81 F2

Spring La *WGSTN* LE18............. **46** B5
The Springs
 RLEIW/BAR LE9 *................. **74** B3
Springway Cl *LEIE* LE3............. **29** E5
Springwell Cl *RLEIS/BBY* LE8... **67** E2
Springwell Dr *RLEIS/BBY* LE8... **66** C3
Springwell La *RLEIS/BBY* LE8... **65** H5
Spruce Wy *LUTT* LE17............. **85** F2
The Square *END/NAR* LE19...... **55** E5
 LEIE LE3.......................... **23** H1
 MKTHBORO LE16................. **81** H1
 RLEIS/BBY LE8................... **59** H5
 RLEIS/BBY LE8................... **67** F3
 RLEIW/BAR LE9................... **51** E3
Squire's Ride *RLEINE/SYS* LE7... **5** G1
Squirrel Cl *END/NAR* LE19........ **54** C4
Squirrel's Cnr *RLEINE/SYS* LE7.. **5** F1
Stable Cl *WGSTN* LE18............. **55** E4
Stablegate Wy
 MKTHBORO LE16................. **82** B1
Stackley Rd *RLEIS/BBY* LE8...... **60** D2
Stadium Pl *LEIN* LE4............... **19** E5
Stadium Ri *LEIN* LE4................ **25** H1
Stadon Rd *RLEINE/SYS* LE7...... **17** F1
Stafford Dr *WGSTN* LE18.......... **57** F2
Stafford Leys *LEIE* LE3............. **32** D2
Stafford St *LEIN* LE4............... **20** A4
 RLEIW/BAR LE9................... **50** A5
Staindale *WGSTN* LE18............ **58** C3
Stainburn Rd *LEIN* LE4............. **22** A1
Stamford Cl *GBY/RBY* LE6......... **22** C1
 LEIW LE3.......................... **23** H2
 MKTHBORO LE16................. **81** H2
Stamford Dr *GBY/RBY* LE6........ **16** B5
 RLEINE/SYS LE7................... **5** E2
Stamford Rd *LEIW* LE3............. **8** A4
Stamford Rd *RLEIW/BAR* LE9.... **32** C1
Stamford St *GBY/RBY* LE6........ **22** B3
 LEI LE1........................... **3** F5
 LEIW LE3.......................... **23** H2
Stanbrig *WGSTN* LE18 *........... **58** C3
Stancliff Rd *LEIN* LE4.............. **22** A1
Stanfell Rd *LEIS* LE2................ **36** B5
Stanhope Rd *WGSTN* LE18....... **58** C2
Stanhope St *LEIS* LE2.............. **27** F5
Stanier Dr *LEIN* LE4................. **21** E3
Stanier Rd *RLEIW/BAR* LE9....... **74** C3
Stanley Dr *LEIE* LE5................. **28** A2
Stanley Rd *LEIS* LE2................ **36** C2
Stanley St *RLEIW/BAR* LE9....... **50** A5
Stanton La *RLEIW/BAR* LE9...... **62** D2
Star Cots *RLEIW/BAR* LE9 *...... **62** B2
Starmer Cl *RLEIW/BAR* LE9...... **72** B1
Station Cl *RLEIW/BAR* LE9....... **32** C1
Station Dr *RLEIW/BAR* LE9....... **32** C1
Station La *LUTT* LE17.............. **76** A3
 RLEINE/SYS LE7................... **5** E1
Station Rd *END/NAR* LE19....... **55** E4
 GBY/RBY LE6...................... **22** C2
 LEIN LE4........................... **24** A1
 LUTT LE17......................... **77** G2
 LUTT LE17......................... **85** H4
 MKTHBORO LE16................. **79** E4
 RLEINE/SYS LE7................... **10** A1
 RLEINE/SYS LE7................... **13** E2
 RLEINE/SYS LE7................... **29** F5
 RLEIS/BBY LE8.................... **60** C4
 RLEIS/BBY LE8.................... **66** D5
 RLEIW/BAR LE9................... **22** D5
 RLEIW/BAR LE9................... **32** C1
 RLEIW/BAR LE9................... **51** G2
 RLEIW/BAR LE9................... **63** G2
 RLEIW/BAR LE9................... **74** B3
 WGSTN LE18....................... **57** H1
Station St *LEIS* LE2................. **3** H5
 RLEIS/BBY LE8.................... **70** A3
 RLEIS/BBY LE8.................... **70** A3
 WGSTN LE18....................... **57** F1
Staveley Cl *WGSTN* LE18.......... **58** C1
Staveley Rd *LEIE* LE5.............. **36** D2
Staythorpe Rd *LEIN* LE4........... **21** E2
Steadman Av *RLEIW/BAR* LE9.. **65** C3
Stebbings Rd *LEIS* LE2............. **44** D3
Steele Cl *LEIE* LE5.................. **28** A5
Steeple Cl *WGSTN* LE18........... **55** E4
 LEIS LE2........................... **28** B2
Stelle Wy *RLEINE/SYS* LE7....... **17** F4
Stemborough La *LUTT* LE17...... **76** B3
Stenor Cl *RLEIS/BBY* LE8......... **68** A3
Stenson Rd *LEIN* LE4............... **21** E4
Stephenson Cl *GBY/RBY* LE6.... **16** A4
 RLEIW/BAR LE9................... **74** C5
Stephenson Dr *LEIE* LE5.......... **17** E5
Stephenson Dr *LEIW* LE3.......... **35** G3
Stephenson Wy
 GBY/RBY LE6...................... **16** A4
Stevens Cl *RLEIW/BAR* LE9...... **62** C2
Stevenson Gdns
 RLEIW/BAR LE9................... **65** F2
Stevens St *MKTHBORO* LE16.... **81** H1
Stevenstone Cl *LEIS* LE2.......... **47** H3
Stewards Cl *RLEIW/BAR* LE9.... **30** B2
Stewart Av *END/NAR* LE19....... **54** C2
Stevning Crs *LEIS* LE2............. **24** B1
Stiles Cl *RLEIW/BAR* LE9......... **74** B4
The Stiles *RLEINE/SYS* LE7....... **5** E5
Stinford Leys
 MKTHBORO LE16................. **82** C1
Stirling Dr *RLEIW/BAR* LE9....... **29** F4
Stockland Rd *LEIS* LE2............ **45** E4
Stocks Rd *RLEIW/BAR* LE9....... **74** C3
Stockton Rd *LEIN* LE4............. **27** F1
Stockwell Cl
 MKTHBORO LE16................. **82** C1

Stockwell Rd *LEIS* LE2............. **46** A2
Stokes Dr *LEIW* LE3................. **25** F2
Stonebridge St *LEIE* LE5.......... **27** F4
Stonechat Wk *LEIE* LE5 *......... **27** E4
Stone Cl *LEIN* LE4................... **18** A1
Stonecroft *RLEIS/BBY* LE8........ **66** C3
Stonecrop Rd *LEIS* LE2............ **21** G5
Stonehaven Rd *LEIN* LE4.......... **20** B3
Stonehill Av *LEIN* LE4.............. **11** C4
Stonehill Dr *RLEIS/BBY* LE8...... **61** E2
Stonehurst Rd *LEIS* LE2........... **34** B5
Stoneleigh Wy *LEIW* LE3.......... **25** C3
Stonelodge Rd *GBY/RBY* LE6.... **16** B4
Stonesby Av *LEIS* LE2.............. **45** E3
Stoneycroft Rd
 RLEIW/BAR LE9................... **50** D4
Stoneygate Av *LEIS* LE2.......... **36** C4
Stoneygate Ct *LEIS* LE2........... **36** C3
Stoneygate Rd *LEIS* LE2........... **36** D5
Stoney Hollow *LUTT* LE17......... **85** C4
Stoneywell Rd *LEIN* LE4........... **17** H2
Stores La *RLEIS/BBY* LE8......... **68** B4
Storey Cl *LEI* LE1.................... **3** F5
Storey St *LEIW* LE3................. **25** E1
Stornaway Rd *LEIE* LE5............ **28** C3
Stoughton Av *LEIS* LE2............ **36** C4
Stoughton Cl *LEIS* LE2............ **47** F2
Stoughton Dr *LEIE* LE2............ **37** F2
Stoughton Dr North
 LEIE LE5........................... **36** D2
Stoughton Dr South
 LEIS LE2........................... **37** F4
Stoughton La *LEIS* LE2............ **38** B4
Stoughton Rd *LEIE* LE2........... **38** C2
 LEIS LE2........................... **36** C3
Stoughton St *LEIS* LE2............ **3** K5
Stoughton St South *LEIS* LE2... **3** K5
Stour Cl *LEIS* LE2................... **47** H2
Stowe Cl *LEIW* LE3.................. **25** E1
Strasbourg Dr *LEIN* LE4........... **18** D4
Stratford Rd *LEIW* LE3............. **34** B4
Strathaven Rd *LEIN* LE4.......... **20** B3
Strathern Rd *LEIS* LE2............ **17** H5
Strathmore Av *LEIN* LE4.......... **20** D3
Stratton Cl *MKTHBORO* LE16.... **81** C3
Streamside Cl
 RLEIW/BAR LE9................... **74** B4
Strensall Hall Dr *LEIS* LE2........ **44** D3
Stretton Cl *LEIE* LE5............... **48** B5
Stretton La *RLEINE/SYS* LE7..... **39** H5
Stretton Rd *LEIW* LE3.............. **25** C5
 RLEIS/BBY LE8.................... **60** D1
Stroma Wy *RLEIS/BBY* LE8....... **56** A3
Stroud Rd *LEIS* LE2................. **27** F3
Strudwick Wy
 RLEIS/BBY LE8.................... **56** A3
Stuart Rd *LEIN* LE4................. **81** G2
 MKTHBORO LE16................. **81** G2
Stuart St *LEIW* LE3................. **35** F2
 RLEIS/BBY LE8.................... **70** A3
Stubbs Rd *LEIN* LE4................ **26** D2
Sturdee Cl *LEIS* LE2................ **44** D5
Sturdee Gn *LEIS* LE2............... **44** D5
Sturdee La *LEIS* LE2............... **44** C4
Sturrock Cl *RLEINE/SYS* LE7..... **29** F4
Styon Rd *LEIN* LE4.................. **24** C1
Sudeley Av *LEIN* LE4............... **19** E5
Suffolk Cl *WGSTN* LE18........... **45** G5
Suffolk St *LEIE* LE5................. **4** D5
Suffolk Wy *RLEIW/BAR* LE9...... **30** B3
Sulgrave Rd *LEIE* LE5.............. **28** C4
Summerlea Rd *LEIS* LE2.......... **28** C4
Summers Wy
 MKTHBORO LE16................. **81** G2
Sunbury Gn *LEIE* LE5.............. **29** E3
Sunbury Ri *RLEIS/BBY* LE8....... **56** A3
Sundew Rd *LEIE* LE5............... **21** G5
Sundial Rd *LEIE* LE5............... **21** G5
Sunningdale Rd *LEIW* LE3........ **33** F1
Sunnycroft Rd *LEIN* LE4.......... **25** C5
Sunnyfield Cl *LEIE* LE5............ **28** C5
Sunny Side *LEIS* LE2............... **47** G4
Sunnyside Cl *RLEIS/BBY* LE8.... **56** A3
Sun Wy *LEIW* LE3.................... **33** H2
Surrey St *LEIN* LE4.................. **26** D1
Susan Av *LEIE* LE5.................. **37** H1
Sussex Av *WGSTN* LE18........... **45** F5
Sussex St *LEIE* LE5................. **3** J2
Sutherington Wy
 RLEINE/SYS LE7................... **9** G5
Sutherland St *LEIS* LE2........... **36** C1
Sutton Av *LEIN* LE4................. **27** E1
Sutton Cl *LEIN* LE4................. **74** A1
Sutton Dr *RLEIW/BAR* LE9....... **74** A1
Sutton Pl *LEIN* LE4................. **20** A5
Sutton Rd *LEIS* LE2................. **45** C1
 MKTHBORO LE16................. **79** F3
Swainson Rd *LEIN* LE4............ **27** G2
Swain St *LEI* LE1.................... **3** H4
Swallowdale Dr *LEIN* LE4......... **18** B1
Swallow Dr *RLEINE/SYS* LE7..... **4** C5
Swallows Cl *LEIE* LE5.............. **32** C4
Swan Cl *LEIE* LE5................... **56** A1
Swannington Rd *LEIW* LE3....... **25** C3
 RLEIW/BAR LE9................... **74** C5
Swanscombe Rd *LEIS* LE2....... **35** H4
Swan St *LEI* LE1.................... **2** C2
Swan Wy *RLEINE/SYS* LE7 *...... **4** B5
Sweetbriar Rd *LEIE* LE5........... **35** E2
Swift Cl *RLEINE/SYS* LE7......... **4** C5
Swift Wy *LUTT* LE17............... **85** C2
Swindale Cl *LEIS* LE2.............. **2** D7
Swinford Av *LEIE* LE5.............. **28** B4
Swinford La *LUTT* LE17............ **85** H5
Swinstead Rd *LEIN* LE4............ **27** H1
Swithland Av *LEIN* LE4............ **26** A1
Swithland Cl *COAL* LE67........... **6** C4
Sword Cl *LEIW* LE3.................. **34** A3
Sybil Rd *LEIW* LE3.................. **34** D4
Sycamore Cl *RLEINE/SYS* LE7... **28** C3
 LEIS LE2........................... **48** C5
 RLEINE/SYS LE7................... **13** F2

Sycamore Dr *GBY/RBY* LE6....... **16** B5
 LUTT LE17......................... **85** E3
Sycamore Gv *GBY/RBY* LE6...... **16** B4
Sycamore La *LEIN* LE4............. **11** C4
Sycamore Rd *RLEIS/BBY* LE8.... **56** B3
Sycamore Wy
 END/NAR LE19................... **54** D5
Sykefield Av *LEIW* LE3............ **35** E1
Sylvan Av *LEIE* LE5................. **27** F4
Sylvan St *LEIW* LE3................. **25** C4
Sylvan Wy *LEIW* LE3............... **33** F1
Symington Wy
 MKTHBORO LE16................. **81** H1
Syston Rd *RLEINE/SYS* LE7...... **4** C2
Syston St East *LEI* LE1............ **26** D5
Syston St West *LEI* LE1........... **26** C2
Sywell Dr *WGSTN* LE18............ **58** C1

T

Tadcaster Av *LEIS* LE2............ **44** D3
Tailby Av *LUTT* LE17............... **27** C2
Talbot La *LEI* LE1................... **2** C4
Talbot St *LEIN* LE4.................. **19** C4
Talbott Cl *RLEIW/BAR* LE9........ **74** C5
Talbot Wd *MKTHBORO* LE16..... **81** H1
Tamar Rd *LEIN* LE4................. **18** C2
 LEIS LE2........................... **47** H3
Tamerton Rd *LEIS* LE2............ **45** E3
Tansey Av *WGSTN* LE18........... **57** G2
Tansley Av *WGSTN* LE18........... **58** D3
Tarbat Rd *LEIE* LE5................. **28** C5
Tarragon Rd *LEIE* LE5............. **21** G5
Tatlow Rd *LEIN* LE4................. **24** A4
Tatton Cl *LEIW* LE3................. **25** E1
Taunton Cl *WGSTN* LE18.......... **58** A2
Taunton Rd *LEIN* LE4............... **34** D1
Taurus Cl *LEIS* LE2................. **3** K4
Taverner Dr *GBY/RBY* LE6........ **22** D3
Taverners Rd *LEIN* LE4............ **10** C5
Tavistock Dr *LEIE* LE5............. **37** F2
Taylor Cl *RLEINE/SYS* LE7........ **13** E1
Taylor Rd *LEI* LE1.................. **26** C3
Taylor's Bridge Rd
 WGSTN LE18...................... **57** G2
Taylors Cl *RLEIW/BAR* LE9....... **62** B4
Teal Cl *WGSTN* LE18 *............. **32** C3
Teasel Cl *END/NAR* LE19......... **54** C5
Tebbs Cl *RLEIS/BBY* LE8......... **66** C2
Tedder Cl *LUTT* LE17............... **85** E4
Tedworth Gn *LEIN* LE4............ **18** D2
Teignmouth Cl *LEIE* LE5.......... **37** F2
Telford Wy *LEIE* LE5................ **29** F1
Temple Rd *LEIN* LE4................ **19** F4
Tempie St *LEIN* LE4................. **27** C5
Tendring Dr *WGSTN* LE18......... **46** D5
Tennis Court Dr *LEIE* LE5......... **28** A3
Tennyson Rd *LUTT* LE17.......... **85** C2
Tennyson St *END/NAR* LE19..... **54** C2
 LEIS LE2........................... **36** C1
Tentercroft Av
 RLEINE/SYS LE7................... **5** F5
Tetuan Rd *LEIW* LE3............... **25** G4
Tewkesbury St *LEIW* LE3.......... **2** A3
Thackeray St *LEIS* LE2............ **35** H4
Thames St *LEI* LE1.................. **2** C2
Thatcher Cl *LEIN* LE4.............. **18** B3
Thatchers' Cnr
 RLEINE/SYS LE7................... **5** G2
Thatch Meadow Dr
 MKTHBORO LE16................. **82** C1
Theddingworth Rd
 MKTHBORO LE16................. **80** A2
Thirlmere Rd *WGSTN* LE18....... **46** C5
Thirlmere St *LEIS* LE2............. **35** G2
Thistle Cl *END/NAR* LE19......... **54** C3
 RLEINE/SYS LE7................... **9** H2
Thistley Cl *LEIW* LE3............... **33** C3
Thomas Cl *LEIW* LE3............... **34** C5
Thomasson Rd *LEIE* LE5.......... **28** B4
Thomson Cl *LEIN* LE4.............. **20** B1
Thoresby St *LEIN* LE4.............. **27** G4
Thornborough Cl
 RLEINE/SYS LE7................... **54** B4
 MKTHBORO LE16................. **82** B2
Thornby Gdns *WGSTN* LE18...... **58** C1
Thorndale Rd *LEIN* LE4............ **12** D5
Thorneycroft Cl
 RLEINE/SYS LE7................... **74** D5
Thornfield Sq *LEIN* LE4............ **54** B1
Thornhills Gv *END/NAR* LE19.... **54** A1
Thornholme Cl *LEIE* LE5........... **18** C3
Thornton Cl *LEIW* LE3............. **33** H2
 RLEINE/SYS LE7................... **74** C5
Thornton La *COAL* LE67........... **17** C5
Thorntree Cl *LEIW* LE3............ **17** C5
Thornville Cl *LEIN* LE4............. **27** C1
Thorpe Dr *WGSTN* LE18........... **46** B4
Thorpe Field Dr *LEIN* LE4......... **12** C4
Thorpe St *LEIW* LE3................ **13** H5
Thorpe St *LEIW* LE3................ **2** D5
Thorpe Wy *END/NAR* LE19....... **43** F4
Thorpewell *LEIE* LE5............... **27** H4
Threadgold Cl *LEIN* LE4........... **18** B1
Thurcaston Rd *LEIN* LE4.......... **10** D5
Thurcroft Cl *LEIS* LE2.............. **44** D5
Thurlaston La
 RLEIW/BAR LE9................... **41** H4
 RLEIW/BAR LE9................... **51** H2
Thurlby Rd *LEIE* LE5............... **27** F3
Thurlington Rd *LEIW* LE3......... **34** B5
Thurlow Cl *LEIE* LE5................ **28** D2
Thurlow Rd *LEIS* LE2............... **36** A4
Thurmaston Bvd *LEIN* LE4........ **12** D4
Thurmaston La *LEIE* LE5.......... **28** A1
Thurnby Hl *LEIE* LE5............... **38** C4
Thurnby La *LEIE* LE5............... **38** C4
Thurncourt Cl *LEIE* LE5............ **28** C3

Thurncourt Gdns *LEIE* LE5....... **29** F3
Thurncourt Rd *LEIE* LE5........... **28** C3
Thurnview Rd *LEIE* LE5............ **38** A2
Thyme Cl *LEIS* LE2.................. **2** B7
Tiber Wy *END/NAR* LE19.......... **33** H5
Tichborne St *LEIS* LE2............. **3** K3
Tigers Cl *WGSTN* LE18............ **57** E1
Tigers Rd *WGSTN* LE18............ **57** E1
Tigers Wy *LEI* LE1................... **36** A2
Tilbury Crs *LEIN* LE4............... **21** F2
Tilford Crs *LEIE* LE5................ **28** C5
Tillett Rd *LEIS* LE3.................. **33** H3
Tilley Cl *LEIW* LE3.................. **33** H4
Tillingham Rd *LEIE* LE5............ **27** H2
Tilling Rd *LEIN* LE4................. **18** C3
Tilton Dr *LEIS* LE2.................. **47** E5
Timber St *WGSTN* LE18........... **57** F2
Timberwood Dr
 GBY/RBY LE6...................... **16** A5
Timson Cl *MKTHBORO* LE16..... **78** B4
Tinker's Dell *RLEINE/SYS* LE7... **5** C1
Tiptree Cl *LEIN* LE4................. **18** D5
Tithe St *LEIE* LE5................... **27** C5
Tophall Dr *RLEIS/BBY* LE8........ **67** E3
Torch Wy *MKTHBORO* LE16...... **82** A4
Torcross Cl *LEIW* LE3.............. **24** C2
Toronto Cl *LEI* LE1.................. **3** H1
Torridon Cl *LEIN* LE4............... **18** D4
Torrington Cl *WGSTN* LE18....... **58** B3
Totland Rd *LEIN* LE4............... **25** G2
Tournament Rd *LEIW* LE3......... **23** E5
Tovey Crs *LEIS* LE2................. **44** D4
Tower Ct *MKTHBORO* LE16....... **80** C1
Tower Rd *RLEIW/BAR* LE9........ **51** F2
Towers Cl *LEIW* LE3................ **32** C1
Towers Dr *RLEIW/BAR* LE9....... **32** C1
Towie Cl *LEIW* LE3 *............... **24** C2
Townend Rd *RLEIW/BAR* LE9.... **50** A4
Townsend Cl *LEIN* LE4............. **20** B2
 RLEIW/BAR LE9................... **74** D4
Townsend Rd *END/NAR* LE19... **42** C5
Towpath Link *WGSTN* LE18....... **57** G5
Trafalgar Wy *LEIS* LE2............. **56** D2
Trafford Rd *LEIW* LE3.............. **27** H3
Tranter Pl *LEIN* LE4................. **20** B5
Treasure Cl *LEIW* LE3.............. **24** A3
Treaty Rd *LEIW* LE3................. **23** E5
Tredington Rd *LEIN* LE4........... **24** B1
Treetops Cl *LEIE* LE5............... **28** A3
Trefoil Cl *LEIS* LE2.................. **21** G5
 RLEIW/BAR LE9................... **74** D5
Tremaine Dr *WGSTN* LE18........ **58** A2
Tremant Rd *LEIS* LE2.............. **44** D5
Trent Av *LEIN* LE4................... **10** C5
Trent Cl *LEIS* LE2.................... **47** H3
 RLEIW/BAR LE9................... **74** C3
Trescoe Ri *LEIW* LE3............... **24** C5
Tressell Wy *LEIW* LE3.............. **33** H5
Trevanth Rd *LEIN* LE4............. **20** B2
Trevino Dr *LEIN* LE4................ **20** B2
Trevose Gdns *LEIE* LE5............ **28** D3
Trigo Cl *LEIN* LE4................... **18** A3
Trillium Cl *LEIE* LE5................ **21** G4
Trinity Cl *RLEINE/SYS* LE7....... **13** F1
Trinity La *LEI* LE1.................... **2** B5
Trinity Rd *END/NAR* LE19........ **55** C1
Tristram Cl *LEIW* LE3............... **33** E3
Triumph Rd *LEIW* LE3.............. **24** A3
Trojan Wy *RLEINE/SYS* LE7...... **12** C2
Troon Wy *LEIW* LE3................ **37** E5
Truro Cl *WGSTN* LE18.............. **58** B2
Truro St *WGSTN* LE18............. **57** E3
Tuckey Cl *RLEIW/BAR* LE9....... **72** B1
Tudor Cl *LEIW* LE3.................. **2** A1
Tudor Dr *LEIS* LE2.................. **47** F2
Tudor Gv *GBY/RBY* LE6........... **23** E1
Tudor Rd *LEIW* LE3................. **2** A1
Tuffleys Wy *LEIW* LE3.............. **33** C4
Tungstone Wy
 MKTHBORO LE16................. **81** H3
Tunstall Crs *LEIS* LE2.............. **34** B5
Turnbull Dr *LEIW* LE3.............. **34** A3
Tunbury Wy *LEIE* LE5.............. **37** E5
Turner Rd *LEIS* LE2................. **47** H4
Turner St *LEI* LE1................... **3** F7
Turnpike Cl *LUTT* LE17............ **85** H1
 MKTHBORO LE16................. **78** B4
Turnpike Wy *COAL* LE67.......... **6** C4
Turnstone Wk *LEIE* LE5 *......... **27** E4
Turn St *RLEINE/SYS* LE7......... **4** D5
Turville Cl *WGSTN* LE18........... **58** C3
Turville Rd *LEIW* LE3............... **34** D2
Tuskar Rd *LEIE* LE5................. **28** D1
Tuxford Rd *LEIN* LE4............... **21** E4
Twickenham Rd *LEIS* LE2......... **56** C1
Twycross St *LEIS* LE2.............. **36** C1
Tyburn St *LEIS* LE2................. **17** H4
Tyes End *LEIN* LE4.................. **41** H5
Tyler Rd *GBY/RBY* LE6............ **22** D2
Tymecrosse Gdns
 MKTHBORO LE16................. **78** B4
Tyndale St *LEIW* LE3............... **35** E1
Tynedale Cl *LEIS* LE2.............. **47** H3
Tynedale Rd *LEIS* LE2............. **47** H3
Tyringham Rd *WGSTN* LE18...... **58** C1

Tyrrell St *LEIW* LE3................. **2** A2
Tysoe Hl *LEIW* LE3.................. **24** B1
Tythorn Dr *WGSTN* LE18.......... **45** G3

U

Ullswater Dr *RLEIW/BAR* LE9.... **51** F4
Ullswater Dr *LEIS* LE2............. **47** C3
Ullswater St *LEIS* LE2............. **2** C7
Ulverscroft Dr *GBY/RBY* LE6.... **16** B5
Ulverscroft Rd *LEIN* LE4.......... **27** E2
Ulvers Croft Wy *COAL* LE67...... **6** C3
Una Av *LEIW* LE3.................... **34** C5
Underwood Ct *LEIW* LE3.......... **23** H2
Underwood Crs
 RLEIW/BAR LE9................... **72** C1
Underwood Dr
 RLEIW/BAR LE9................... **62** A5
Unicorn St *LEIN* LE4............... **12** G4
Unity Rd *LEIW* LE3.................. **24** A2
University Cl *RLEINE/SYS* LE7... **13** F1
University Rd *LEI* LE1.............. **36** A2
Upex Cl *RLEIS/BBY* LE8........... **65** H2
Upland Cl *COAL* LE67.............. **6** B3
Upland Dr *COAL* LE67.............. **6** B3
Uplands Rd *LEIS* LE2.............. **45** F5
 LEIS LE2........................... **47** F2
Upper Brown St *LEI* LE1.......... **2** E5
Upper Charnwood St
 LEIS LE2........................... **3** K2
Upper Church St
 RLEINE/SYS LE7................... **5** E5
Upper George St *LEI* LE1......... **3** G1
Upper Green Pl
 MKTHBORO LE16................. **78** D2
Upper Hall Cl *LEIE* LE5............ **28** C2
Upper Hall Gdn *LEIE* LE5......... **28** C2
Upper King St *LEI* LE1............. **3** F7
Upper New Wk *LEI* LE1............ **3** J7
Upper Tichborne St *LEIS* LE2.... **3** K6
Upperton Ri *LEIW* LE3............. **34** D1
Upperton Rd *LEIW* LE3............ **35** E1
Uppingham Cl *LEIE* LE5........... **28** C5
Uppingham Dr
 RLEIW/BAR LE9................... **73** H1
Uppingham Rd *LEIE* LE5.......... **27** F3
 RLEINE/SYS LE7................... **58** D1
Upton Dr *WGSTN* LE18............ **58** D1
Utah Cl *LEIW* LE3................... **24** A3
Uttoxeter Cl *LEIN* LE4............. **20** B2
Uxbridge Cl *LEIN* LE4.............. **19** H3

V

Vale Cl *LEIS* LE5.................... **28** C3
Vale End *RLEINE/SYS* LE7........ **29** E5
Valence Rd *LEIW* LE3.............. **34** D1
Valentine Dr *LEIE* LE5............. **46** D2
Valentine Rd *LEIE* LE5............. **28** D5
Valiant Cl *LEIW* LE3................ **24** B3
Valjean Crs *RLEIW/BAR* LE9..... **32** C3
Valley Cl *LEIW* LE3.................. **33** G3
Valley La *LUTT* LE17................ **85** F1
Valley Rd *COAL* LE67............... **6** C4
 LEIS LE2........................... **21** F3
Valley Wy *MKTHBORO* LE16...... **79** F5
Vancouver Rd *LEI* LE1............. **26** C3
Vandyke Rd *LEIS* LE2.............. **47** H4
Vaughan Cl
 MKTHBORO LE16................. **81** H4
Vaughan Rd *LEIS* LE2.............. **45** E1
Vaughan St *LEIW* LE3.............. **2** A3
Vaughan Wy *LEI* LE1............... **2** D3
Vaults St *LEIN* LE4.................. **20** D4
Ventnor Rd *LEIE* LE5............... **46** B1
Ventnor Rd South *LEIS* LE5 *.... **46** B2
Ventnor St *LEIE* LE5 *............. **27** F5
Ventor St *LEIE* LE5................. **27** F5
Verdale Av *LEIN* LE4............... **20** D2
Vernon Rd *LEIS* LE2............... **45** E1
Vernon St *LEIW* LE3................ **2** A3
Vestry St *LEI* LE1.................... **3** G5
Vetch Cl *END/NAR* LE19.......... **54** B3
Vicarage Cl *RLEINE/SYS* LE7.... **5** E5
 RLEIW/BAR LE9................... **23** E3
Vicarage La *LEIE* LE5.............. **28** B2
 LEIN LE4.......................... **19** C4
Vicarage St *LEIN* LE4.............. **54** D3
Vicarage St *RLEIW/BAR* LE9..... **51** F3
Victoria Av *LEIS* LE2............... **3** J7
 MKTHBORO LE16................. **78** B5
Victoria Ct *GBY/RBY* LE6......... **16** B5
Victoria Gdns *LEIS* LE2........... **36** C2
Victoria Pde *LEI* LE1............... **2** C3
Victoria Park Rd *LEIS* LE2........ **36** B3
Victoria Pas *LEI* LE1............... **3** J7
Victoria Rd *RLEIS/BBY* LE8...... **55** H3
Victoria Rd East *LEIE* LE5........ **27** G2
Victoria Rd North *LEIN* LE4...... **19** C4
Victoria St *END/NAR* LE19....... **54** C4
 LEIN LE4.......................... **12** C4
 RLEIS/BBY LE8................... **68** B4
 WGSTN LE18...................... **46** B5
Victor Rd *LEIW* LE3................. **24** B2
Victors Cl *LEIS* LE2................. **44** C4
Viking Rd *WGSTN* LE18............ **45** G4
Villers Ct *RLEIS/BBY* LE8......... **56** B3
Vincent Cl *LEIW* LE3............... **25** F4
Vinehouse Cl
 RLEINE/SYS LE7................... **10** B1
The Vineries *RLEIS/BBY* LE8.... **66** D3
Vine St *LEI* LE1...................... **3** E4
Vislok Cl *MKTHBORO* LE16....... **81** H3
Vitruvius Wy *END/NAR* LE19..... **33** G5
Vostock Cl *LEIS* LE2............... **3** K4
Vulcan Rd *LEIE* LE5................. **3** K1
Vyner Cl *LEIW* LE3.................. **33** G3

W

Wade St LEIN LE4 19 F4
Wadkins Wy RLEINE/SYS LE7 29 G5
Wagtail Cl RLEIS/BBY LE8 68 C5
Wainwright Av LEIE LE5 21 G4
Wakefield Pl LEIN LE4 20 A5
Wakeley Cl END/NAR LE19 54 C4
Wakeling Cl RLEIS/BBY LE8 65 H1
Wakerley Rd LEIE LE5 37 F1
Wakes Cl LUTT LE17 77 F2
Wakes Rd WGSTN LE18 46 B5
Walcote Rd LEIN LE4 20 C5
Walcot Rd MKTHBORO LE16 81 H2
Waldale Dr LEIS LE2 36 C3
Waldron Dr LEIS LE2 47 G3
Wale Rd RLEIS/BBY LE8 55 H4
Wales Orch LUTT LE17 76 A3
Walker Cl RLEIW/BAR LE9 * 74 C5
Walker Manor Ct LUTT LE17 85 H3
Walker Rd LEIN LE4 19 F1
Walkers Wy RLEINE/SYS LE7 5 E5
Wallace Dr GBY/RBY LE6 15 G2
Wallingford Rd LEIN LE4 19 F5
Wallis Cl RLEINE/SYS LE7 10 B1
Walnut Av LEIN LE4 11 F4
Walnut Cl COAL LE67 6 B4
LEIS LE2 47 E3
RLEIW/BAR LE9 74 B3
Walnut Gv LEIS LE2 44 B4
Walnut Leys RLEIW/BAR LE9 65 F4
Walnut St LEIS LE2 35 G2
Walnut Wy RLEIS/BBY LE8 56 B5
Walpole Ct LEIW LE3 24 D5
Walsgrave Av LEIE LE5 28 D5
Walshe Rd LEIE LE5 28 B4
Walsingham Crs LEIW LE3 33 F2
Waltham Av LEIW LE3 34 C3
Walton Cl RLEIW/BAR LE9 32 D1
Walton St LEIW LE3 35 E2
Wand St LEIN LE4 26 C1
Wanlip Av LEIN LE4 11 G5
Wanlip La LEIN LE4 11 H5
Wanlip Rd RLEINE/SYS LE7 12 B1
Wanlip St LEI LE1 26 C3
Wansbeck Gdns LEIE LE5 28 C2
Wanstead Rd LEIW LE3 23 G5
Ward Cl LEIS LE2 44 C1
Wardens Wk LEIW LE3 33 F2
Wards Closes WGSTN LE18 58 C3
Wareham Rd RLEIS/BBY LE8 56 B5
Warmsley Av WGSTN LE18 46 A4
Warner Cl COAL LE67 6 B3
RLEIS/BBY LE8 66 A1
Warren Av LEIN LE4 21 E2
Warren Cl COAL LE67 6 C4
LEIE LE5 28 A2
Warren Dr LEIN LE4 21 E2
Warren La LEIW LE3 32 C3
Warren Park Wy
END/NAR LE19 42 C3
Warren Rd END/NAR LE19 55 F2
Warren St LEIW LE3 2 A3
The Warren RLEINE/SYS LE7 5 F2
Warren Vw LEIN LE4 21 E2
Warrington Dr GBY/RBY LE6 16 A5
Wartnaby St
MKTHBORO LE16 81 F1
Warwick Cl MKTHBORO LE16 78 D4
RLEIW/BAR LE9 30 A3
Warwick Rd END/NAR LE19 55 F5
RLEIS/BBY LE8 55 G5
RLEIS/BBY LE8 69 F3
RLEIW/BAR LE9 73 H1
WGSTN LE18 45 H5
Warwick St LEIW LE3 2 A3
Washbrook La LEIS LE2 46 D4
RLEIS/BBY LE8 61 G2
Washington Cl
RLEIW/BAR LE9 50 A5
Watchcrete Av
RLEINE/SYS LE7 5 G4
Waterfield Cl LEIE LE5 28 B5
Waterfield Pl
MKTHBORO LE16 * 78 D4
Waterfield Rd
RLEINE/SYS LE7 9 H2
Watergate RLEINE/SYS LE7 5 H2
Watergate La END/NAR LE19 43 F1
Waterloo Crs RLEIS/BBY LE8 66 D3
WGSTN LE18 46 C4
Waterloo Wy LEI LE1 3 G7
Watermead Wy LEIN LE4 19 H3
Waterside Rd LEIE LE5 21 E3
Waterville Cl LEIW LE3 24 A4
Watery Gate La
RLEIW/BAR LE9 52 C3
Watkin Rd LEIS LE2 35 F2
Watling St LEI LE1 26 B3
Watson Av MKTHBORO LE16 81 F3
Watson Rd LEIN LE4 20 A5
Watts Cl LEIN LE4 18 A4
Waudby Cl END/NAR LE19 55 E5
Waveney Ri LEIS LE2 47 H2
Waverley Rd RLEIS/BBY LE8 56 C5
WGSTN LE18 57 F1
Wavertree Cl
RLEIW/BAR LE9 65 F2
Wavertree Dr LEIN LE4 19 H4
Wayfarer Dr RLEINE/SYS LE7 5 H1
The Wayne Wy LEIE LE5 27 H4
LEIN LE4 11 G5
Wayside Dr LEIN LE4 20 B1
LEIS LE2 47 G3
Weake Cl RLEINE/SYS LE7 5 E5
Weaver Rd LEIE LE5 28 D3
RLEIW/BAR LE9 51 F3
Webb Cl LEIW LE3 33 F3
Webbs Wy RLEIW/BAR LE9 62 B4
Webster Rd LEIW LE3 34 A1
Weir Cl WGSTN LE18 57 H3
Weir Rd RLEIS/BBY LE8 70 A4
Welbeck Av LEIN LE4 19 E5
Welbeck Cl RLEIS/BBY LE8 56 C5
Welcombe Av LEIW LE3 34 B4
Weldon Rd WGSTN LE18 46 B5
Welford Ct LEIS LE2 45 H1
Welford Pl LEI LE1 2 E5
Welford Rd LEIS LE2 3 F6
RLEIS/BBY LE8 56 B3
WGSTN LE18 58 B2
Welham Rd
MKTHBORO LE16 79 E2
Welland Ct
MKTHBORO LE16 79 E5
Welland Park Rd
MKTHBORO LE16 81 G2
Welland St LEIS LE2 3 K6
Welland Vale Rd LEIE LE5 38 B1
Wellesbourne Dr LEIW LE3 24 B1
Welles St LEIW LE3 2 C4
Wellgate Av LEIN LE4 11 F4
Wellhouse Cl WGSTN LE18 58 A3
Wellinger Wy LEIW LE3 34 A1
Wellington Cl LEIW LE3 33 G3
Wellington Pkwy LUTT LE17 84 A4
Wellington St LEI LE1 3 F5
RLEINE/SYS LE7 13 E1
Well Spring Hl WGSTN LE18 58 C3
Welton Cl RLEIS/BBY LE8 69 H3
Wembley Rd LEIW LE3 23 H5
Wendys Cl LEIE LE5 28 D3
Wenlock Wy LEIN LE4 21 E4
Wensleydale Rd
WGSTN LE18 58 D2
Wensley Ri LEIS LE2 56 C1
Wentbridge Rd LEIN LE4 20 B4
Went Rd LEIN LE4 19 G1
Wentworth Cl
RLEIS/BBY LE8 70 B4
Wentworth Gn
RLEIW/BAR LE9 32 B1
Wentworth Rd LEIW LE3 25 G4
RLEIS/BBY LE8 68 C4
Wesley Cl GBY/RBY LE6 22 C2
RLEIW/BAR LE9 72 C2
Wesley St LEIN LE4 19 F4
Wesley Wy COAL LE67 6 C4
Wessex Dr LEIW LE3 24 C5
West Av LEIS LE2 36 B3
WGSTN LE18 45 H5
Westbourne St LEIN LE4 26 C2
West Br LEIW LE3 2 C4
Westbridge Cl LEIW LE3 2 C5
Westbury Rd LEIS LE2 36 A4
Westcotes Dr LEIW LE3 25 G5
West Ct MKTHBORO LE16 82 B3
Westdale Av LEIS LE2 56 A1
Westdown Dr LEIN LE4 20 C2
West Dr LEIE LE5 28 A2
Westerby Cl WGSTN LE18 46 B4
Westerby La RLEIS/BBY LE8 69 H5
Westerdale Rd WGSTN LE18 58 D1
Western Av MKTHBORO LE16 81 G3
RLEIS/BBY LE8 68 B5
Western Bvd LEIS LE2 2 C7
Western Dr RLEIS/BBY LE8 56 B4
Westernhay Rd LEIS LE2 36 C4
Western Park Rd LEIW LE3 25 E5
Western Rd LEIW LE3 2 B6
Westfield Av RLEIS/BBY LE8 66 C2
WGSTN LE18 45 H4
Westfield Cl
MKTHBORO LE16 81 F1
Westfield Rd LEIW LE3 25 E5
Westgate Av LEIN LE4 11 E4
Westgate La
MKTHBORO LE16 80 B1
Westgate Rd LEIS LE2 45 H2
Westhill Rd LEIW LE3 25 E4
West Holme St LEIW LE3 2 A5
Westland Cl
MKTHBORO LE16 80 B1
West Langton Rd
RLEIS/BBY LE8 71 E4
Westleigh Av LEIW LE3 35 E2
Westleigh Rd LEIS LE2 57 E2
LEIW LE3 35 E2
Westmeath Av LEIE LE5 28 B4
Westminster Dr LEIS LE2 56 D2
Westminster Rd LEIS LE2 37 E4
Westmorland Av LEIN LE4 20 A5
WGSTN LE18 57 F1
Weston Cl LEIS LE2 48 A4
Westover Rd LEIW LE3 33 H3
West St END/NAR LE19 54 C1
LEI LE1 3 F7
LEIW LE3 17 E5
RLEINE/SYS LE7 4 D5
RLEIS/BBY LE8 56 A2
RLEIW/BAR LE9 51 F2
West View Av LEIS LE2 44 B5
West Wk LEI LE1 3 H7
Wetherby Cl RLEINE/SYS LE7 5 G3
Wetherby Rd LEIN LE4 20 B4
Wexford Cl LEIS LE2 47 H4
Weymouth Cl WGSTN LE18 58 B3
Weymouth St LEIN LE4 26 D2
Wharf St LEIN LE4 12 B4
Wharf St North LEI LE1 3 G1
Wharf St South LEI LE1 3 G2
Wharf Wy LEIS LE2 56 B1
Wheatfield Cl LEIW LE3 24 A3
Wheatland Cl LEIS LE2 47 H3
Wheatland Rd LEIN LE4 18 D2
Wheatlands Dr
RLEIS/BBY LE8 66 D2
Wheatley Rd LEIN LE4 18 D3
Wheatley's Rd LEIN LE4 20 B1
Wheat St LEI LE1 3 G2
Wheeldale WGSTN LE18 58 D1
Wheeler Cl LUTT LE17 85 G4
Whetstone Gorse La
RLEIS/BBY LE8 66 A4
Whiles La LEIN LE4 11 H5
Whinchat Rd LEIE LE5 27 E4
Whinham Av RLEIW/BAR LE9 73 H2
Whitby Cl RLEIW/BAR LE9 74 A1
Whitcroft Cl COAL LE67 6 C4
Whiteacres RLEIS/BBY LE8 65 G1
White Barn Dr
RLEIW/BAR LE9 65 F3
Whitebeam Cl
END/NAR LE19 54 C3
Whitebeam Rd LEIS LE2 47 E1
White Cl RLEIW/BAR LE9 74 C3
Whitefield Rd LEIN LE4 19 F4
Whitegates Fld WGSTN LE18 58 C2
Whitehall Rd LEIE LE5 37 H1
Whitehead Crs WGSTN LE18 45 H5
White Horse La LEIN LE4 19 H1
White House Cl
GBY/RBY LE6 16 A4
LUTT LE17 76 A2
Whiteoaks Rd LEIS LE2 47 G5
Whitesand Cl LEIW LE3 24 B1
White St RLEIS/BBY LE8 69 H3
Whitley Cl LEIW LE3 25 F2
Whitman Cl LEIW LE3 24 B4
Whitteney Dr LEIS LE2 44 D4
Whittier Rd LEIS LE2 45 F1
Whittington Dr
GBY/RBY LE6 22 C1
Whittington Rd LEIW LE3 17 H4
Whittle Cl RLEIS/BBY LE8 55 H5
Whittle Rd LUTT LE17 85 F4
Whitwell Rw LEIS LE2 45 E3
Whitwick Rd COAL LE67 6 B1
Whitwick Wy LEIW LE3 25 G2
Wicken Ri WGSTN LE18 46 C4
Wickham Rd LEIS LE2 47 F4
Wicklow Dr LEIE LE5 28 A4
Wiclifway LUTT LE17 85 G2
Widford Cl LEIE LE5 28 A2
Wightman Cl
RLEIW/BAR LE9 62 B3
Wightman Rd
RLEIW/BAR LE9 50 C4
Wigley Rd LEIE LE5 28 C2
Wigston La LEIS LE2 44 D2
Wigston Rd LEIS LE2 46 D4
RLEIS/BBY LE8 56 B3
Wigston St LEI LE1 3 G4
RLEIS/BBY LE8 67 F2
Wilberforce Rd LEIW LE3 35 F2
Wileman's Cl RLEIW/BAR LE9 51 E5
Wiley Wy LEI LE1 3 F7
Wilf Brown Cl
RLEIW/BAR LE9 51 G3
Wilkes Wy RLEINE/SYS LE7 12 D2
Wilkinson La RLEIW/BAR LE9 51 E5
William Cl RLEINE/SYS LE7 5 H3
Williams Cl END/NAR LE19 54 D5
William St END/NAR LE19 54 D4
LEI LE1 3 H3
Willoughby Gdns LEIW LE3 33 E2
Willoughby Rd
RLEIS/BBY LE8 66 C3
Willow Brook Cl LEIW LE3 17 E5
Willowbrook Cl
RLEINE/SYS LE7 5 H3
RLEIW/BAR LE9 74 B2
Willow Brook Rd LEIE LE5 27 E3
Willowbrook Vw LEIE LE5 29 E4
Willowbrook Wy
RLEINE/SYS LE7 5 H2
Willow Cl END/NAR LE19 55 E5
Willow Ct LEIS LE2 3 J5
Willow Crs MKTHBORO LE16 81 F2
Willowdene Wy
RLEIW/BAR LE9 50 B5
Willow Dr GBY/RBY LE6 23 E1
RLEIS/BBY LE8 67 E2
Willow Herb Cl LEIS LE2 48 A4
Willow Park Dr WGSTN LE18 46 A5
Willow Pl WGSTN LE18 58 B1
Willow Rd RLEIS/BBY LE8 56 B4
Willow St LEI LE1 26 C3
RLEIW/BAR LE9 30 A2
Willowtree Cl LEIE LE5 21 G5
Willow Tree Cl
RLEIW/BAR LE9 50 B3
Willow Tree Crs LUTT LE17 85 E3
Willow Wk RLEINE/SYS LE7 12 D1
Willsmer Cl RLEIW/BAR LE9 74 C4
Willson Cl MKTHBORO LE16 82 B1
Wilmington Ct LEIS LE2 37 E5
Wilmington Rd LEIW LE3 34 D2
Wilmore Crs LEIW LE3 33 H2
Wilne St LEIS LE2 36 C1
Wilnicott Rd LEIW LE3 34 B4
Wilsford Cl WGSTN LE18 58 A3
Wilshere Cl RLEIW/BAR LE9 22 D5
Wilson Cl LEIW LE3 33 H3
Wilson Rd WGSTN LE18 57 E2
Wilson St LEIS LE2 27 E5
Wilton St LEI LE1 3 F1
Wiltshire Rd LEIN LE4 18 D5
WGSTN LE18 45 H5
Wimbledon St LEI LE1 3 G3
Wimborne Cl WGSTN LE18 58 A2
Wimborne Rd LEIS LE2 46 B2
Winchendon Cl LEIE LE5 27 G3
Winchester Av LEIW LE3 34 D2
RLEIS/BBY LE8 56 A2
Winchester Rd
RLEIS/BBY LE8 66 C2
Windermere Cl
RLEIW/BAR LE9 51 F3
Windermere Dr
RLEIW/BAR LE9 63 H2
Windermere Rd
WGSTN LE18 46 D5
Windermere St LEIS LE2 35 G2
Winder's Wy LEIS LE2 44 D3
Windley Rd LEIS LE2 45 F2
Windmill Av LEIN LE4 11 H4
Windmill Bank WGSTN LE18 58 C2
Windmill Cl GBY/RBY LE6 22 D2
LEIN LE4 12 D4
Windmill Gdns
RLEIS/BBY LE8 70 A1
Windmill Ri GBY/RBY LE6 16 A4
Windrush Dr LEIS LE2 47 H3
Windsor Av GBY/RBY LE6 16 A5
LEIN LE4 19 H5
LEIS LE2 57 E2
Windsor Cl LEIS LE2 47 G5
Winforde Crs LEIW LE3 33 H1
Wingfield St LEIN LE4 19 H5
Winifred St LEIS LE2 2 D7
Winslow Dr WGSTN LE18 46 C4
Winslow Gn LEIE LE5 28 C2
Winstanley Dr LEIW LE3 34 B1
Winster Dr LEIN LE4 12 C4
Winston Av RLEIW/BAR LE9 63 H2
Winterburn Gdns
RLEIS/BBY LE8 55 H4
Winterfield Cl LEIW LE3 23 H3
Wintergreen Cl LEIE LE5 21 G4
Wintersdale Rd LEIE LE5 28 C4
Winterton Cl LEIN LE4 12 D4
Winton Av LEIW LE3 34 D3
Wistow Rd RLEIS/BBY LE8 59 H5
RLEIS/BBY LE8 69 F1
WGSTN LE18 58 B2
Withcote Av LEIE LE5 28 C5
Withens Cl LEIW LE3 25 E3
Witherdell LEIN LE4 18 A4
Withers Wy END/NAR LE19 33 H4
LEIW LE3 33 H3
Withington Cl LEIW LE3 33 H3
Woburn Cl LEIS LE2 44 C4
MKTHBORO LE16 82 B1
WGSTN LE18 58 C1
Wodehouse Rd LEIW LE3 34 C1
Wokingham Av LEIS LE2 56 D1
The Wolds RLEINE/SYS LE7 5 H1
Wollaton Cl LEIW LE3 23 H2
Wolsey Cl GBY/RBY LE6 16 A5
LEIW LE3 32 D3
RLEIS/BBY LE8 68 B3
Wolsey Dr GBY/RBY LE6 22 B1
Wolsey La RLEIS/BBY LE8 68 B3
Wolsey St LEIN LE4 26 A2
Wolsey Wy RLEINE/SYS LE7 12 D1
Wolverton Rd LEIW LE3 35 E3
Woodbank LEIS LE2 56 B1
Woodbank Rd GBY/RBY LE6 15 H4
LEIS LE2 46 A2
Woodbine Av LEIS LE2 3 K7
Woodbine Crs LUTT LE17 85 G4
Woodborough Rd LEIE LE5 37 G1
Woodboy St LEI LE1 26 C3
Woodbreach Dr
MKTHBORO LE16 82 C1
Wood Br LUTT LE17 84 D4
Woodbridge Rd LEIN LE4 19 H4
Woodbury Ri RLEIS/BBY LE8 61 E2
Woodby La LUTT LE17 84 D1
Woodcote Rd LEIW LE3 43 G1
Woodcroft Av LEIS LE2 45 G2
Wood End LEIW LE3 25 E3
Woodfield Cl END/NAR LE19 54 D3
Woodfield Rd LEIS LE2 47 F1
Woodford Cl WGSTN LE18 58 A3
Woodford Rd LEIS LE2 35 F2
Woodgate LEIW LE3 25 H3
Woodgate Cl
MKTHBORO LE16 82 C2
Woodgate Dr LEIN LE4 11 F4
Woodgon Rd
RLEINE/SYS LE7 17 F1
Woodgreen Rd LEIN LE4 27 F1
Woodgreen Wk LEIN LE4 27 F1
Woodhall Cl LEIW LE3 24 B5
Wood Hl LEIE LE5 27 E4
Woodhouse Cl COAL LE67 6 C3
Woodhouse Rd
END/NAR LE19 54 B4
Woodland Av END/NAR LE19 54 D3
LEIS LE2 36 C4
Woodland Cl COAL LE67 6 C4
Woodland Dr LEIW LE3 33 H3
Woodland Rd LEIE LE5 27 F3
Woodlands Ct LEIS LE2 48 A4
Woodlands Dr GBY/RBY LE6 15 H3
Woodlands La
RLEIW/BAR LE9 23 E4
The Woodlands
MKTHBORO LE16 78 A5
RLEIS/BBY LE8 66 D2
WGSTN LE18 46 D4
Woodlea Av LUTT LE17 85 E3
Woodley Rd GBY/RBY LE6 22 C2
Woodman's Cha
RLEINE/SYS LE7 5 G2
Woodmarket LUTT LE17 85 G4
Woodnewton Dr LEIE LE5 38 B1
Woodpecker Cl LEIW LE3 32 C3
Woods Cl LEIS LE2 47 G2
Woodshawe Ri LEIW LE3 34 A2
Woodside Cl END/NAR LE19 54 B3
LEIN LE4 27 F1
Woodside Rd LEIS LE2 47 H5
Woodstock Cl LEIN LE4 19 E3
Woodstock Rd LEIN LE4 19 E3
Wood St LEI LE1 3 F1
RLEIW/BAR LE9 51 E3
Woodville Gdns WGSTN LE18 46 A3
Woodville Rd LEIW LE3 25 F5
Woodway Rd LUTT LE17 85 F4
Woodyard La RLEIS/BBY LE8 55 H3
Wooldale Cl RLEINE/SYS LE7 9 G5
Wootton Cl RLEIS/BBY LE8 55 H5
Wootton Ri LEIS LE2 44 D3
Worcester Av LEIN LE4 11 H3
Worcester Cl RLEIW/BAR LE9 50 A4
Worcester Dr
MKTHBORO LE16 78 C4
WGSTN LE18 57 F1
Worcester Rd LEIS LE2 44 D1
Wordsworth Crs
END/NAR LE19 54 C2
Wordsworth Rd LEIS LE2 36 A4
Worrall Cl LEIW LE3 33 H1
Worrall Rd LEIW LE3 33 H1
Worsh Cl RLEIS/BBY LE8 65 H1
Worsley Wy RLEIS/BBY LE8 56 A5
Worthington St LEIS LE2 27 E5
The Wranglands
RLEIS/BBY LE8 68 C4
Wreake Rd LEIN LE4 12 C4
Wreford Crs LEIE LE5 29 E3
Wren Cl LEIS LE2 45 E1
RLEINE/SYS LE7 4 B5
Wright Cl RLEIS/BBY LE8 65 H2
Wright La LEIS LE2 47 H4
Wroxall Wy LEIW LE3 25 G2
Wyatt Cl LEIW LE3 33 G1
Wych Elm Cl RLEIS/BBY LE8 60 D2
Wych Elm Rd LEIS LE2 47 E1
Wychwood Rd
RLEIS/BBY LE8 66 A1
Wycliffe St LEI LE1 2 E4
Wycombe Rd LEIE LE5 27 G2
Wye Dean Dr WGSTN LE18 58 B1
Wykeham Cl RLEIS/BBY LE8 56 B5
Wylam Cl LEIW LE3 25 E2
Wymar Cl LEIN LE4 18 C4
Wyndale Dr RLEINE/SYS LE7 5 E4
Wyndale Rd LEIS LE2 45 H1
Wyndham Cl LEIS LE2 47 G1
Wynfield Rd LEIW LE3 25 F5
Wyngate Dr LEIW LE3 25 F5
Wynthorpe Ri LEIW LE3 34 C1
Wynton Cl RLEIS/BBY LE8 56 C5
Wyvern Av LEIN LE4 20 B4
Wyvern Cl RLEIW/BAR LE9 * 74 C4
Wyville Rw LEIW LE3 34 C4

Y

Yardley Dr WGSTN LE18 45 H3
Yarmouth St LEI LE1 3 F1
Yarrow Cl LEIE LE5 28 C1
Yarwell Dr WGSTN LE18 58 C1
Yaxley Cl RLEINE/SYS LE7 29 F4
Yeats Cl LEIW LE3 33 H4
Yelverton Av LEIE LE5 38 A2
Yeoman La LEI LE1 3 F3
Yeomanry Ct
MKTHBORO LE16 81 H1
Yeoman's Dl RLEINE/SYS LE7 5 G1
Yeoman St LEI LE1 3 G3
Yew Cl LEIW LE3 32 D4
The Yews LEIS LE2 47 F2
Yew Tree Cl LUTT LE17 85 E3
RLEIW/BAR LE9 50 C3
Yew Tree Dr LEIW LE3 24 A4
York Cl LEIS LE2 57 E2
York Rd LEI LE1 2 E5
Yorkshire Rd LEIN LE4 27 E1
York St LEI LE1 3 F5
MKTHBORO LE16 82 A1
Yukon Wy LEI LE1 3 H1

Abbey Business Park
 LEI LE1 .... 26 A3
Abbey Community
 Primary School
 LEIN LE4 .... 26 C1
Abbey Pumping Station
 LEIN LE4 .... 19 F5
Abington High School
 WGSTN LE18 .... 58 A1
Al Aqsa Primary School
 COAL LE67 .... 6 C5
Alderman Richard Hallam
 Primary School
 LEIN LE4 .... 25 C1
Al-Islamia Primary School
 .... 3 J3
All Saints CE Primary School
 RLEINE/BAR LE9 .... 72 B2
 WGSTN LE18 .... 58 A1
Alpha Tutorials
 LEIN LE4 .... 20 A3
Anstey Nomads FC
 RLEINE/SYS LE7 .... 9 H5
Ashfield School
 LEIE LE5 .... 37 F1
Auster Industrial Estate
 LEIN LE4 .... 20 D1
Avenue Primary School
 LEIS LE2 .... 36 B4
Aylestone Leisure Centre
 LEIS LE2 .... 35 H5
Babington Community
 College
 LEIN LE4 .... 18 B4
Badgerbrook
 Primary School
 RLEIS/BBY LE8 .... 65 H1
Barley Croft
 Primary School
 LEIN LE4 .... 18 C4
Barrington Park
 Industrial Estate
 LEIN LE4 .... 18 B2
Barwell CE Junior School
 RLEIW/BAR LE9 .... 50 A5
Barwell Infant School
 RLEIW/BAR LE9 .... 50 A5
Barwell Medical Centre
 RLEIW/BAR LE9 .... 50 A5
The Beauchamp College
 .... 47 F5
Beaumont Leys
 Health Centre
 LEIN LE4 .... 18 C4
Beaumont Leys School
 LEIN LE4 .... 18 B5
Beaumont Lodge
 Primary School
 LEIN LE4 .... 18 B1
Bede Island Business Park
 LEIS LE2 .... 2 B6
Beedles Lake Golf Centre
 RLEINE/SYS LE7 .... 5 F1
Belgrave Cemetery
 LEIN LE4 .... 19 F3
Belgrave CE Primary School
 LEIN LE4 .... 19 F3
Belgrave Hall & Gardens
 LEIN LE4 .... 19 G4
Belgrave Industrial Centre
 LEIN LE4 .... 19 G5
Belgrave RFC
 LEIN LE4 .... 19 F3
Best Western Belmont
 House Hotel
 LEI LE1 .... 3 H6
Best Western Stage Hotel
 WGSTN LE18 .... 46 A3
Best Western
 Three Swans Hotel
 MKTHBORO LE16 .... 81 H1
Birkett House School
 & Hostel
 WGSTN LE18 .... 58 A1
Birstall Cemetery
 LEIE LE4 .... 11 F5
Birstall Golf Club
 LEIN LE4 .... 19 F2
Bishop Ellis Catholic
 Primary School
 LEIN LE4 .... 12 D4
Blaby Industrial Park
 RLEIS/BBY LE8 .... 56 A2
Bosworth Community
 College
 RLEIW/BAR LE9 .... 30 C2
Bradgate Park
 Country Park
 RLEINE/SYS LE7 .... 8 D1
Braunstone Community
 Primary School
 LEIW LE3 .... 34 A1
Braunstone Frith
 Industrial Estate
 LEIW LE3 .... 23 H5
Braunstone Frith J & I
 School
 LEIW LE3 .... 24 B4
Bridge Business Park
 LEIN LE4 .... 12 B5
Bridge Junior School
 LEIE LE5 .... 27 E3
Brockington College
 END/NAR LE19 .... 55 F1
Brocks Hill Country Park
 WGSTN LE18 .... 47 E5
Brocks Hill Primary School
 LEIS LE2 .... 47 F5
Brooke House College
 MKTHBORO LE16 .... 78 C5
Brooke House Day School
 RLEIW/BAR LE9 .... 65 E4

Brookside Primary School
 LEIS LE2 .... 47 H1
Brookvale High School
 GBY/RBY LE6 .... 15 H5
Broomfield Primary School
 RLEINE/SYS LE7 .... 5 H2
Bushloe High School
 WGSTN LE18 .... 57 H1
BUSM Business Park
 LEIN LE4 .... 26 C1
Buswells Lodge
 Primary School
 LEIN LE4 .... 18 A4
Caldecote Community
 Primary School
 LEIW LE3 .... 34 C4
Campanile Hotel
 LEI LE1 .... 3 G1
Castle Hill Country Park
 LEIN LE4 .... 10 A5
Catherine Infant School
 LEIN LE4 .... 26 D2
Catherine Junior School
 LEIN LE4 .... 26 D2
Catherine Street
 Industrial Estate
 LEIN LE4 .... 20 B5
Charnwood Health Centre
 LEIE LE5 .... 27 E3
Charnwood
 Primary School
 LEIS LE2 .... 3 K2
Chartwell Drive
 Industrial Estate
 WGSTN LE18 .... 45 G5
Christ the King RC
 Primary School
 LEIW LE3 .... 25 F4
Church Hill CE Junior School
 LEIW LE3 .... 12 D5
The City Gallery
 LEI LE1 .... 3 G4
City of Leicester College
 LEIE LE5 .... 38 B1
Clarendon Park
 Medical Centre
 LEIS LE2 .... 36 A4
Clyde Street Medical Centre
 .... 3 H2
Cobden Street
 Industrial Estate
 LEIE LE5 .... 27 E3
Coleman Primary School
 LEIE LE5 .... 37 E1
Cosby Golf Club
 RLEIW/BAR LE9 .... 65 F5
Cosby Primary School
 RLEIW/BAR LE9 .... 65 F2
Cossington Street
 Sports Centre
 LEIN LE4 .... 26 D1
Cottage Lane
 Industrial Estate
 RLEIW/BAR LE9 .... 74 C3
Countesthorpe College
 RLEIS/BBY LE8 .... 66 C2
Croft CE Primary School
 RLEIW/BAR LE9 .... 63 G3
The Croft Medical Centre
 LEIS LE2 .... 47 G4
Cropston Cemetery
 RLEINE/SYS LE7 .... 10 A1
Crown Hills Community
 College
 LEIE LE5 .... 37 F1
Darul Arqam Educational
 Institute
 LEIE LE5 .... 27 F4
Darul Uloom School
 LEIN LE4 .... 19 G5
Days Inn
 LEI LE1 .... 3 F2
 LEI LE1 .... 33 F3
De Montfort Hall
 LEI LE1 .... 36 A2
De Montfort University
 .... 2 D5
Desford Primary School
 RLEIW/BAR LE9 .... 30 A3
Dovelands Primary School
 LEIW LE3 .... 25 F5
Dowry Furlong
 Wildlife Area
 GBY/RBY LE6 .... 16 A3
Dunton Bassett
 Primary School
 LUTT LE17 .... 77 E2
Earls Close Industrial Estate
 LEIN LE4 .... 12 D4
Eastfield Primary School
 LEIN LE4 .... 12 D4
The Elizabeth Woodville
 Primary School
 GBY/RBY LE6 .... 16 A5
Ellesmere College
 LEIW LE3 .... 34 D3
Emily Fortey School
 LEIW LE3 .... 24 D4
Enderby Danemill
 Primary School
 END/NAR LE19 .... 54 D1
Enderby Leisure Centre
 & Golf Club
 END/NAR LE19 .... 54 D1
Enderby Road
 Industrial Estate
 RLEIS/BBY LE8 .... 55 G2
English Martyrs RC School
 LEIW LE3 .... 25 F1
Euro Business Park
 LEI LE1 .... 79 F5
Evington Pool
 LEIE LE5 .... 38 A2

Evington Valley
 Primary School
 LEIE LE5 .... 36 D2
Express by Holiday Inn
 LEIE LE5 .... 35 G2
Eyres Monsell
 Primary School
 LEIS LE2 .... 44 D4
Faircharm Industrial Estate
 LEIE LE5 .... 35 F3
The Fairfield
 Primary School
 WGSTN LE18 .... 45 G5
Farndon Fields
 Primary School
 MKTHBORO LE16 .... 81 H4
Feilding Cottage Hospital
 LUTT LE17 .... 85 H3
Fernvale Primary School
 RLEINE/SYS LE7 .... 29 F4
Field Head Hotel
 COAL LE67 .... 6 D3
Fleckney CE Primary School
 RLEIS/BBY LE8 .... 68 A3
Fleckney Industrial Estate
 LEIE LE5 .... 68 C4
Fleckney Leisure Centre
 RLEIS/BBY LE8 .... 68 B2
Folville Junior School
 LEIW LE3 .... 34 C3
Forest Lodge
 Primary School
 LEIW LE3 .... 24 C2
Fosse Medical Centre
 LEIN LE4 .... 25 G4
Fosse Park Shopping Centre
 END/NAR LE19 .... 43 H3
Fosse Primary School
 LEIN LE4 .... 25 H3
Foxbank Industrial Estate
 RLEIW/BAR LE9 .... 62 B3
Freemens Common
 Trading Estate
 LEIS LE2 .... 35 H3
Friar Lane FC
 LEIS LE2 .... 35 H5
Fullhurst Community
 College
 LEIW LE3 .... 34 D2
Gartree High School
 LEIE LE5 .... 47 F5
Gateway Sixth Form
 College
 LEIS LE2 .... 2 D5
Gilbros Business Centre
 LEI LE1 .... 3 G2
Gilroes Cemetery
 LEIW LE3 .... 18 A5
Gilroes Crematorium
 LEIW LE3 .... 18 A5
Glebelands Primary School
 LEIN LE4 .... 10 C4
Glenfield Hospital
 LEIW LE3 .... 17 G5
Glenfield Primary School
 LEIW LE3 .... 23 H2
Glen Gorse Golf Club
 LEIS LE2 .... 47 H5
Glen Hills Primary School
 LEIS LE2 .... 44 A5
Glenmere Primary School
 WGSTN LE18 .... 46 D5
Gorse Hill Hospital
 RLEINE/SYS LE7 .... 17 H3
Granby Primary School
 LEIS LE2 .... 44 D1
Grange Business Park
 RLEIS/BBY LE8 .... 55 H2
Great Bowden Cemetery
 MKTHBORO LE16 .... 79 F3
Great Bowden CE
 Primary School
 MKTHBORO LE16 .... 79 E3
Great Central Railway
 RLEINE/SYS LE7 .... 10 D2
Greenfield Primary School
 RLEIS/BBY LE8 .... 67 G2
Greengate Medical Centre
 LEIN LE4 .... 11 G4
Green Lane Infant School
 LEIE LE5 .... 27 E3
The Green Surgery
 .... 6 B4
Greyfriars Sports Club
 LEIS LE2 .... 35 G2
Greystoke Primary School
 END/NAR LE19 .... 55 E3
Groby Community College
 GBY/RBY LE6 .... 15 H5
Groby Trade Estate
 GBY/RBY LE6 .... 16 A3
Guthlaxton College
 WGSTN LE18 .... 57 H2
Hallbrook Primary School
 GBY/RBY LE6 .... 74 B5
The Hall Primary School
 LEIW LE3 .... 24 C1
Hamilton Business Park
 LEIE LE5 .... 21 F4
Haramead Business Centre
 LEI LE1 .... 3 H1
Harborough Athletic Club
 MKTHBORO LE16 .... 79 E5
Harborough Leisure Centre
 MKTHBORO LE16 .... 82 A3
Harborough Theatre
 MKTHBORO LE16 .... 81 H1
Haymarket Shopping Centre
 LEI LE1 .... 3 F3
Haymarket Theatre
 LEI LE1 .... 2 E2
Hazel Primary School
 LEIS LE2 .... 35 H2

Heatherbrook
 Primary School
 LEIN LE4 .... 17 H1
Heathfield High School
 RLEIW/BAR LE9 .... 50 C4
Herrick Primary School
 LEIN LE4 .... 20 B3
Highcliffe Primary School
 LEIN LE4 .... 11 F5
Highfield Rangers FC
 LEIN LE4 .... 20 C3
Highfields Primary School
 LEIS LE2 .... 3 K5
Hill Lane Industrial Estate
 COAL LE67 .... 6 A2
HM Prison
 LEIS LE2 .... 3 F7
HM Young Offenders
 Institution & Remand
 Centre (Glen Parva)
 LEIS LE2 .... 56 D1
Holmfield Primary School
 LEIE LE5 .... 33 F2
Holy Cross Catholic
 Primary School
 LEIS LE2 .... 45 F4
Hope Hamilton CE
 Primary School
 LEIE LE5 .... 21 F4
Humberstone Heights
 Golf Club
 LEIE LE5 .... 28 A1
Humberstone Junior School
 LEIE LE5 .... 28 B1
Huncote Cemetery
 RLEIW/BAR LE9 .... 53 H3
Huncote Community
 Primary School
 RLEIW/BAR LE9 .... 53 H3
Huncote Leisure Centre
 RLEIW/BAR LE9 .... 53 G3
Hunters Lodge Medical
 Centre
 LEIN LE4 .... 32 D3
Ibis Hotel
 LEI LE1 .... 3 H4
Imperial Avenue Infant
 School
 LEIW LE3 .... 34 D2
Inglehurst Infant School
 LEIW LE3 .... 25 F3
Inglehurst Junior School
 LEIW LE3 .... 25 F3
Innkeeper's Lodge
 RLEIW/BAR LE9 .... 32 D2
Jewry Wall Museum
 .... 2 C4
John Doran Gas Museum
 LEIS LE2 .... 35 G3
John Wycliffe Primary
 School
 LUTT LE17 .... 85 F4
Judgemeadow Community
 College
 LEIE LE5 .... 38 A2
Kestrels Field Primary
 School
 LEIE LE5 .... 21 H5
Keyham Lodge School
 LEIE LE5 .... 21 H5
Kibworth CC
 RLEIS/BBY LE8 .... 69 G3
Kibworth Cemetery
 RLEIS/BBY LE8 .... 70 B2
Kibworth CE Primary
 School
 RLEIS/BBY LE8 .... 69 H2
Kibworth Golf Club
 RLEIS/BBY LE8 .... 70 B4
Kibworth High School
 RLEIS/BBY LE8 .... 70 A4
Kibworth RUFC
 MKTHBORO LE16 .... 82 A4
King Richard III Infant
 School
 LEIW LE3 .... 2 A5
Kingsway Primary School
 LEIE LE5 .... 34 A3
Kirby Muxloe Castle
 RLEIW/BAR LE9 .... 23 E4
Kirby Muxloe Cemetery
 RLEIW/BAR LE9 .... 22 D4
Kirby Muxloe Golf Club
 RLEIW/BAR LE9 .... 32 B1
Kirby Muxloe Primary
 School
 RLEIW/BAR LE9 .... 23 E5
Kirby Muxloe Sports Club
 RLEIW/BAR LE9 .... 23 E4
Knighton Fields Primary
 School
 LEIS LE2 .... 35 H5
Lady Jane Grey Primary
 School
 GBY/RBY LE6 .... 16 A5
Lakeside Business Park
 LEIN LE4 .... 12 B5
The Lancaster School
 LEIE LE5 .... 45 G1
Langmoor Primary School
 LEIS LE2 .... 46 D3
Latimer Primary School
 RLEINE/SYS LE7 .... 17 G2
Launde Primary School
 LEIS LE2 .... 47 F2
Leeson Clinic
 LEIW LE3 .... 35 E2
Leicester Airport
 LEIS LE2 .... 48 C1
Leicester Castle
 LEIS LE2 .... 2 C5
Leicester Cathedral
 LEI LE1 .... 2 D4

Leicester City FC
 (Walkers Stadium)
 LEIS LE2 .... 35 G3
Leicester College
 (Abbey Park Campus)
 LEIN LE4 .... 26 B2
Leicester College
 (Bede Island Campus)
 LEIW LE3 .... 35 F2
Leicester College
 (Freemen's Park Campus)
 LEIS LE2 .... 35 H2
Leicester College
 (St Margaret's Campus)
 LEI LE1 .... 26 B3
Leicester Exhibition Centre
 LEIE LE5 .... 3 G3
Leicester Frith Hospital
 LEIW LE3 .... 17 H5
Leicester General Hospital
 LEIE LE5 .... 28 A5
Leicester Grammar
 Junior School
 LEIE LE5 .... 38 A1
Leicester Grammar School
 LEI LE1 .... 2 D4
Leicester High School
 Junior Department
 LEIS LE2 .... 37 E5
Leicester Ivanhoe CC
 LEIW LE3 .... 32 B3
Leicester Leys Leisure
 Centre
 LEIN LE4 .... 18 A2
Leicester Market
 LEI LE1 .... 2 E4
Leicester Museum
 of Technology
 LEIN LE4 .... 19 F5
Leicester Racecourse
 LEIS LE2 .... 46 C2
Leicester Royal Infirmary
 LEIS LE2 .... 2 E7
Leicestershire CCC
 (Grace Road)
 LEIS LE2 .... 35 G5
Leicestershire Golf Club
 LEIE LE5 .... 37 F3
Leicester Tigers RFC
 (Welford Road Ground)
 LEIS LE2 .... 35 H2
Leysland Clinic
 RLEIS/BBY LE8 .... 66 C2
Leysland High School
 RLEIS/BBY LE8 .... 66 B2
Lime Leigh Medical Centre
 LEIE LE5 .... 35 E2
Linden Primary School
 LEIE LE5 .... 37 G2
Little Bowden Primary
 School
 MKTHBORO LE16 .... 82 A2
Little Hill Primary School
 WGSTN LE18 .... 58 A2
The Little Theatre
 LEI LE1 .... 3 G5
London Road Private
 Hospital
 LEIS LE2 .... 36 D4
Longslade Community
 College
 LEIN LE4 .... 11 H3
Long Street Surgery
 WGSTN LE18 .... 58 A1
Lubenham All Saints
 Primary School
 MKTHBORO LE16 .... 80 C1
Lutterworth Golf Club
 LUTT LE17 .... 85 G5
Lutterworth Grammar
 School & Community
 College
 LUTT LE17 .... 85 F3
Lutterworth Health Centre
 LUTT LE17 .... 85 H3
Lutterworth High School
 LUTT LE17 .... 85 F4
Lutterworth Sports Centre
 LUTT LE17 .... 85 F3
Madani High School
 LEIS LE2 .... 36 D3
Magazine Gatehouse
 .... 2 D5
Magna Park Distribution
 Centre
 LUTT LE17 .... 84 A3
Manorfield CE Primary
 School
 RLEIW/BAR LE9 .... 62 B4
Manor High School
 LEIS LE2 .... 47 H1
Market Harborough
 Cemetery
 MKTHBORO LE16 .... 82 A3
Market Harborough CE
 Primary School
 MKTHBORO LE16 .... 78 B5
Market Harborough
 District Hospital
 MKTHBORO LE16 .... 81 G1
Market Harborough
 Golf Club
 MKTHBORO LE16 .... 81 H5
Market Harborough
 Medical Centre
 MKTHBORO LE16 .... 81 H1
Markfield Cemetery
 COAL LE67 .... 6 C3
Marlow Road
 Industrial Estate
 LEIW LE3 .... 35 F3
Marriott Primary School
 LEIS LE2 .... 45 E2

Martin High School
 RLEINE/SYS LE7 .... 9 F5
Martinshaw Primary School
 GBY/RBY LE6 .... 15 H3
Mayflower Primary School
 LEIE LE5 .... 37 F1
Meadowdale Primary School
 MKTHBORO LE16 .... 79 F5
The Meadow Primary School
 WGSTN LE18 .... 46 C5
Medway Community
 Primary School
 LEIS LE2 .... 36 C1
Mellor Primary School
 LEIN LE4 .... 19 H4
Mercenfeld Primary School
 COAL LE67 .... 6 B4
Meridian Business Park
 END/NAR LE19 .... 33 H5
Meridian Leisure Park
 LEIW LE3 .... 34 A4
Merridale Medical Centre
 LEIE LE5 .... 34 D4
Merrydale Junior School
 LEIE LE5 .... 27 G2
The Merton Primary School
 RLEINE/SYS LE7 .... 13 F2
Millfield Community
 Primary School & Centre
 LEIW LE5 .... 34 A5
Millgate School
 LEIS LE2 .... 36 A5
Mill Hill Industrial Estate
 END/NAR LE19 .... 42 C4
Mill Lane Industrial Estate
 LEIW LE3 .... 23 C1
The Mill on the Soar Hotel
 RLEIW/BAR LE9 .... 73 F1
Moat Community College
 LEIE LE5 .... 3 J4
Montrose Primary School
 LEIS LE2 .... 44 D2
Mowmacre Community
 & Sports Centre
 LEIN LE4 .... 19 E1
Mowmacre Hill Primary
 School
 LEIN LE4 .... 18 D2
Narborough Health Centre
 END/NAR LE19 .... 55 E3
National Space Centre
 LEIN LE4 .... 19 F5
Nether Hall School
 LEIE LE5 .... 28 D1
Newarke Houses Museum
 LEIS LE2 .... 2 D5
New College Leicester
 LEIW LE3 .... 24 D3
Newlands Primary School
 RLEIW/BAR LE9 .... 50 C3
New Parks Leisure Centre
 LEIW LE3 .... 24 C1
Newtown Linford Primary
 School
 GBY/RBY LE6 .... 7 H4
New Walk Centre
 LEI LE1 .... 2 E5
New Walk Museum
 & Art Gallery
 LEI LE1 .... 3 G6
Northfield House Primary
 School
 LEIN LE4 .... 27 G1
Nuffield Hospital Leicester
 LEIE LE5 .... 28 B2
Oadby Golf Club
 LEIS LE2 .... 46 C2
Oadby Health Centre
 LEIS LE2 .... 47 E3
Oadby Industrial Estate
 LEIS LE2 .... 46 D3
Oadby Town FC
 LEIS LE2 .... 46 D4
Oak & Ash Business Park
 LEI LE1 .... 27 E5
Oakberry Road
 Industrial Estate
 LUTT LE17 .... 85 H1
Oaklands School
 LEIE LE5 .... 37 H1
Oaks Industrial Estate
 END/NAR LE19 .... 54 C4
 RLEIW/BAR LE9 .... 51 E3
Oakwood School
 LEIW LE3 .... 23 H1
Odeon Cinema
 LEIS LE2 .... 35 H3
Old John Tower
 GBY/RBY LE6 .... 8 B1

Old Mill CP School
 RLEIW/BAR LE9 .... 74 B3
Old Wyggestonians
 Sports Club
 LEIS LE2 .... 46 D4
Orchard CE
 Primary School
 RLEIW/BAR LE9 .... 73 H3
The Osiers
 Business Centre
 END/NAR LE19 .... 43 G2
Overdale J & I School
 LEIS LE2 .... 46 A2
The Parkland Primary
 School
 WGSTN LE18 .... 57 F2
Parks Primary School
 LEIE LE5 .... 25 E2
Pasley Road Health Centre
 LEIS LE2 .... 44 D4
The Pastures Primary
 School
 END/NAR LE19 .... 54 B1
Peckleton Lane
 Business Park
 RLEIW/BAR LE9 .... 40 A1
Phoenix Arts Centre
 LEI LE1 .... 2 E5
Piccadilly Cinema
 LEI LE1 .... 3 F1
Piper Way School
 LEIW LE3 .... 24 D4
Pochin Primary School
 RLEINE/SYS LE7 .... 13 H4
Premier Inn
 END/NAR LE19 .... 33 H4
 LEIS LE2 .... 60 A2
 LEIW LE3 .... 17 F5
 LEIW LE3 .... 25 E1
 LEIW LE3 .... 33 F2
Queensmead Community
 Primary School
 LEIW LE3 .... 34 C1
Queniborough Industrial
 Estate
 RLEINE/SYS LE7 .... 5 G4
Ramada Hotel
 LEI LE1 .... 3 F4
Rana Academy
 LEIN LE4 .... 19 G5
Ratby Primary School
 GBY/RBY LE6 .... 22 C1
Ratby Sports Club
 GBY/RBY LE6 .... 22 C2
Ravenhurst Primary School
 LEIW LE3 .... 34 B5
The Record Office for
 Leicestershire
 WGSTN LE18 .... 46 A5
Red Hill Field Primary
 School
 END/NAR LE19 .... 54 C3
Regency Hotel
 LEIS LE2 .... 36 D4
Regent College
 LEI LE1 .... 36 A2
Regent Street Industrial
 Estate
 END/NAR LE19 .... 55 F3
Richard Hill CE Primary
 School
 RLEINE/SYS LE7 .... 10 B2
Ridgeway Primary School
 MKTHBORO LE16 .... 78 D4
Riverside Community
 College
 LEIW LE3 .... 34 D5
Riverside Community
 Primary School
 LEIN LE4 .... 11 H5
The Robert Smyth School
 MKTHBORO LE16 .... 78 C4
Rockingham Industrial
 Estate
 MKTHBORO LE16 .... 79 E5
Rolleston Primary School
 LEIS LE2 .... 56 D1
Rose Farm Business Park
 RLEIS/BBY LE8 .... 57 F5
Roundhill Community
 College
 LEIE LE5 .... 12 D3
Rowlatts Hill Primary School
 LEIE LE5 .... 28 A4
Rushey Mead Health Centre
 LEIN LE4 .... 20 B3
Rushey Mead Primary
 School
 LEIN LE4 .... 20 A5

Rushey Mead Recreation
 Centre
 LEIN LE4 .... 20 A3
Rushey Mead School
 LEIN LE4 .... 20 A3
Sacred Heart RC Primary
 School
 LEIE LE5 .... 27 E4
Saffron Hill Cemetery
 LEIS LE2 .... 45 F4
Saffron Lane Sports Centre
 LEIS LE2 .... 35 H4
Saffron Lane Stadium
 LEIS LE2 .... 35 H4
St Barnabas Primary School
 LEIE LE5 .... 27 G3
St Crispins School
 LEIE LE5 .... 36 B3
St Cuthberts CE Primary
 School
 RLEIS/BBY LE8 .... 61 E2
St George's Retail Park
 LEI LE1 .... 3 J3
St John Fisher Catholic
 Primary School
 WGSTN LE18 .... 46 C4
St John the Baptist CE
 Primary School
 LEIE LE5 .... 36 C3
St Josephs RC Primary
 School
 LEIE LE5 .... 28 D2
 MKTHBORO LE16 .... 81 H1
St Lukes CE Primary School
 RLEINE/SYS LE7 .... 29 F5
St Lukes Hospital
 MKTHBORO LE16 .... 78 B4
St Margarets Baths
 LEI LE1 .... 2 D2
St Margarets Business
 Centre
 LEI LE1 .... 2 E1
St Margarets Bus Station
 LEI LE1 .... 2 E2
St Margarets Sports Centre
 LEI LE1 .... 26 A2
St Martins Shopping Centre
 LEI LE1 .... 2 E4
St Mary de Castro Church
 LEI LE1 .... 2 C5
St Marys Business Park
 MKTHBORO LE16 .... 78 D5
St Marys CE Primary School
 LUTT LE17 .... 85 F1
St Marys Fields Infant
 School
 LEIW LE3 .... 35 E3
St Matthews Sports Hall
 LEI LE1 .... 3 H1
St Matthews Business Centre
 LEI LE1 .... 3 F1
St Patricks RC Primary
 School
 LEIN LE4 .... 19 H5
St Pauls RC School
 LEIE LE5 .... 38 A1
St Peter & St Paul CE
 Primary School
 RLEINE/SYS LE7 .... 4 D4
St Peters CE Primary School
 RLEIS/BBY LE8 .... 55 H4
St Peters Health Centre
 LEI LE1 .... 3 J5
St Peters RC Primary School
 RLEIW/BAR LE9 .... 51 G2
St Thomas More
 Catholic School
 LEIS LE2 .... 36 C5
Sandfield Close Primary
 School
 LEIN LE4 .... 20 C2
Satha Sai School
 LEIN LE4 .... 27 E2
Scraptoft Valley Primary
 School
 LEIE LE5 .... 28 D2
Shaftesbury Junior School
 LEIW LE3 .... 2 A6
Sharnford CE Primary
 School
 HINC LE10 .... 72 A4
Shenton Primary School
 LEIE LE5 .... 27 E3
The Sherrier Centre
 LUTT LE17 .... 85 G3
Sherrier CE Primary School
 LUTT LE17 .... 85 G2
Shires Shopping Centre
 LEI LE1 .... 2 E3

Shonki Business Centre
 LEI LE1 .... 26 B3
Sir Jonathan North
 Community College
 LEIE LE5 .... 45 G1
Slater Primary School
 LEIW LE3 .... 2 C1
Soar Valley College
 LEIN LE4 .... 20 A4
Southfields Infant School
 LEIE LE5 .... 45 F3
South Leicester RFC
 WGSTN LE18 .... 58 B3
South Leicestershire
 College
 WGSTN LE18 .... 57 H1
South Wigston Health
 Centre
 WGSTN LE18 .... 57 G1
South Wigston High School
 LEIS LE2 .... 57 E2
Sparkenhoe Community
 Primary School
 LEIS LE2 .... 3 K5
Spence Street Sports Centre
 LEIE LE5 .... 3 K5
Spinney Hill Primary School
 LEIE LE5 .... 27 F5
Springfield Road Health
 Centre
 LEIS LE2 .... 36 C3
Stafford Leys Primary
 School
 LEIW LE3 .... 32 D3
Stokes CE Primary School
 RLEIS/BBY LE8 .... 56 A4
Stokes Wood Primary
 School
 LEIW LE3 .... 25 F2
Stonehill High School
 LEIE LE5 .... 11 G3
Stoneygate FC
 RLEINE/SYS LE7 .... 29 G2
Stoneygate School
 LEIS LE2 .... 36 C3
Sunningdale Industrial Park
 LEIW LE3 .... 33 G1
Superbowl
 LEI LE1 .... 2 D2
Syston Cemetery
 RLEINE/SYS LE7 .... 13 C1
Syston Health Centre
 RLEINE/SYS LE7 .... 5 E5
Taylor Road Primary School
 LEIE LE5 .... 26 D3
Thistly Meadow Primary
 School
 RLEIS/BBY LE8 .... 56 C4
Thomas Estley
 Community College
 RLEIW/BAR LE9 .... 74 B3
Thurlaston CE Primary
 School
 RLEIW/BAR LE9 .... 41 E5
Thurmaston Cemetery
 LEIE LE5 .... 12 C5
Thurnby Lodge Primary
 School
 LEIE LE5 .... 28 D4
Thythorn Field Primary
 School
 WGSTN LE18 .... 58 B4
Townlands CE Primary
 School
 RLEIW/BAR LE9 .... 51 F4
Travelodge
 LEI LE1 .... 2 C3
Trinity Hospital
 LEI LE1 .... 2 C5
Troon Industrial Estate
 LEIN LE4 .... 21 E3
Troon Way Business Centre
 LEIN LE4 .... 20 C3
Tropical Birdland
 RLEIW/BAR LE9 .... 30 B1
University Exhibition Centre
 LEIW LE3 .... 2 C4
University of Leicester
 LEI LE1 .... 36 A3
 LEI LE1 .... 36 D5
University of Leicester
 Harold Martin
 Botanic Garden
 LEIS LE2 .... 37 F5
University of Leicester
 Sports Ground
 LEIS LE2 .... 37 G5

Uplands Junior School
 LEIS LE2 .... 27 E5
Uppingham Road
 Health Centre
 LEIE LE5 .... 27 G3
Victoria Clinic
 LEIS LE2 .... 36 B3
Vipers RFC
 RLEIS/BBY LE8 .... 56 A4
VUE Cinema
 END/NAR LE19 .... 34 A4
Vulcan Business Centre
 LEIE LE5 .... 27 E4
Walnut Street
 Medical Centre
 LEIS LE2 .... 35 G2
Wanstead Industrial Park
 LEIN LE4 .... 23 H5
Water Leys Primary School
 WGSTN LE18 .... 45 H4
Watermead Country Park
 LEIN LE4 .... 12 B4
Weavers Close CE Primary
 School
 RLEIW/BAR LE9 .... 51 F3
Welford Road Cemetery
 LEIS LE2 .... 36 A2
Welland Industrial Estate
 MKTHBORO LE16 .... 79 F5
Welland Park Community
 College
 MKTHBORO LE16 .... 81 H2
Westbridge Industrial Park
 LEIW LE3 .... 2 C4
Westcotes Health Centre
 LEIW LE3 .... 35 E1
Western Golf Club
 LEIW LE3 .... 23 H4
Westfield House Hotel
 RLEIS/BBY LE8 .... 56 B3
Westleigh Business Park
 RLEIS/BBY LE8 .... 56 B2
Westleigh RFC
 RLEIS/BBY LE8 .... 66 A1
Whetstone Golf Club
 RLEIW/BAR LE9 .... 65 G2
Whitehall Primary School
 LEIE LE5 .... 37 H1
Wigston Cemetery
 WGSTN LE18 .... 58 B3
Wigston Swimming Pool
 WGSTN LE18 .... 57 H2
Wilberforce Road Surgery
 LEIW LE3 .... 2 A7
William Bradford
 Community College
 RLEIW/BAR LE9 .... 50 C3
Willowbrook Primary
 School
 LEIE LE5 .... 29 E4
Winstanley High School
 LEIW LE3 .... 34 A4
Wolsey House Primary
 School
 LEIN LE4 .... 19 E4
Woodland Grange Primary
 School
 LEIE LE5 .... 47 H4
Woodlands Day Hospital
 END/NAR LE19 .... 54 D3
Woodstock Primary School
 LEIN LE4 .... 19 E3
Woolden Hill CP School
 RLEINE/SYS LE7 .... 9 G4
Wreake Valley Community
 College
 RLEINE/SYS LE7 .... 5 F4
Wycliffe Industrial Estate
 LUTT LE17 .... 85 H2
Wyggeston Hospital
 LEIE LE5 .... 35 E1
Wyggeston & Queen
 Elizabeth I College
 LEI LE1 .... 36 A3
Wygston's House Museum
 of Costume
 LEI LE1 .... 2 D4
Wyvern CP School
 LEIN LE4 .... 20 B5

Acknowledgements

Schools address data provided by Education Direct.

Petrol station information supplied by Johnsons.

Garden centre information provided by:

Garden Centre Association  Britains best garden centres

Wyevale Garden Centres

The statement on the front cover of this atlas is sourced, selected and quoted
from a reader comment and feedback form received in 2004